POWER, PARTICIP
POLITICAL RENEWAL

Case studies in public participation

Marian Barnes, Janet Newman and Helen Sullivan

ONE WEEK LOAN

First published in Great Britain in 2007 by

The Policy Press
University of Bristol
Fourth Floor
Beacon House
Queen's Road
Bristol BS8 1QU
UK

Tel +44 (0)117 331 4054
Fax +44 (0)117 331 4093
e-mail tpp-info@bristol.ac.uk
www.policypress.org.uk

© Marian Barnes, Janet Newman and Helen Sullivan 2007

British Library Cataloguing in Publication Data
A catalogue record for this book is available from the British Library.

Library of Congress Cataloging-in-Publication Data
A catalog record for this book has been requested.

ISBN 978 1 86134 667 4 paperback
ISBN 978 1 86134 668 1 hardcover

Cover design by Qube Design Associates, Bristol.
Front cover image kindly supplied by Cristopher Potter
(cspcreative@yahoo.com.au).
Printed and bound in Great Britain by Hobbs the Printers, Southampton.

Contents

Acknowledgements   iv

one   Introduction   1
two   Participation in context   7
three   Inclusive democracy and social movements   33
four   Shaping public participation: public bodies and their publics 53
five   Re-forming services   71
six   Neighbourhood and community governance   99
seven   Responding to a differentiated public   135
eight   Issues and expertise   165
nine   Conclusion: power, participation and political renewal   183

References   207
Index   221

Acknowledgements

We would like to thank the participants in the case studies discussed in this book for agreeing to let us watch them and talk to them about their engagement. Our thanks are also due to Andrew Knops, who was a member of the team who carried out this research. The work was funded by the Economic and Social Research Council as part of the Democracy and Participation Programme, award no. L215252001.

ONE

Introduction

Recent developments in public policy have emphasised the need for greater public participation in decision making and for new forms of democratic practice. More and better public participation is viewed as capable of improving the quality and legitimacy of decisions in government, health services, local government and other public bodies, as well as having the potential to address the 'democratic deficit' (Stewart, 1999) and to build community capacity and social capital. The aspirations are high:

> Public participation could radically improve our quality of life. It can contribute to creating more active citizens, help manage complex problems in public service design and delivery, help build the new relationships and shifts of power and resources required for 21st century governance, and develop individuals' skills, confidence, ambition and vision. For these and other reasons, public participation has become an essential ingredient in public policy decision-making and delivery. (Mulgan, 2005, p 2)

Consequently, there has been an explosion of participative forums, including citizens' juries, area committees, neighbourhood forums, tenant groups, user groups and groups reflecting what are viewed as communities of interest or identity. Some have been established by public bodies in order to facilitate dialogue with the public, while others have independent origins, often based on voluntary, charitable or political activity.

The result of this explosion is that channels of access to the political system are widening, new opportunity structures being opened up, and more active forms of dialogue being fostered. In the process not only are some 'lay' publics becoming more expert in how to navigate the public policy system, but public service workers are being exposed to new experiences and encounters that have the capacity to change their orientations to what they do. How can we understand the significance of all this? How far does it represent a fundamental change in governance? And what is the potential of any such change to address inequalities of power, overcome social exclusion or to foster political renewal?

This book addresses such questions through an empirical and theoretical analysis of public participation, offering a critical perspective on its capacity to empower citizens, lead to public service change and enhance democracy. It addresses the way in which public policy discourses construct notions of the public and engage with a diversity of publics in a plural polity. It examines the motivations of participants and the ways in which the identities and interests of officials and citizens are negotiated. It explores the ways in which institutions enable and constrain the development of public participation initiatives, including the way in which debate and dialogue can take place within participation forums, and what consequences such deliberations may have for public policies. It considers whether participation makes a difference to the conduct of officials or to the processes of delivering public services. And it explores the dynamics produced as groups that have their origins in voluntary or community activity encounter public bodies seeking to engage in dialogue with them.

In order to address these issues the book draws on and discusses different ways of theorising collective action and governance processes. We adopt a sceptical stance that questions some of the uncritical claims that have been made for public participation. Many academic and policy perspectives on this subject are based in theories of deliberative democracy. We acknowledge the value of this work in distinguishing the potential of dialogic processes from representative democracy that seeks to assess public views through the aggregation of preferences. But we also agree with critics of deliberative democracy that it is naïve to suggest that deliberative processes themselves are not subject to power relationships that shape the way in which they work. Thus we also draw on new institutional theory to understand the way in which institutional rules and norms that operate within the public bodies sponsoring such initiatives influence what it is possible to achieve, and how such processes themselves develop their own rules (both formal and informal) that determine who can take part and how participation can be performed. Our approach also differs from much other work on public participation by using social movement theory to address the relationship between independently organised collective action with policy or service development objectives and action from within public agencies to engage citizens in dialogue.

The book draws substantially on research carried out as part of the Economic and Social Research Council's (ESRC's) Democracy and Participation programme as well as related work by the authors. The research project involved in-depth analysis of 17 examples of public involvement across a range of policy contexts in two English cities. These included, for example, initiatives designed to enable users of health and social care services to have their say about services, to engage young people in a regeneration initiative, to consult with older people in relation to policy affecting their lives, and to increase the level of citizen involvement in decision making at a neighbourhood level. The selection of case studies followed an initial mapping of public participation initiatives in each city that was carried out by means of a snowballing questionnaire sent to contacts in local government, the National Health Service (NHS) and the voluntary sector. As well as enabling us to review participation across a range of policy domains, case studies were chosen to take account of initiatives whose origins lay outside the public sector as well as officially sponsored initiatives. We conducted interviews with both citizens and officials engaged in these initiatives and with officials holding strategic roles in public bodies – people who were likely to have had some influence in shaping participation policies and strategies and others who might need to be convinced by the arguments resulting from such participation. We also observed examples of deliberative forums in action in order to see at first hand the dialogue that took place within them.

In the following three chapters of the book we address the conceptual and theoretical perspectives that we use subsequently to discuss case studies of participation in practice. In Chapter Two we explore the ways in which different discourses of public participation and user and citizen empowerment have developed and evolved in UK public policy, and place this in the context of similar international developments. We then explore how New Labour's approach to public participation engaged with these discourses and examine the evidence on the impact of public participation on public decision making, governance practice and service outcomes.

In Chapter Three we consider the way in which concerns about the management and government of public services have intersected with concerns about a decline in political participation. Such concerns have prompted the development of experiments in deliberative forms of decision making across the public sector. We then compare this with the move toward more participative modes of decision making that have been promoted by action among autonomous groups of service users and citizens, reflecting on issues such as motivations for participation, the objectives that are sought and the opportunity structures that provide a context within which such action takes place.

Chapter Four sets out two different frameworks through which the micro-politics of case studies is analysed in later chapters. Questions drawn from new institutional theory focus on the importance of studying how the rules and norms of deliberative practice are developed, negotiated and contested within forums, and with what consequences. The chapter goes on to consider 'the public', 'the community', 'the citizen-consumer' and other images as social constructions formed out of a range of discourses and ideologies that are historically embedded in institutional practice. It raises questions about the ways in which such constructions might inform common-sense conceptions about the nature of democratic debate, the processes of representation on which membership may be based, and the interaction between 'lay' and 'official' identities.

We then turn to a discussion of the 17 case studies of public participation, drawing on the issues introduced in Chapters Two to Four to analyse and explain our findings. Case studies are grouped thematically. Chapter Five discusses participation initiatives that are designed to contribute to the development of public services that are more responsive to their users. Chapter Six is concerned with neighbourhood-based participation, a major feature of public policy under the New Labour governments in the UK. Chapter Seven focuses on ways in which public bodies attempt to engage with or respond to a socially differentiated public, including groups whose origins lay in social or political movements. Finally, in Chapter Eight we turn our attention to activist, issue-based groups engaged in dialogue with officials in an attempt to directly influence public policy. Each chapter reflects on who the participants were and how and why they came to take part; the nature of the deliberative processes that developed; the way in which these interacted with issues of representation and legitimacy; how institutional norms and rules enabled or constrained participation; and the possible development of new relationships and identifications that transcended the lay/official divide.

In our conclusion (Chapter Nine) we reflect on what our evidence suggests about the transformatory potential of public participation, and its capacity to contribute to a process of political renewal. Our analysis indicates that the aspirations highlighted earlier may need to be tempered by an awareness of the institutional practices that constrain agency or produce a loss of trust. We highlight the power of official discourses to define and delimit notions of 'the public' and of 'legitimate participants', but also suggest ways in which such meanings are contested and negotiated. We explore how relationships and identities are shaped in the context of power inequalities, and explore the tensions that exist when those engaged in autonomous collective action find themselves engaging in dialogue with public bodies. Our micro-analysis of what actually happens within participative forums enables us to offer a nuanced reflection on these processes: how they operate and with what consequences. It also produces new insights into the dilemmas experienced by public service workers exposed to new encounters with the public.

TWO

Participation in context

Introduction

Securing the participation of citizens in the governance of their societies is currently presenting a challenge to governments worldwide. In many western democracies public participation rates are falling and cynicism about government and politics is the dominant feature. The resultant concern about low levels of public participation reflects an underlying unease about the health of western liberal democracies and the legitimacy of their modes of governance (Daemen and Schaap, 2000; Smith, 2005). Further afield, evidence from recent studies undertaken in the southern hemisphere reveals concern among citizens about institutional corruption, a disconnection between governing bodies and the lives of citizens and a lack of attention to the needs of the poorest (Commonwealth Foundation, 1999; Narayan et al, 2000; Gaventa, 2004).

For some observers the problem lies with the role played by the state. So, Ostrom (2000) argues that Scandinavian governments exhibit centralising tendencies that turn citizens into 'passive observers' and 'crowd them out' of participation in public policy (2000, p 12). For others the problem is linked to the state's subjugation to global capital, diluting the act of citizenship to an exercise in making choices about consumption (Klein, 2000; Monbiot, 2000). Limited public participation is also attributed to a wider societal malaise in which economic, social and technological changes have reduced citizens' capacity to participate – what Putnam (1993, 2000) terms their 'social capital'. Linked to all of these is an acknowledgement that some groups or communities are more adversely affected by this malaise in participation. For example, in both northern and southern hemispheres, poor people are identified as in need of special attention from the state and voluntary sector bodies to ensure their 'inclusion' in governance and 'to build their capacity to participate'; both of the latter features have been evident in various UK regeneration programmes over the past 20 years.

According to Gaventa (2004), in "both South and North, there is growing consensus that the way forward is found in focusing on *both* a more active and engaged citizenry *and* a more responsive and effective state which can deliver needed public services" (2004, p 4; emphasis in original). One of the consequences of this is the recent articulation of citizens as 'partners' with state institutions and private and voluntary sector bodies in the identification and resolution of public policy problems (Sullivan and Skelcher, 2002). For example, in Southern Africa and Asia a programme of 'community-based natural resource management' devolves control of particular resources to local communities working in partnership with relevant public authorities and interests. Partner status is afforded to the local communities partly on the basis that they are at least as knowledgeable as professionals about how to manage such natural resources (Fortmann et al, 2001). Elsewhere in the US and the UK local communities have long been considered partners in the processes of neighbourhood revitalisation or regeneration and service users have been claimed as partners in service development, even though in practice their relative lack of resource power renders them as less than equal partners (Hastings et al, 1996; Barnes et al, 1999; Peterman, 2000). Behind the façade of the language of partnership it is possible to identify a range of ways in which governments and state institutions have attempted to stimulate public participation in specific contexts and to regenerate the relationship between the state and citizens (Fung and Wright, 2003; Wainwright, 2003; Cornwall and Coelho, 2004).

This chapter traces the development of the different discourses of public participation and user and citizen empowerment in UK public policy and situates each in its international context, identifying core themes and drivers. It discusses developments in English local governance under New Labour, describing the key elements of public participation policy and locating the impulses for public participation in a number of different discourses. These will be explored in more depth in the case study chapters that form the latter part of this book. The chapter concludes with some reflections on emerging evaluation evidence about the impact on public bodies and citizens of some of New Labour's public participation initiatives.

Public participation discourses

This analysis of official public participation discourses in the UK, that is, those generated by the state, takes as its starting point Gyford's (1991) assertion that in the 1960s and 1970s the default position adopted and expected of the British public, in relation to public policy and public service provision, was that of 'passive recipients'. Indeed Gyford goes further, arguing that the combination of representative democracy, bureaucratic organisation and the privileging of professionals as the guardians of the public interest, in effect created an 'infantilised public'. However, the roots of revitalisation were also present at this point, and nourished by challenges to and among the political elites, they developed over time to support a number of different normative discourses of the public's role in relation to the state. Each was based around the core idea of the 'active citizen', and each in turn presented its own challenge to the dominance of representative democracy, bureaucratic organisation and professional judgement.

Here we review the development of four different official discourses of public participation that have proved particularly influential in directing public policy and service provision. In brief these are:

- 'empowered public' discourse
- 'consuming public' discourse
- 'stakeholder public' discourse
- 'responsible public' discourse.

We present the core elements of each discourse, examine its historical and theoretical underpinnings and discuss examples of the impact of this discourse on public policy and public service provision in the UK and internationally. It is important to emphasise here that what we focus on is how the state has responded to prompts about public participation in order to develop strategies for engaging with and creating 'active citizens'. What is not considered here, but is central to the discussions in the following two chapters, is the impact on public participation of the prompts and pressures emanating from outside the organised state sector, from voluntary organisations, grass roots bodies and individual activists. These generated their own discourses that sometimes contributed to, but more often conflicted with, those of the organised state. The contribution made by these and their significance to the wider debate about democratic, state and civil renewal are considered in the next two chapters, while the case study chapters present empirical data on the interaction between state and civil society discourses.

'Empowered public' discourse

The 'empowered public' discourse focuses on consistently marginalised and/or disadvantaged groups or communities. The term 'community' has become ubiquitous in public policy debates but very often its use serves to confuse. This is because there are numerous meanings attached to the use of the word, and it is not always clear which is meant. Taylor (2003) outlines a helpful way of classifying 'community': as a *descriptive* term denoting those who share interests in common; as a *normative* term pointing to a set of values and conditions that should inform how we live but which have been challenged by developments such as globalisation; and as an *instrumental* term, which combines elements of the other two to attach agency to communities and to associate particular values with more localised service provision. In this volume, references to the ways in which public sector agents use the term will largely reflect this instrumental use and our empirical work will discuss the consequences of this use of the term on public participation. We will also explore alternative conceptions of community, those that are claimed by citizens themselves, and consider the implications of these on interactions with public bodies.

The 'empowered public' discourse is a good example of the instrumental use of the term 'community'. It conceives of communities' disadvantage as deriving from institutionalised discrimination or neglect and seeks to address this by supporting interventions that will act to empower these communities to enable them to act on their own behalves. The analysis that supports this discourse is one that locates the core problem in the unequal power relations that prevail between the state and particular communities or groups. Consequently proposed solutions are based on communities becoming empowered and then challenging the state to operate in a different way. The 'empowered public' discourse is a site of struggle between different views of power, inequality and political agency. In Chapter Three we consider the way in which civil society groups and movements have initiated and shaped their own strategies for empowering the public and challenging the state. Here we focus on state-sponsored empowerment activity, supported through targeted policy initiatives and resources.

The UK roots of the 'empowered public' discourse stem from the 1960s when there was a growing awareness that despite the creation of the welfare state and government intervention in economic policy, levels of poverty and inequality were still unacceptably high. A new consensus emerged that rejected the argument that the persistence of inequality and poverty could be explained through individual and collective pathology. It proposed instead that the persistence of poverty and inequality among particular communities was as a direct result of the failure of public bodies to respond to the particular needs of these communities and to cooperate with each other in order to deliver services more effectively. This interpretation was similar to, and informed by, the ideas that underpinned the War on Poverty in the US in the 1960s (Marris and Rein,1972;Taylor, 2003).

In the UK this debate led to the creation of spatially targeted education priority areas (EPAs) and community development projects (CDPs) among other initiatives. Each sought to develop and test interventions to combat urban poverty and to involve citizens as empowered partners in their dealings with the state.These ultimately failed to shift the prevailing balance of power (Cockburn, 1977), although the critical analysis of capitalism and the role of the state developed by the CDP teams, and the strong association with local struggles of some of the community workers and academics involved, led to tensions in the CDP teams' relationship with their sponsors and funders (Loney, 1983; Mainwaring, 1988).

In the UK in the 1980s, the participation of local communities in centrally sponsored programmes to address their poverty and deprivation gave way to the fascination with the private sector as a key resource to support area regeneration. Initially private sector partners were involved in programmes that focused on improving the physical environment. However, in the 1990s the emphasis was broadened to include economic and social regeneration and local communities were granted a new role as partners in regeneration alongside private, voluntary and public sector bodies. City Challenge and the Single Regeneration Budget (SRB) were both examples of this approach and in both cases considerable resources were allocated to 'capacity building' activity within the host communities, although subsequent evaluations of the initiatives found such interventions only partially successful in shifting the balance of power among partners (for example, Russell et al 1996; Brenna et al, 1998; Rhodes et al, 2002). Similar conclusions can be drawn from attempts in the US and mainland Europe to facilitate state-sponsored neighbourhood revitalisation in the 1980s and 1990s (Peterman, 2000;Allen and Cars, 2002).

The election of New Labour in 1997 led to some important changes in direction for regeneration policy but retained and intensified the 'empowered public' discourse.The principle of competition for funds was replaced by targeting spending on specific areas based on indices of deprivation. Importantly for our purposes partnerships *with* communities gave way to the idea of partnerships *led* by communities. Finally regeneration policy was recast to strengthen joined-up action in key policy areas – namely education and employment, health, crime and the physical environment – although this 'joining up' also needed to demonstrate efficacy in engaging with and responding to citizens' views and concerns.

The 'empowered public' discourse is not exclusively associated with spatially located communities despite being the focus of much government policy. Attention has also been paid by state agencies (locally and nationally) to interventions that seek to 'empower' communities of interest or identity, for example, Black and minority ethnic groups, women, young people, older people, disabled people and carers (for example, Barnes, 1997). For Gyford (1991) the changing demography of Britain was an important contributor to the transformation of the public from 'passive' to 'active' citizens, the emerging social diversity generating a more 'assertive public'. This also seemed to be borne out by trend data collected by the Central Statistical Office, which, in the mid-1970s, reported that public participation was a "significant social characteristic of the present age in British society" (in Gyford, 1991, p 195).

Early interventions by the local state included the development of policies of inclusion, initially employment-related policies but latterly policies that covered service delivery to diverse communities. These were accompanied in local government by the establishment of various combinations of equalities committees. Most common were those that sought to address the needs of women and black and minority ethnic communities, although over time some authorities also added committees for disability. These provided both a means of scrutinising the local authority's activities (and sometimes those of other bodies) and a way of connecting more directly to specific communities, via the 'race' and women's units that were established by local authorities to support both organisational development and community development. High profile in the late 1980s and 1990s, these committees, units and their work became 'mainstreamed' in the 21st century, although with varying degrees of success (Gibbon, 1992; Edwards, 1995; Creegan et al, 2003; Squires and Wickham-Jones, 2004).

This focus on the 'empowerment' of marginalised communities is also evident internationally. Gaventa (2004) describes the way in which constitutional changes in India were designed to make local councils more representative of traditionally excluded populations by reserving seats for women, for those of lower castes and tribes. Following these changes about one million women and about 600,000 lower caste or tribal members were elected to local government office. Others describe the way in which specific policy levers might be identified as instruments of empowerment. For example, Groenewald and Smith (2002) discuss the introduction of an integrated approach to development planning at the local level in South Africa. Here there were hopes that, through the participation of the public in the process, individuals would become empowered and civil society organisations might become established, so furthering the country's transition to democracy.

'Consuming public' discourse

The 'consuming public' discourse is focused on the expectations and experiences of individuals in their use of public services. Underpinned by neoliberal thinking and heavily influenced in practice by the contributions of US writers such as Peters and Waterman (1982) and Osborne and Gaebler (1992), the 'consuming public' discourse characterises individuals as free agents able to exercise choice in their use of public services, facilitated by the operation of a market in goods and services. This has implications for both the public and service providers. Individuals are no longer considered passive recipients of services over which they have no control, but active consumers in the process of service selection and delivery, with rights and opportunities for redress. Service providers in turn are required to 'open up' to the choices and aspirations of consumers, to become responsive and to compete with others in the provision of services. The state acts to enable the interactions between consumers and providers and to regulate activity to protect the public interest.

The emergence of the 'consuming public' discourse in the 1980s had a significant impact on western democracies, particularly in the UK where it was adopted and promoted by successive Conservative governments. Latterly its influence has been felt in the southern hemisphere, not least through the interventions of the World Bank in supporting the liberalisation of public services as core elements of 'reconstruction' programmes. In the UK in the 1980s the privatisation of the relationship between the citizen and the state took a number of forms. A new language emerged borrowed from the private sector including such terms as consumers, customers, value for money and quality. New mechanisms were developed through which consumers could be made more aware of the level and standard of service they should be able to expect and what should happen if these standards were not met. Similarly market research–type techniques became more common as the vehicle for finding out how service users felt about service quality and choice. Alongside this, waves of public sector reform opened up public services to the market, for example through compulsory competitive tendering, and private sector bodies began to develop portfolios of activities in the public sector. Public sector organisations adopted private sector modes of operating including performance-related pay and customer care training to help with the new orientation to the consumer. The state also sought to support this orientation through the development of processes of audit and scrutiny, such as independent inspections of services and the publication of 'league tables' of performance, for example in relation to schools (Ferlie et al, 1998; Gaster and Squires, 2003).

A key symbol of the 'consuming public' discourse in the UK was the establishment of the Citizens Charter initiative in 1991. According to John Major, the Prime Minister who introduced the scheme, the Charter initiative was an important opportunity to reverse the domination of the service provider over the user. "They give the citizen published standards and results; competition as a spur to quality improvement; responsiveness; and value for money.... They give more power to the citizen and more freedom to choose" (quoted in Prior et al, 1995, pp 23-4). By 1994 the Charter initiative had developed apace with charters associated with public services as diverse as the operation of the courts, the London Underground, the NHS, schools and job centres. In local government, while not all local authorities signed up to this initiative, the majority of local authorities began to develop and adopt their own sets of service standards designed to improve relationships with their consumers. Charters have also proved popular in other democracies as part of reform programmes stimulated by the 'new public management' philosophy. For example, Rose and Ståhlberg (2005) describe their application in the Nordic countries alongside means of generating 'customer' feedback such as service-related surveys. They also illustrate how Denmark and to a lesser extent Sweden have developed their consumer orientation further through the establishment of user boards in schools that afford parents particular powers in relation to service design and delivery.

Some British commentators including Corrigan (1997) argued that this new consumer discourse was valuable as it provided citizens with a meaningful expression of their citizenship, not previously expressed through voting. Others were less convinced, seeing the discourse as a dilution rather than an enhancement of citizenship. For example, Prior et al argued that the "logical outcomes of the privatisation of citizenship seem clear: an ever decreasing capacity to deal with needs and problems that can only be resolved through collective commitment and action, and an ever increasing division between, on the one hand, those citizens who are able to compete and succeed in the market place and, on the other hand, those who are either unable to compete in the first place or who lose out, and for whom little in the way of a safety net of public provision exists" (1995, p 167).

Following the election of New Labour in 1997 some commentators saw in the government's early interventions a move away from the exclusive focus on consumers. For example Gaster and Squires (2003) identified in the policies on social exclusion and citizen education a governmental perspective that "public service providers need to think beyond current users, and to involve their whole communities" (p 43). Nonetheless a range of early initiatives including Best Value in local government, the establishment of Patient Advice and Liaison Services (PALS) in the NHS and the development of specialist schools all reinforced the consumer discourse. This has been emphasised by a resurgence of interest in the mantra of 'choice' as the dominant feature of public services (Leadbeater, 2004; Clarke et al, 2006). The influence of these and other debates relating to the 'consuming public' discourse on the way in which the public is constituted for the purposes of public participation will be considered in Chapter Four.

'Stakeholder public' discourse

The 'stakeholder public' discourse is built around the idea of the public (as individuals or via groups) having a stake in the good governance of the public realm. This may be expressed in different ways: for example, as users of services, as indirect beneficiaries of the provision of services to others or as taxpayers. The concept of stakeholding is considered to be particularly valuable in complex and diverse societies because it "enables us to recognise a diversity of legitimate entitlements to representation within the public as well as the private sphere" (Rustin, 1997, p 80), through the articulation of the different kinds of stakes that individuals and groups may have in relation to different institutions and interests. According to Rustin this "has the great advantage of realism. It allows the recognition of the real differences of position, interest and claims that have to be taken account of in any actual polity" (pp 75-6). Along with this legitimation of a role comes the responsibility to exercise that role: as Hirst indicates, a "stake implies a voice, and the right to voice implies the obligation to use it, to steward our own assets. In that sense the concept helps us to restore the robust democracy of free people governing themselves" (1997, p 71).

Proponents of a 'stakeholder public' discourse may hold very different views about the kind of democratic system that can best support its realisation. For some a 'stakeholder public' discourse is entirely consistent with the operation of representative democracy, offering a way of complementing and strengthening it through the introduction of new 'voices' and modes of engagement in public decision making (for example, see Hutton, 1997). For others, however, the 'stakeholder public' discourse implies a fundamental challenge to representative democracy, suggesting instead an approach to governing that privileges citizen control through discussion and consensual decision making over voting and the relinquishing of decision making to representatives (Cunningham, 2002). In these 'participatory democracies' decentralisation of decision making is vital (in both economic and political spheres). An alternative expression of the 'stakeholder public' discourse is that articulated by Hirst, who proposes a version of 'associative democracy' in which there is a preference for governing through a network of voluntary associations (that may be neighbourhood-based or based on interest or identity), but an acknowledgement that the state has an albeit limited role, for example, in fulfilling tasks that are society wide or where there are gaps in voluntary provision (Hirst, 1994; and see below).

The concept of a 'stakeholder public' is evident in the (in some cases long-standing) attempts to initiate and embed public participation in the governance of the societies of the southern and northern hemispheres (Cornwall and Coelho, 2004; Smith, 2005). Decentralisation of government has often been used as a means of operationalising the concept of the 'stakeholder public', but the introduction of decentralisation schemes is frequently problematic as the experiences of Barcelona in the 1980s (Blakeley, 2002), neighbourhood committees in Mexico (Flores, 2002) and the new municipal level councils in Brazil in the 1990s (Coelho, 2004) reveal. One of the difficulties such schemes often face is the differences of view that prevail among stakeholders about the kind of democracy that the schemes are designed to promote; some stakeholders may perceive them as a means of enhancing a representative system of democracy by bringing decision making *closer* to the people, while others may see them as a means of stimulating participative democracy through decision making *by* the people. Examples of both may be found in the development of tenant participation programmes and participatory planning initiatives in the UK in the late 1960s and

1970s (limited decision making by the people), and early attempts at decentralising local government in Tower Hamlets and Islington (decision making closer to the people). Examinations of local government decentralisation schemes in the UK since the 1960s suggest that a hybrid of the above approaches predominates, in which decision making is *informed by* the people (Burns et al, 1994, Sullivan et al, 2001).

The idea of the 'stakeholder public' is also apparent in the attempts to intervene in relationships in the economic sphere; for example the involvement of workers in the decision-making processes of major employers in Germany reflected the belief that if employees' stake in the enterprise was acted on, economic and social benefits would result; while the changes to the operation of the pensions system in Australia to build in significant commitments from both employers and employees were based on the principle that all had a stake in securing the future wellbeing of people in retirement.

In the UK in the 1990s there was a concerted attempt by some academics, politicians and commentators to develop the idea of a 'stakeholder society' in which the social, political and economic dimensions were brought together. Hutton (1997) argued that "social and economic inclusion, rather than equality, should be the overriding objective for the contemporary left. Inclusion implies membership; you cannot be included if you are not a member. But membership entails obligations as well as rights. So a stakeholder society and a stakeholder economy exist where there is mutuality of rights and obligations constructed around the notion of economic, social and political inclusion" (p 3). The implications of this aspiration were wide-ranging, with Barnett arguing that the "idea of a stakeholder democracy is more radical in the British context because the British state is founded not on democracy, in which citizens are sovereign, but on consent orchestrated from above to protect the parliamentary rule of the elite" (1997, p 85). The inclusivity of stakeholding would challenge this through the introduction of new voices and forms of expression as well as new roles for the public as stakeholders. However, the challenge would also need to be met by the institutions of the state itself. For Hirst (1997a) the central problem was the executive power of government. The realisation of stakeholding, he argued, required proportional representation, the decentralisation of power and greater control over politicians by society.

Kuttner (1997) argues that this new concept of stakeholding in the UK "splits the difference between the new individualism of the 1990s and the need for a more inclusionary or collectivist society ...

[attempting to] marry the fashionable rhetoric of the former with the practical politics of the latter" (1997, pp 32-3). However, Rustin (1997) reminds us of alternative understandings of the stakeholder public in the UK, citing the historical link between property and voting in the country, a link challenged by the idea of universal citizenship in the 1950s but then cleverly reversed by the Conservatives in the 1980s through the promotion of the Right to Buy, the privatisation of public services and the ambition to transform local government into a local 'company' in which residents became 'shareholders' (Adam Smith Institute, 1989).

Hirst (1994) opts for the collectivist position. His work on associationalism, "a mixture of social crusading by those 'haves' who care and the empowerment of the 'have nots'" (p 10), demonstrates the way in which he sees a 'stakeholder public' operating. For Hirst, "associationalism makes accountable representative democracy possible again by limiting the scope of state administration, without diminishing social provision. It enables market-based societies to deliver the substantive goals desired by coordinative and regulatory institutions" while the "concept of the governance of social affairs through voluntary associations can enable groups to build their own social worlds in civil society ... and compete politically by soliciting the voluntary choices of individuals" (1994, pp 12-13).

Once elected New Labour made some attempt, formally at least, to deliver on the kind of inclusionary stakeholding that Kuttner describes. While use of the language of 'stakeholding' was short-lived New Labour utilised a 'stakeholder public' discourse in its programmes for democratic and civil renewal. Decentralisation became a popular vehicle again, mirroring similar developments in other countries of the northern and southern hemispheres, such as 'interactive governance' in the Netherlands, where the direct participation of citizens and other stakeholders in decision making is often combined with a neighbourhood approach (Denters and Klok, 2005). In England this commitment to decentralisation is articulated in government ambitions to devolve power and control from Whitehall to the regions, localities and even neighbourhoods (ODPM, 2006). It is also evident among local authorities and their partners who are developing new area-based institutions that involve the public as 'stakeholders' in local governance (Sullivan and Howard, 2005).

'Responsible public' discourse

The 'responsible public' discourse emphasises the role of individuals and groups in owing a duty to others and to the state in their conduct. Informed both by the communitarian movement in the US and the development of New Right ideas about personal liberty and responsibility in the UK, the 'responsible public' discourse acknowledges the vital importance of family and civil society in fostering reciprocal relationships between individuals and groups. It also highlights the importance of self-governing, although this can be expressed in different ways: as self-discipline at an individual level, as communities governing themselves through the institutionalisation of accepted rules and norms, and/or as the relationship of individuals and communities with instruments of the state, regulated by commonly accepted standards and codes of conduct.

One manifestation of the 'responsible public' discourse emerged in the 1980s with the UK Conservative government's promotion of the term 'active citizens' to mean individuals acting philanthropically and generating links and resources between themselves underpinned by a legitimate self-interest. The Conservative notion of 'active citizens' focused on two particular features – as taxpayers, citizens had a right to demand value for money from their local authorities and other public service providers and to hold them to account on this basis; and as responsible individuals, citizens were obliged to engage in self-help, to take responsibility for themselves, their property and their families. In the US there was little tolerance for the idea that some may not be able to take responsibility for themselves; instead the debate was constructed in terms of those who wilfully chose not to be responsible. This position was powerfully articulated by Murray (1990) who argued that the consequence of this in the US was the emergence of an 'underclass', and this argument had some resonance with commentators in the UK.

In the 1980s in the UK the 'responsible public' discourse supported the development of particular Conservative policies including the drive for private health insurance and education. The discourse also informed the Conservatives' approach to other public priorities, for example, emphasising the role of residents in Neighbourhood Watch schemes as a contribution to community safety (Gilling, 1997). For Gyford, this interpretation of the responsible public discourse may also have proved useful for the state as "the public confined to individual roles may be easier to handle than the public as actual or potential groups making organised demands and intruding as a political force into the policy making process" (1991, p 184).

By contrast, the Left's orientation to a 'responsible public' was borne out of a perception of citizenship as more social, with bonds arising from collective action in communities. This was influenced by the work of communitarians such as Etzioni (1998) and latterly via the interpretation of communitarian thinking for the British context by Tam. He equated communitarianism with inclusive communities that "are to be distinguished from other forms of community by their operative power relations, which enable all their members to participate in collective processes affecting their lives" (Tam, 1998, p 8, quoted in Taylor, 2003, p 39). This prescription proved attractive to those outside government and informed the development of community self-governing initiatives, such as that in Balsall Heath in Birmingham (Atkinson, 1994).

Echoes of the communitarian approach are apparent in the policy programmes of New Labour, although the language of communitarianism was quickly dropped. In the early work of the Social Exclusion Unit and latterly in the Home Office's programme for civil renewal led by David Blunkett (2003), the importance of self-discipline, family life, strong communities and a relationship based on rights and responsibilities with the state are all apparent. According to Barnes et al (2004a) the role of public participation in the civil renewal agenda is both to stimulate the emergence of active citizens and to help generate stronger and more cohesive communities.

Active citizens are those who are ready and prepared to take on the obligations of citizenship by contributing directly or indirectly to the good governance of their communities. Different levels of support may be needed to enable 'hard to reach' groups, refugee communities and others to take on these obligations, but there is a clear assumption inherent in the civil renewal agenda that acceptance of these obligations is non-negotiable.

The generation of stronger and (crucially) more cohesive communities is to be achieved through the exercise of collective action within and between communities. Much collective action will be built around assumed shared interests within a locality, but it could also be based in identities as members of a specific ethnic or faith group. Working collectively, it is argued, will enable the breaking down of suspicion between different cultures. Thus while ethnic and faith groups might be a basis for collective action, the expectation is that such groups will work for cohesion, and in order to reveal shared values, rather than to strengthen separate identities.

The state has a (largely facilitative) role to play in the creation of active citizens and cohesive communities by providing education for citizenship, by supporting the building of community capacity, by acting to overcome barriers that divide communities and by developing an evidence base of 'what works' that can be shared widely. However, Driver and Martell (1997) have criticised New Labour's approach, arguing that it identifies with a "conditional, morally prescriptive, conservative and individual communitarianism, rather than a less conditional and redistributional, social-economic, progressive and corporate communitarianism" (cited in Taylor, 2003, p 40). While more recent developments in the civil renewal agenda do allow for the emergence of a more collective and state-supported communitarianism, other initiatives, such as the high priority given to initiatives such as Anti-social Behaviour Orders, continue to reflect a much harder edge to the civil renewal agenda and the expectations of a 'responsible public' than some on the Left may have anticipated.

It is possible to link each of the four discourses to different elements of policy that contribute to New Labour's approach to public participation. This is potentially problematic as the discourses are not necessarily complementary but may generate tensions should they be deployed together. For example, the 'empowered public' and the 'stakeholder public' both emphasise the role of the collective, while the 'consuming public' focuses primarily on the individual, and the 'responsible public' provides coverage of both. Each discourse claims a different role for the state, with the 'empowered public' and the 'stakeholder public' identifying the state as having significant involvement in generating public participation, compared to the 'consuming public' and the 'responsible public' discourses that envisage a lesser role for the state. Power relationships between the state and the citizen need to be challenged in the 'empowered public' and the 'stakeholder public' discourses, while they rarely feature in the 'consuming public' and the 'responsible public' discourses. In three out of the four discourses decentralisation is a potentially important strategy for realising public participation, while in the 'consuming public' discourse it is largely irrelevant. Similarly while three out of the four discourses have universal application, the 'empowered public' discourse is very deliberately aimed at particular disadvantaged or marginalised publics. Finally the discourses also contain normative implications for the kind of democracy that would best suit them. For example, the 'empowered public' and the 'consumer public' assume the operation of a system of representative democracy. However, versions of the 'stakeholder public' and 'responsible public' (communitarianism) discourses suggest the possibility of an alternative system of participatory democracy.

Consequently it is likely that in practice different discourses will dominate at different points in time and in different policy areas. In the next section this is explored in relation to New Labour's programme for public participation.

New Labour and public participation

The perceived inadequacy of the Conservatives' individualised conceptualisation of citizens as consumers led to an emphasis, in the latter years of the 20th century, on the responsibilities of citizens to contribute to creating their own and others' welfare (Barnes and Prior, 2000). This position was developed under the New Labour administration that took power in 1997. It promoted a broader interpretation of citizenship (as multi- rather than uni-dimensional) and emphasised the role of public participation in local governance as a means of developing a more involved and responsible local citizenship. The aim of public participation was to create a 'virtuous circle' whereby participation in specific local initiatives led to increased levels of public interest in, involvement with and influence over local affairs. In contrast to the Conservatives' attempted 'managerialisation' of local politics, New Labour promoted the local arena as a space for democratic renewal, urging local agencies to experiment with new forms of public engagement and deliberation, to contribute to the building of responsive and accountable governance across the board (DETR, 1998).

Objectives, purposes and discourses

In practice public participation initiatives were directed at supporting the achievement of the government's overarching objectives of improving local services and outcomes and achieving democratic renewal (DETR, 1998). Barnes et al (2004a) identified multiple purposes associated with the promotion of public participation in relation to these objectives. These and the linkages with the four public participation discourses are described in the table below and explored further in the following text.

Public participation in the improvement of local services is dominated by the 'consumer public' and 'stakeholder public' discourses. This is exemplified by the introduction of 'Best Value' in local government, described as a "duty that local authorities ... owe to local people". Best Value in services was intended to be secured via the active

Table 2.1: Objectives, purposes and discourses of public participation

Government objectives	Public participation purposes	Dominant official discourse(s)
Improved services	Improving the responsiveness of public services and outcomes for service users both collectively and individually	Consumer/ stakeholder publics
	Enabling services to be designed and delivered by community organisations and/or 'local people'	Empowered public
Improved outcomes	Reducing social exclusion	Empowered public
	Achieving social order and social cohesion	Responsible public
	Improving health and reducing health inequalities	Empowered public
Democratic renewal: Institutional	Improving the quality and legitimacy of decisions in government, health services, local government and other public bodies	Stakeholder public
	Removing or reducing the 'democratic deficit' evidenced by low turnout in parliamentary, local and European elections	Stakeholder/ responsible publics
Democratic renewal: Individual/ community	Generating 'positive freedom', civic virtues, mutuality and trust	Stakeholder/ responsible publics
	Building community capacity and empowerment	Empowered public
	Building individual skills and capacity	Empowered/ responsible publics

involvement of citizens (as taxpayers, business people, service users and community representatives) in reviewing local services and considering alternative means of delivery – including partnerships. The role of public participation here was as a means of raising standards and ensuring the best possible fit between local services and local needs, although the capacity of Best Value to achieve this in practice has been disputed (Martin and Davis, 2001). The same principle lay behind the government's promotion of patient and public involvement initiatives in the NHS. Here particular mechanisms were introduced to 'improve the experience of patients' in the NHS, including PALs. At the same time the wider public was identified as having a legitimate voice in the operation of the health service. Consequently patient and public health forums were established in NHS trusts, local health services became subject to 'scrutiny' by local authorities on behalf of the wider population and places were reserved for 'lay' representatives on the governing bodies of the new foundation hospitals (DH, 2004).

While some public participation initiatives focused on a single policy area or service, drawing on the citizen's expertise as a consumer, such as the development of tenants' compacts within social housing, other initiatives were oriented towards service improvement across policy domains within a given geographical area. For example, the Neighbourhood Management Pathfinder initiative focused on 'joining up' local services within a locality via the appointment of a neighbourhood manager supported by a board comprised of local residents, voluntary representatives, local professionals and others, all of whom were considered to have a stake in the delivery of locally appropriate services (SEU, 2001). Here the lived experience of citizens in that neighbourhood was what qualified them to sit as legitimate members of the neighbourhood management board.

In addition to being involved in the decision-making process, public participation initiatives have developed to include the promotion of 'social entrepreneurship' where services can be delivered directly by citizens themselves through community organisations. Evident mainly in localities targeted for regeneration, this option has also been taken up by service user groups in relation to particular services, for example, tenant management organisations. In both cases the dominant discourse is that of the 'empowered public'.

New Labour also conceived of a role for public participation in the achievement of improved local outcomes that might require additional interventions beyond the delivery of mainstream services, for example in relation to the tackling of policy concerns that were beyond the purview of a single organisation, but required concerted action from a range of public and possibly private, voluntary and community organisations. At a strategic level such interventions included the duty placed on local authorities to develop an overarching community strategy identifying the key long-term priorities for the local area, and the Local Strategic Partnership (LSP), a cross-sector, multiagency grouping of the key strategic players in the locality brought together in order to better 'join up' local policies and programmes. In both cases it was expected that the deliberations and decision making would be informed by the public in their role as governance stakeholders, and specific mechanisms had to be developed to secure this participation.

In addition a range of 'special projects' known as area-based initiatives (ABIs) were established by New Labour. These were targeted at geographical areas that were experiencing significant levels of deprivation or inequality. While varied both in scale and scope ABIs held in common the need to involve the public in the development and delivery of their interventions. In the case of Sure Start (an initiative aimed at improving the life chances of children aged 0-4) public participation was centred on the engagement of parents, while in the New Deal for Communities Programme (small area regeneration focusing on crime, education, worklessness, health and environment), public participation embraced anyone resident in the local area (DETR, 1998, 1999a 1999b). The 'empowered public' discourse sits alongside the 'responsible public' discourse in many ABIs, as the emphasis is both on helping communities to help themselves, accompanied by an expectation that communities acknowledge their responsibility to help themselves.

Finally public participation was central to New Labour's ambition to renew democracy in localities. Enhanced public participation – the more frequent and deeper engagement of citizens – was seen as contributing to 'greater democratic legitimacy' for elected local authorities, allowing them to develop their potential as 'community leaders' within the context of partnership approaches to local delivery. There were institutional and 'public' dimensions to this aspect of the reform agenda. Early initiatives focused on the institutional via the development of innovations in voting, such as the extension of postal voting and experiments with alternative sites for polling booths. There were also reforms to local government institutions. Here, while New Labour determined the parameters of reform, it hoped to encourage the public to play an active part in deciding the specific shape of reform in its locality. For instance, local authorities were required under the 2000 Local Government Act to consult with citizens over new arrangements for councillor decision making (for example, the introduction of a directly elected mayor). Local authorities were also given the discretion to develop 'sub-local' institutional arrangements, such as area committees or area forums, as a way of bringing decision making closer to the public and offering new opportunities to become involved in local deliberations. These developments played to both a 'stakeholder public' discourse (for example, through devolving influence over decisions) and a 'responsible public' discourse (for example, through emphasising the duties attached to citizenship).

In addition to developing new ways in which citizens exercised 'voice' in the democratic process, work on democratic renewal also focused on building the capacity of citizens and communities to take advantage of new opportunities to exercise 'voice' and 'choice'. Early interventions emerged as part of the National Strategy for Neighbourhood Renewal (NSNR) and included the establishment of the Community Empowerment Network (CEN) and the Community Empowerment Fund (CEF), both of which were designed to enable community organisations and groups to engage with and influence the workings of the LSP (SEU, 2001).

Subsequent initiatives included the Russell Commission's National Framework for Youth Action and Engagement' (2005), which outlined an approach to reinvigorating volunteering in the 21st century, the Active Learning for Active Citizenship initiative that sought to build on the citizen education programme under way in schools by extending it to the wider public and communities, and the Together We Can initiative that aimed to support the development of capacity within communities and within government to enable the two sides to work together more productively to achieve shared outcomes. The importance of this capacity building element to the New Labour programme has been a consistent theme since 1997. Its significance is evidenced in the recent review of capacity building by the Home Office (Home Office, 2004) which identified 22 major policy reforms across six government departments, all of which contributed to/relied on community capacity. These initiatives all display elements of both the 'empowered public' discourse and the 'responsible public' discourse.

As suggested by the above discussion, the four discourses of public participation cut across New Labour's reform programme in complex ways. They also operate at different scalar levels, an important factor in a multilevel governance environment.

Multilevel governance can be defined as "negotiated, non-hierarchical exchanges between institutions at the transnational, national, regional and local levels ... [which] do not have to operate through intermediary levels but can take place directly between, say the transnational and regional levels, thus bypassing the state level" (Peters and Pierre, 2001, p 132). In the UK the central state played an important role in relation to multilevel governance most obviously through New Labour's establishment of sub-national institutions such as the Scottish Parliament and Welsh Assembly. In England it introduced a sub-local dimension via its focus on urban regeneration through targeted neighbourhood action (see Chapter Six). This proved significant in the development of public participation and early initiatives reflected the 'empowered public' and 'stakeholder public' discourses (Sullivan, 2001d, 2002). The neighbourhood obtained a higher profile with the publication of *Citizen engagement and public services: Why neighbourhoods matter* (ODPM/HO, 2005). This document outlined a role for neighbourhoods in securing responsive and appropriate public services and it reflected the discourses of the 'consumer public' and 'responsible public' in its proposals. It paid close attention to the role of community leaders – emphasising that neighbourhood developments should work with the democratic processes of local government, but it also emphasised the contribution of other public and private bodies in the process of neighbourhood renewal.

New Labour's focus on public participation has attracted a number of critiques. One concerns the implications of broadening and deepening public involvement in governance on representative democracy. While it is now widely accepted that representative democracy is insufficient as a means of reconnecting citizens with governing institutions (Stoker, 1996; Lowndes and Sullivan, 2004) and the development of more participative activities, particularly at the local level, is plentiful and increasing (ODPM, 2002), there remain important unresolved tensions in this policy agenda. At one level these are practical tensions about how decisions should be made, for example how to reconcile the recommendations emerging from participative processes with the formal decision-making mechanisms of representative democracy (Stoker, 1996). However, at another level, the increase and intensity of public participation in local governance might suggest the existence of more normative tensions pertaining to the kind of local democratic system that is desired, for example the promotion of a participatory rather than representative democracy (Pratchett, 1999).

Another important critique relates to the way in which New Labour sought to overcome social exclusion by building capacity within communities to enable them to better help themselves. 'Social capital' became shorthand for what that capacity could be. A relationship-oriented concept focusing on levels of civic engagement, it pointed to the ways in which the norms of reciprocity and trust developed in civic relationships could create the capacity among citizens for collective action and expectations of responsive government (Putnam, 2000). The New Deal for Communities Programme introduced by New Labour in 1998 identified the development of social capital as centrally linked to its success (DETR, 1999b). However, for Lowndes and Wilson (2001) the development of social capital may be compromised by the limits of the institutional framework, for example if decision-making structures and processes remain impervious to citizen views. Therefore it is important to examine the extent to which the institutional context acts to facilitate or constrain the development of social capital within communities (see Chapter Four).

Public participation in practice

There is little doubt that the reform programme and orientation of New Labour has facilitated an upsurge in the focus on, and activity in relation to, public participation. The range of initiatives described in the previous section gives some indication of the way in which public participation has become an accepted part of public policy and public services. This is perhaps best exemplified in the breadth and depth of public participation activity under way in local authorities. Surveys commissioned by central government in 1998 and 2002 have shown a rapid increase in both the volume and range of non-electoral participation initiatives used by local government – whether of a traditional form (public meetings, consultation documents), or a 'consumerist' type (such as questionnaires and focus groups), or a more innovative nature (such as interactive websites or citizens' juries) (Lowndes et al, 1998; ODPM, 2002). Each local authority uses an average of 10.5 different participation initiatives, and it is estimated that 14 million people took part in such exercises during 2001 (ODPM, 2002). However, as Wilson (1999) has pointed out, more participation does not necessarily equate to more democracy and, in relation to public participation initiatives more widely, closer examination is needed to determine their impact on services, outcomes and democratic renewal.

Available evidence is mixed[1]. A recent study for the Active Citizenship Centre (Rogers and Robinson, 2004) reviewed the evidence of the benefits of community engagement for community safety, health, education, employment, housing, regeneration and local government. Its coverage was broader than that of New Labour's terms in office, although many of its examples were from 1997 onwards. The study found positive examples of the benefits of community engagement in relation to each of the areas studied. Some of these examples formed part of the mainstream of service or policy delivery, such as tenant participation 'compacts' in housing and the role of school governors in education. Elsewhere, examples of good practice were the exception rather than the norm, for example the use of citizens' juries in informing health services and the development of Local Exchange Trading Systems (LETS) in supporting local entrepreneurship. The study concluded that "*at its best*, community engagement can empower citizens; make a significant difference to the way services are designed and run and secure widely valued policy outcomes" (2004, p 7; emphasis added). Evidence from other research and evaluations suggests that ensuring that public participation operates 'at its best' is no easy matter and that very often attempts at public participation do not influence services and outcomes in the way participants wished (see, for example, Burton et al, 2004 and Barnes et al, 2005).

A variety of reasons are given for this mismatch in intention and outcome. Chanan (2003), in his review of community involvement and urban policy for the Office of the Deputy Prime Minister (ODPM) identified what he terms the 'ambiguity' that surrounds the aims, purposes and targets linked to community involvement as a fundamental limiting factor. This is endorsed by the findings from the national evaluation of LSPs, which, in its examination of LSP–neighbourhood relationships found that the "purpose of LSPs' engagement with 'sub-localities' and neighbourhoods is frequently ill-defined. At its most general, interaction is concerned with enhancing public involvement in the workings of the LSP, usually through the engagement of voluntary and community groups. The rationale for promoting enhanced public involvement can be about ensuring that different view points are represented in LSP deliberations and/or that the decisions arrived at by the LSP are somehow 'better' as a result of this public involvement" (Sullivan and Howard, 2005, p 39).

Barnes et al (2005), in their study of community involvement in Health Action Zones (HAZs) (an ABI seeking to improve health and reduce health inequalities through partnership and community-based interventions) found that despite instances of 'good practice', overall the impact of the public on the workings of the HAZ was limited as the public had little influence where it really mattered, over the strategic direction of HAZ, partly because the attention of the HAZ was drawn upwards rather than outwards, and,

> HAZ became more of a top-down initiative than initial hopes and aspirations might have suggested. Priorities were set centrally in a way that was not originally anticipated; the need to respond to changes in the structure of the NHS and other policy and governance initiatives meant that more energy was expended in negotiating the place of HAZ in the context of the statutory system than in establishing community objectives and priorities. (Barnes et al, 2005, p112)

The LSP evaluation drew attention to the issue of infrastructure and resourcing, identifying this as a key factor in enabling effective engagement from among the community and voluntary sectors (ODPM/DfT, 2006). These findings support those of Taylor et al (2005) and the National Audit Office (2004), whose research into the workings of the Community Participation Programme (CPP) both concluded that the existence of a separate, discrete source of funding for community sector engagement was a vital part of the infrastructure necessary to secure effective public participation. The CPP was subsequently absorbed into a larger 'Safer and Stronger Communities Fund' by the Home Office.

Taylor (2003) considered the role of public servants in creating the conditions for public participation to flourish, suggesting that they can present important obstacles through their practiced resistance to change and the perpetuation of doing what they have always done. The consequences of this institutional inertia on public participation is explored in our case studies, and the important contribution that professionals can make to opening up as well as closing down opportunities for deliberation in public participation initiatives, is highlighted.

Two common issues emerge from the findings of these research and evaluation activities that endorse the conclusion drawn by Gaventa (2004) (see the introduction to this chapter): first, that citizens need to be willing and able to participate, and second, that public bodies need to be prepared to do what is necessary to make the most of the potential of public participation including addressing institutional inertia and tackling the power relationship between public bodies and public participants (Jones, 2002; Rogers and Robinson, 2004; Lowndes et al, 2006). It is this interface that forms the substance of the case studies in Chapters Five to Eight of this volume.

Conclusion

This chapter has explored the context within which public participation has become at once more important and more difficult to achieve. Focusing on the UK, but with reference to the experiences of other democracies in the northern and southern hemispheres, it has tried to explain the urgency of purpose that underpins governmental initiatives to reinvigorate democratic practice through public participation. In their attempts to re-engage the public with the institutions of governance, governments and state agencies have developed a number of official discourses of public participation. These conceptualise the relationship between the citizen and the state in different ways and propose distinctive strategies and practices for public participation. In the remainder of this book we will be exploring how those different discourses inform the public participation practice under way in localities.

New Labour's own programme of public participation draws on all of these discourses of the public, even though in practice these discourses may not prove complementary. Through the cases that provide the empirical basis for this book we will be able to better understand how participation practices relate to different discourses within New Labour policies, and where the points of complementarity and tension arise.

Finally the implications of recent research and evaluation findings about the fate of New Labour's public participation interventions suggest that institutional resistance effectively limits any meaningful exchange taking place between the public and relevant government bodies, and ultimately prevents any wholesale transformation of local outcomes. Through the cases presented in this book we will be able to examine the nature of institutional resistance, explore the link between institutional resistance and the quality of exchange and follow through the consequences of local exchanges on the emerging outcomes.

But before we turn to a detailed discussion of public participation in practice, as evidenced in our case studies, in Chapters Three and Four we explore some of the more theoretical approaches to understanding the nature and dynamics of such participation. In Chapter Three we focus on ways in which ideas about more participative approaches to public policy making have been framed and consider how this relates to autonomous action among community and user groups and social movements. In Chapter Four we consider the way in which notions of 'the public' have been constructed and shaped participation, and also what shapes the way in which the 'rules of the game' of participation are determined.

Note

[1] Studies also focus their attention in a variety of linked but different ways, for example, on public participation, community involvement, voluntary and community sector engagement.

THREE

Inclusive democracy and social movements

In Chapter Two we discussed the way in which the discourse of public participation has evolved within public policy in the UK and beyond, and described the way in which the practice of participation has developed in relation to this. In this chapter we consider other influences on these processes of democratisation. First, we discuss how concerns about the way in which public services are managed and governed, and about the decline of political participation through voting, have led to an advocacy of more deliberative forms of politics and policy making as key elements of modern governance (for example, Newman, 2001). Second, we discuss the move to more inclusive forms of politics and decision making that have derived from autonomous action among community, identity and user groups. We discuss the significance of social movement theory in understanding such action, and relate this to conceptualisations of social justice as requiring recognition as well as redistribution (for example, Young, 1990, 2000; Fraser, 1997). This body of literature is also helpful in considering the extent to which new opportunities for public participation represent processes of empowerment or incorporation.

Governance, participation and deliberative democracy

We begin by relating theories of deliberative democracy to ideas about changes in the nature of governance. The focus here is on the process of decision making – how should policy decisions be reached in advanced democracies and what does this imply for the way in which public involvement in policy making should be designed?

From a governance perspective, opening up decision making about public policies and services to wider influence is seen as a means both of improving the legitimacy of decisions and enhancing the responsiveness of the services that are provided. Action to secure user and public involvement has been prompted by evidence of loss of faith in formal politics and evidence of declining trust in public services (Barnes and Prior, 1996; Coulson, 1998), and is also driven by more positive commitments to public accountability based on consent achieved through public discourse (Ranson and Stewart, 1994). As we saw in Chapter Two, a wide range of purposes and aspirations are suggested for improving public participation in public services. Such participation is perceived to offer a solution to diverse ills affecting the public realm and to be capable of producing positive outcomes for the participants themselves.

The normative assumptions underpinning more participative approaches to policy decision making are that such decisions will be both better and be seen to be more legitimate if they draw on lay knowledge based in personal experience as well as on the expert knowledge of professionals and other public officials. This is particularly the case in complex and diverse societies in which 'expertise' is widely distributed and social and cultural differences generate multiple perspectives on public policy issues.

Different commentators highlight different aspects of the dilemma facing democracy in complex societies. For example, Dietz (1995) focuses on the impact of *technological development*: "However sound the democratic tradition, it is under pressure in the contemporary world. One source of pressure is the power of science and technology to change the world. We can produce changes that are not easily related to the daily experience of most people and thus not linked to our moral sense. Most of us lack the moral context to understand the implications of artificial life, genetic engineering or other new technologies and thus have trouble making informed ethical judgments about them" (Dietz, 1995, p xviii)[1]. Gutmann and Thompson (1996) also emphasise the *moral* context for decision making about issues of public policy and the necessity for finding ways of reaching agreement in conditions where conflicts about fundamental values exist. These conflicts could relate to technological innovations, but, as Gutmann and Thompson illustrate, also concern issues such as abortion, Income Support, surrogate motherhood and waste disposal. Another focus for those arguing for more participative approaches to policy making is the perceived *expansion of government* (including the service delivery arm of government) into all aspects of people's lives and the accompanying processes of bureaucratisation that render individuals powerless to control their own affairs.

Responses to these dilemmas take different forms. Hirst (1994, 1997b) argues for what he terms 'associative democracy', which he claims "offers a principle of administrative renewal, a way of restoring the ideal of committed public service in the face of widespread bureaucratic failure and retreat" (1994, p 6). He outlines a welfare system based on associational principles in which service provision would be by voluntary, self-governing organisations, which are themselves partnerships between the providers and recipients of the service. Linked to this are proposals intended to counteract the 'atrophied' nature of representative democracy (1997, p 29) and the failure of both economic liberalism and collectivism. In relation to the political system Hirst argues that political authority should be decentralised and become pluralistic. The building blocks of democracy for Hirst would be groups into which individuals enter on the basis of voluntary association and which would not only replace the state as the providers of welfare services (residential care, hospitals, schools, etc), but also, because of their internal democratic structures, form the basis on which social affairs are organised and individuals are able to exercise influence.

But the analysis that has most influenced the development of more participative forms of governance is based on what is known as 'deliberative democracy'. Stewart (1999) discussed examples of practical developments based on this approach within local government, while Coote and Lenaghan (1997), Davie et al (1998) and Barnes (1999b) have addressed similar initiatives in the health service. Deliberative democracy is claimed to have both political and educative purposes. It is concerned not only with creating a more active participative democracy, but also a more informed citizenry who are better able to engage with the complex issues that form the substance of policy making. It aims to bring decision making out of the hidden back rooms in which bargaining takes place between interest groups, and enable 'ordinary citizens' to engage in dialogue with both the issues and the decision makers. Dryzek (1990) contrasts liberal notions of democracy, which are associated with voting, strategy, private interests, bargaining, exchange, spectacle and limited involvement with participatory modes of democracy that emphasise a politics that is discursive, educational, oriented to truly public interest and "needful of active citizenship" (Dryzek, 1990, p 13). Fishkin (1991) suggests that the closer a democracy gets to the ideal of deliberation at every level within the political process the more complete it is.

Deliberative democracy and its critics

Deliberative democracy advocates argue it can generate a stronger democracy with citizens empowered in relation to both politicians *and* public officials. The practice of deliberative democracy is intended to open knowledge previously restricted to specific scientific or other communities to lay scrutiny, as well as to open up political arenas to

more direct processes of citizen involvement. For example, citizens'
juries and related deliberative practices have been held on issues such
as genetic technology (Dunkerley and Glasner, 1998); waste disposal
(Petts, 1997, 2001); the future of agriculture and the food system
(Wakeford, 1999); as well as a range of policy issues facing local
government and the NHS (LGMB, 1996; Coote and Lenaghan, 1997;
McIver, 1997; Barnes, 1999). In each case 'experts' are required to
present evidence to lay people who can question, challenge and dispute
the basis on which this is used to reach policy decisions. And lay
people can also deliberate among themselves, drawing on their own
'ordinary wisdom' (Davie et al, 1998) to suggest issues that the experts
may not have considered, as well as factors that might indicate why
the *technically* preferable solution may not be the *democratically* preferred
solution to policy problems. Underlying such initiatives is the belief
that technical or expert knowledge alone is inadequate to the resolution
of policy problems, since the issues such problems raise are also political
and ethical. Renn et al (1993) developed a conceptual model for
participatory decision making that integrates three types of knowledge:
"knowledge based on common sense and personal experience;
knowledge based on technical expertise, and knowledge derived from
social interests and advocacy" (p 190). Exactly how such an integration
happens, including whether it takes place within or between groups
of citizens and 'experts', depends on the precise model being used
(Stewart, 1999).

Deliberative democracy advocates have argued that a process of
rational debate among equals is required if the potential of such models
is to be realised (for example, Fishkin, 1991). The priority accorded to
rationality as a basis on which administrative systems should be built
was accompanied by an objectivist basis for scientific method that
continues to define the way in which evidence is judged in the context
of evidence-based policy making (Nutley and Webb, 2000). The
theoretical underpinning of deliberative democracy derives from
Habermas's work on *communicative rationality* (1984, 1990). As a critical
theorist Habermas's work had a political as well as theoretical objective.
He was interested not only in how the state could improve the
legitimacy of its decision making, but also in how the dominance of
scientific rationality in the organisation of society could be challenged.
'Communicative' rationality was considered to have such a potential
through the development of practices enabling different ways of
knowing to communicate with each other and thus enhance the
potential for cooperation between people. Habermas argued that such
practices require free and equal participation in the public sphere in a

deliberation about socio-political or practical issues. Such participation in turn demands communicative competence: "*Communicative competence* is the ability to use language (more precisely speech acts) to create understanding and agreement (Habermas, 1970), that is to communicate rationally" (quoted in Webler, 1995, p 44). Webler goes on to specify four elements to communicative competence: "*cognitive competence* – the ability of an individual to master the rules of formal logic; *speech competence* – mastery of linguistic rules; *pragmatic competence* – mastery of pragmatic rules; and *role competence* – mastery of rules for interaction" (Webler, 1995, p 44). Habermas prescribes a series of conditions for this deliberative form of communication, designed to promote the use of reason in argument. These require that anyone who is competent to speak and act is allowed to take part in the process of deliberation; that all those taking part in the process of deliberation are allowed to introduce any assertion they wish to make and to question any assertion made by others; all are allowed to express their attitudes and wishes; and no speaker should be prevented from exercising those rights – either as a result of internal or external pressure.

More critical analysts have argued that this deliberative ideal cannot be achieved because it is not possible to assume that power relations can be excluded from deliberative processes. For example, both Nancy Fraser (1997) and Iris Marion Young (2000) have argued that simply 'bracketing' power – assuming that power can be overcome by speech alone – is insufficient to guard against inhibitions on speaking that are due to dominant attitudes towards *styles* of speech, which are often integral to social identities. This does not mean that they dismiss the objective of enabling more inclusive forms of democracy, but rather argue that this cannot be achieved solely on the basis of enabling public argument. Indeed, Young argues for the importance of democratic practices that increase the chances that people will move from positions based in self-interest to those that are more likely to deliver social justice as a result of having to listen directly to others whose positions and circumstances are different from their own. This notion of *transforming* views, rather than simply aggregating preferences (as happens in voting) is central to the concept of deliberative democracy. But Young notes that more attention has been given to what she calls the *external* factors that can exclude people from taking part in decision making about matters that concern them, than to the *internal* processes that can also exclude: "... the terms of discourse make assumptions some do not share, the interaction privileges specific styles of expression, the participation of some people is dismissed as out of order" (2000, p 53).

Young suggests that assuming that deliberation has to be based solely in *reason* – which is usually defined as neutral and dispassionate, and conducted solely through rational argument – will exclude many people. She argues instead for the importance of recognising and valuing other styles of speech in deliberative processes and identifies greeting, rhetoric and storytelling as modes of speech that are excluded by deliberative theorists. For example, the concept of 'greeting' or public acknowledgement is absent in those cases where individuals or groups who have tried to make claims in public forums have found themselves ignored, stereotyped or otherwise insulted; while telling individual stories of experiences (narrating) can often be dismissed as 'mere anecdotes' rather than valid evidence. Our own and others' experience of initiatives to secure the involvement of, for example, older people and mental health service users clearly demonstrates the way in which storytelling can be dismissed and de-legitimised as a basis on which to draw conclusions about policy and service issues (Church, 1996; Barnes, 2004). Rhetoric, a committed and passionate attempt to persuade others, is usually regarded as aiming to manipulate rather than to reflect a genuine expression of the emotional meaning and content of the position being represented. Young argues that situating deliberation, rhetoric, narrative and greeting in relation to one another provides a more sophisticated understanding of the elements that may be necessary to enable dialogue between citizens and public officials to take place in a way that is capable of generating alternative discourses and transforming policy making. Thompson and Hoggett (2001) have also argued that it is not possible to understand the process of deliberative democracy solely in terms of rational debate between free and equal citizens. They suggest it is equally important to address the issue of group emotions within deliberative forums such as citizens' juries. They argue that "This is a little understood area which nevertheless can have a powerful impact on democratic practices, since all groups, including those formed when people come together to deliberate, are characterised in part by emotional dynamics that threaten to undermine such deliberation" (Thompson and Hoggett, 2001, p 352).

The critiques of deliberative democracy offered by Fraser, Young and others alert us to the importance of including an understanding of the processes by which some publics come to be included within such participative policy making, while others may not be. We address the way in which publics are *constituted* for public participation in Chapter Four. Young's work highlights the importance of understanding the way in which assumptions about 'appropriate' ways of debating issues can serve to exclude those with different communication styles.

In the context of this discussion of different theoretical perspectives on participative or inclusive democracy it is also important to consider Anne Phillips' (1995) work, which distinguishes a politics of ideas from what she refers to as a 'politics of presence'. Phillips' work is mainly concerned with the principles and practices associated with elected assemblies and how to ensure that disadvantaged groups are fairly represented within them. However, her discussion of whether such representation requires the actual presence of such groups is also relevant to a consideration of deliberative democracy. Phillips notes that, although the projects of deliberative democracy and that of ensuring better representation of minorities and disadvantaged groups in elected assemblies share objectives of reducing political exclusion, they also run counter to each other on the issue of group interests. A key principle of deliberative democracy is that the process of deliberation can lead to transformation of views and opinions through exposure to other positions. Phillips notes: "Though the arguments for including previously excluded groups and perspectives are rarely couched solely in terms of representing group interest, this is inevitably one part of the whole. In some cases, this becomes the dominant concern, and it then runs up against a deep distaste among deliberative democrats for the politics based around interest" (1995, p 146). This distaste is related to the prioritisation of dispassionate argumentation over committed representation of a particular position or experience.

Iris Marion Young (2000) addresses this issue by distinguishing the basis on which a representative speaks on behalf of others. She acknowledges the impossibility that any representative can be identical to her constituents. She distinguishes three modes of representation: an individual can be represented according to interest, opinion and perspective. *Interest* refers to those things that are important to and affect the life prospects of individuals or goals of organisations, *opinions* refer to the values, principles and priorities held by a person, while *perspective* refers to the experience, history and social knowledge derived from their social positioning. This distinction is important in countering arguments that deliberative processes should explicitly avoid including participants because they have particular perspectives on the issue in question that derive from lived experiences.

A rather different perspective on deliberation in policy making comes from postmodern and social constructionist approaches to public policy (for example, Fischer, 2003; Hajer and Wagenaar, 2003). This work derives from critiques of policy making as the search for technocratic solutions to policy problems. It recognises that not only are social values central to the policy process, but that the process of policy making itself needs to be understood as a dialogic process in which it is less a question of reviewing evidence than negotiating meanings, seeking control over meanings and constructing policies on the basis of this. We can see the effect of this in a number of policy contexts. For example, Jock Young (1999) discusses the way in which certain groups and individuals become 'demonised': black muggers, drug addicts, child murderers; and how this affects thinking and policy in relation to crime (see also Chapter Four). This perspective suggests a way of undertaking policy analysis, as well as a way of thinking about how 'the public' may be engaged in the process of policy making. It questions the way in which policy questions are constructed, the theoretical assumptions that underpin such constructions and the role of discourse in framing the way in which 'allowable alternatives' may be included in policy debate. Fischer suggests that this approach to policy analysis is capable of representing a broader range of interests than those of bureaucratic decision makers: "Part of this is done by emphasizing political choice and citizen participation. It is also done by examining and clarifying the ways in which people's interests are discursively constructed, how they come to hold specific interests. Towards this end, the focus has to include an analysis of the often distorted nature of political communication in Western societies" (2003, p 15). He also suggests that this approach can go beyond analysis to help "decision makers and citizens develop alternatives that speak to their own needs and interests rather than those defined and shaped for them by others" (Fischer, 2003, p 15). This, he suggests, can help promote public discussion.

One example of the way in which this approach to policy analysis has been applied is Sevenhuijsen's application of a feminist ethic of care to an analysis of social policies (for example, Sevenhuijsen, 1998, 2003a, 2003b). Locating her argument within an ideal of active citizenship and a "notion of the public sphere as a special location for beginning new things by acting together" (2003a, p 180), Sevenhuijsen argues for an integration of 'daily care' into democratic practices through which decisions about public services are made. But in addition to offering this as a perspective on the *processes* of policy making, Sevenhuijsen has developed an analytical approach through which policy can be subjected to a discursive analysis that reveals the normative paradigms underpinning it. She notes that such paradigms "confer power upon certain speaking positions and vocabularies, and are thereby instrumental in producing hegemonic discourses, in including and excluding certain modes of speaking" (2003b, p 2).

Yanow (2003) offers another perspective on this approach to policy analysis that is relevant to our argument in this book. She suggests that it is important to understand not only different values and the way in which they affect the way public policies will be evaluated, but also to understand beliefs and feelings. She illustrates this by referring to a study in which different North American 'race'-ethnic groups were surveyed about their views of nursing home care for elderly relatives. Some groups had no conceptual framework within which to understand the questions as they took it for granted that elderly relatives are cared for at home until death. "The analyst anticipates that the policy would mean different things to different policy-relevant publics, and the first step is to begin to identify those different communities of meaning to discover what the policy means for each group.... The policy analyst might recommend that the decision-maker call a public forum on the matter or take some other action to discuss the issues publicly before she decides what action to take" (Yanow, 2003, p 235). Yanow uses the term 'local knowledge' to refer to "the very mundane, but still expert, understanding of and practical reasoning about local conditions derived from lived experience" (p 236).

Deliberative and representative democracy

A key dilemma in relation to both the theory and practice of deliberative and other forms of participative governance is the relationship between such practices and representative democracy – an issue raised in Chapter Two. Representative democracy developed because of the impossibility of enabling all citizens to take part directly in decision making. Elected representatives are intended to act on behalf of citizens and to be accountable to them. If other forums are created in which citizens are engaged directly with public officials to deliberate on policy issues and to come forward with proposals for action, what authority do such proposals carry vis-à-vis those that come from elected representatives? As Rao et al note: "Liberal democracy is founded on the process of representation, yet at the same time it postulates an active, participating citizen. While in theory they can coexist and complement one another, elected representatives may become uneasy about the prospect of community involvement in decisions that have hitherto been seen as their prerogative. Such initiatives require councillors to share their power with others whom they may think ill-informed, lacking legitimacy and scarcely representative of the communities they claim to speak for" (Rao et al, 2000, pp 3-4). Reflecting the critiques of deliberative democracy offered by Fraser (1997) and Young (2000), Aars and Offerdal (2000) suggest that one of the ways in which the principles of representative and deliberative democracy might be seen to be in conflict is that "deliberation seems to be the natural responsibility of those who are best equipped for it" (p 70), whereas taking part in democratic processes by voting does not demand either the particular competences necessary for deliberation, nor does it make the sometimes substantial practical demands of participative democracy. However, they conclude that this does not have to be the case. Political debate is an opportunity to persuade or convince opponents, and thinking and talking through an issue is a necessary prelude to producing just or reasonable decisions. Participation is one means to such an end and to accessing different types of knowledge. Hence the principles of participation and representation should not be considered to be in opposition even if relationships between the two need to be addressed in practice (see also Saward, 2005).

Up to now we have been considering ideas about opening up public decision making that start from the perspective of existing decision makers: the politicians and public officials who, with varying degrees of enthusiasm, are seeking ways of developing more participative relationships with the citizens they serve. But the pressures to change these relationships also come from citizens themselves, particularly when those citizens are involved in some form of collective organisation, whether that be service user organisations, community groups based in localities or identity, or groups campaigning for a particular cause. Political theorists such as Fraser, Young, Phillips and others who address the relationship between democracy and social justice start to engage with the challenges offered by social movements to both the forms of traditional politics, and the substance of the policies that derive from these. For example, many of the challenges to the exclusive nature of political processes have come from feminist politics and from black and minority ethnic groups. In the next section we focus on key issues in the theorisation of social movements and suggest what questions this raises about deliberative or dialogic forms of public participation.

Social movements

Various definitions have been offered of social movements. Our focus here is on collective action that has its origins in shared concerns, usually deriving from dissatisfactions with some aspect of 'the way things are', and a consequent wish to achieve changes in the way life is ordered. The notion of 'a movement' implies that the action is not a one-off activity (such as a demonstration), but a process in which different groups may be engaged over time. Beyond this we will leave the issue of definition alone, preferring Melucci's (1996) approach of using the notion of social movement as an analytic concept rather than an empirical category, and focus instead on the significance of issues such as motivations to take part, collective identity building and forms of action.

Crossley makes a number of claims about the significance of social movements. For our purposes here the key claim is as follows:

> The question of change, particularly change by way of movement politics, is a question about the difference which social agents themselves can make to the various structural dimensions of their life, a question about the form and distribution of power in society and the adequacy and limits of democracy. Social movements are, in effect, natural experiments in power, legitimation and democracy. (Crossley, 2002, p 9)

From this perspective, collective action based on commitments to a cause such as environmentalism, anti-poverty or animal rights, or on shared identities as feminists or gay activists, offers a challenge not only to specific policies and practices, but also to the democratic process itself. Within the spaces created by social movements, new identities can be created, new ideas explored, new solutions proposed and from these official definitions, assumptions and identities can be challenged. But these spaces are not the 'invited spaces' (Cornwall, 2004) created by officials seeking to open up policy-making processes. Rather they are alternative arenas in which what Fraser has termed 'counterpublics' created alternative public spheres because they have been excluded from the official public sphere, or because they reject the norms that operate within this. One example Fraser describes is the way in which African Americans used black churches at a time when they were excluded from 'whites-only' institutions of civil society, to publish newspapers, hold conventions and criticise state policies. Another example can be seen in the mental health service user/survivor movement that is concerned not only with seeking to achieve more responsive services, but more fundamentally with challenging the way in which mental illness and those who live with mental health problems are constructed within both lay and professional discourse (Barnes and Bowl, 2001).

Within these alternative public spheres experiences can be expressed in ways that do not conform to the normative expectations outlined by deliberative democrats. This can enable those who use different forms of communication, such as deaf people, to develop perspectives that are themselves linked to those modes of communication. For example, Davis challenges what he refers to as "one of the foundational ableist myths of our culture: that the norm for humans is to speak and hear, to engage in communication through speaking and hearing" (Davis, 1995, p 15). By questioning the assumptions that the aural/oral method of communicating is totally natural and anything else a deviation, Davis challenges assumptions that equate language with reason – a fundamental tenet of deliberative democracy. Less radically challenging, perhaps, is the recognition that different social groups develop different styles of speaking and that these are differently valued. Young (2000, p 64) cites the way in which Jesse Jackson's attempt to run for nomination as the democratic presidential candidate in the US was undermined by commentators who focused more on his style of speaking, considered too akin to that of a black preacher than was appropriate for a serious presidential candidate, than on the substance of his message. In other contexts quoting the scriptures, cappella singing and audience responses have contributed to the development of a collective consciousness among black voters – in particular tapping into an aspect of black religious culture that "sustained Black resistance and organization since the time of slavery ... the divinely endowed strength that allowed an ordinary person to overcome obstacles to making a difference in the political world" (Harris, 2001, p 51).

The creation of spaces in which groups often excluded from both official decision-making processes and from mainstream civil society could meet to share experience and start to theorise such experiences has led to what Seidman (1998) has called the 'making of new social knowledges'. Two clear examples of this are the way in which feminist theories developed out of the consciousness raising and practical action within the women's movement (such as developing centres for women who have experienced violence from male partners), and the way in which the social model of disability has been articulated by disabled people who have organised to resist the oppressive nature of services and responses based on the individualised medical model. The similarities in the processes involved in the two movements are flagged by Campbell and Oliver (1996) in the introduction to a chapter on disability consciousness: "This chapter will focus on the way disabled people have redefined the problem of disability as the product of a disabling society rather than individual limitations or loss, despite the fact that the rest of society continues to see disabled people as chance victims of tragic fate. We will then consider how this process has required the redefinition of self and a recognition that the personal is political" (p 105). In both cases new knowledges that have been generated through organisation within social movements have been circulated beyond those movements, have influenced official policy makers' and professionals' discourses and practices, and within the academy have "given birth to social knowledges, some of which contest important aspects of the social science disciplines" (Seidman, 1998, p 254). The significance of the discursive space available within social movements to create alternative ways of conceptualising and theorising social issues means their significance extends far beyond the achievement of any individual campaign directed at a specific social policy or practice.

Motivations

An important aspect of social movement theory, which is also highly relevant to our consideration of public participation, concerns motivations for participation. Different social movement theorists offer different explanations for why people take part. We can distinguish three broad types of explanation: first, those deriving from a socio-cultural perspective that emphasises the significance of value systems, the way in which actors make sense of their own situations and their responses to dissatisfactions with institutional or broader social norms; second, those deriving from rational choice theory that focus on the assessment individual agents make concerning the means to achieve their goals, interest and desires; and third, those that focus on the social networks in which individuals are engaged and the way in which they may both prompt and facilitate participation, as well as sustaining social movement action (see, for example, Della Porta and Diani, 1999; Crossley, 2002; Diani and McAdam, 2003).

Melucci suggests (1996, p 43) that it is possible to find empirical evidence that would support a wide range of frameworks that have been offered to explain why social movements emerge. However, the views of early theorists such as Kornhauser (1959) and Gusfield (1963), who argued that activists were primarily people who were dislocated, alienated and isolated, have been discounted by empirical research that has demonstrated that those who are better integrated into social networks are more likely to be recruited to social movements. As is often the case, we may need to draw from different types of explanation to understand best why people get involved. For example, what type of networks are most likely to lead to participation and how do these relate to the way in which people make sense of their own situations and decide it makes sense to act collectively to achieve their desires? For Melucci, networks represent the context in which interactions between individuals produce both the cognitive and affective schema that can connect individuals to collective action (1996, p 65). This suggests we should not look for structural factors to account for involvement, but rather focus on the immediate networks within which people interact on a day-to-day basis. As Diani and McAdam (2003) describe: "Typically, social movement activists and sympathizers are linked through both 'private' and 'public' ties well before collective action develops. Personal friends, relatives, colleagues, and neighbours, may all affect individual decisions to become involved in a movement; so may people who share with prospective participants some kind of collective engagement, such as previous or current participation in other movement activities, political or social organizations, and public bodies" (Diani and McAdam, 2003, p 7). It is within such networks and relationships that we might find the production of *motivations* for participation – a concept that can be distinguished from the 'incentives' that rational choice theorists invoke in explaining the evaluation of costs and benefits of participation.

Motivations to participate can be understood as linked to identities, an active process of making sense of oneself and one's connections to others in order to construct a self that has strong affective elements and that directs the way in which people decide to act. Individuals become motivated to take part in movements with others through a process of deciding that action is worthwhile to achieve change, that it makes sense in terms of their sense of who they are, what they value and how they stand in relation to the world. Many theorists and researchers of social movements argue, then, that it is necessary to draw on both sociological and social psychological theories in order to understand why some people do and others do not get involved (Stryker et al, 2000).

The concept of identity has also been invoked in seeking to explain the sustainability of social movements, that is, how we can account for the difference between one-off protest actions and enduring organisation and action in pursuit of social change. In this context the focus is on the way a process of *collective identity* production takes place (for example, Melucci, 1996). This involves a collective definition of the meaning of the action in which actors are engaged, the field within which change is sought, the means by which objectives may be achieved, and the opportunities and constraints that operate within this field. Such processes are not just cognitive, but also involve an affective investment. This means that the production of a collective identity is not restricted to those movements that may be considered to be based within particular social identities: as women, members of a particular minority ethnic or cultural group, or people who have experienced mental distress. High levels of commitments to goals (such as environmental sustainability or poverty reduction), together with the experience of solidarity through collective action, can create collective identities as activists – what is sometimes called a 'we-ness', which involves distinguishing 'us' from the rest of society. Melucci suggests that the generation of ritual, practices, norms and rules as groups become more institutionalised, forms of organisation, communication and leadership that constitute the network of relationships in which actors are involved, are all important in contributing to this process.

Often such collective identities involve the development of an 'oppositional consciousness', defined by Mansbridge (2001) as follows:

> We say that members of a group that others have traditionally treated as subordinate or deviant have an oppositional consciousness when they claim their previously subordinate identity as a positive identification, identify injustices done to their group, demand changes in the polity, economy or society to rectify those injustices, and see other members of their group as sharing an interest in rectifying those injustices. (Mansbridge, 2001, p 1)

The subordinate groups discussed in the collection from which Mansbridge's introduction is taken include African Americans, disabled people, sexually harassed women, Chicano workers and AIDS activists. White and Fraser's (2001) discussion of personal and collective identities among the oppositional social movement of Republican Sinn Féin in Ireland illustrate how such positions can also link with armed conflict. What is common to these perspectives is that they locate social movement action with struggles against larger systems of domination and oppression. Such struggles seek both material change, such as that demanded by Chicano workers in Texas (Rodriguez, 2001) and cultural change that aims to convince people to see the world differently. The latter objective is evident in, for example, action among psychiatric system survivors to challenge binary distinctions between madness and sanity (Barnes and Bowl, 2001), and in the work of AIDS activists that is not only directed towards supporting sufferers, but also to challenging and subverting dominant perceptions of the disease and those who are infected by it (Altman, 1994; Stockdill, 2001).

Social movement objectives

This brings us to another of the key factors in the theorising of social movements: the objectives and consequences of social movement action. Gamson (1975) has distinguished successful outcomes of social movements in terms of tangible policy changes (such as anti-discrimination legislation), and changes in the system of interest representation. This distinction can also be seen in the distinctions that are sometimes made between 'old' and 'new' social movements. Old movements were often seen to be class-based and as having primarily redistributive objectives. New movements, in contrast, often involved activists from more advantaged sections of society (such as students) who defined their objectives in cultural, expressive or recognition terms (for example, Cohen, 1985). While this binary distinction between old and new movements is now regarded as less important, understanding social movement objectives as relating both to the achievement of tangible policy change and to cultural changes relevant to social rules and norms remains significant.

Della Porta and Diani (1999) discuss the significance of objectives relating to interest representation in terms of the consequences of collective mobilisation for the distribution of power in society. They quote research that has demonstrated that, while disadvantaged groups might achieve improvements in their material circumstances, this is not necessarily accompanied by improvements in access to, or control over, decision-making processes. However, they also suggest that the conditions that can limit social movement potential are changing, and that conclusions drawn from this research on social movements in the 1960s and 1970s may no longer apply. In particular, channels of access to the political system are widening (as the empirical research discussed in this book testifies), and as the number and range of social movements increases, this "larger family of movements" (Della Porta and Diani, 1999, p 253) creates an infrastructure and resource on which newer movements can build and from which they can learn. This also creates channels of access to policy makers that can be utilised by others: "...the substantive gains made by one movement can have beneficial consequences for the demands of other movements and their success encourages further mobilizations. It can be concluded, therefore, that the importance of social movements tends to grow in as much as there is an ever-increasing amount of resources (both technical and structural) available for collective action" (p 254). We can point to evidence of this in the way in which movements of users of health and social care services have developed and expanded in part because of the opening up of service decision making by officials, and because those involved in early user organisations have supported and inspired others (see, for example, Barnes, 1997; Barnes and Bowl, 2001). We consider other examples of this process in Chapters Seven and Eight.

Other commentators offer a more social constructivist analysis. Melucci (1996) talks not only about the symbolic and linguistic resources that social movements take from previous movements but also of the importance of discursive capacity as a resource to reduce costs and maximise benefits of action. For Melucci, discourse is both a strategy and an objective of social movement action: "Contemporary movements strive to reappropriate the capacity to name through the elaboration of codes and languages designed to define reality, in the twofold sense of constituting it symbolically and of regaining it, thereby escaping from the predominant form of representation ..." (1996, pp 357-8). But conceiving social movement objectives in this way does not mean they are uninterested in 'real' changes in the social world. For example, gaining control over the way in which the experience of disability is defined and the language through which this is expressed has substantial implications for the policies, practices and services designed to enable disabled people to live their lives as they want to (Oliver, 1995). In an unusual application of social movement theory Rao et al (2000) have considered ways in which the cultural innovations made possible through social movement action have enabled the creation of new organisational forms: "how entrenched, field-wide authority is collectively challenged and restructured; how new norms, values and ideologies are infused into social structures via political contestation; and how institutional entrepreneurs and activists play key roles in framing new practices, mobilizing resources (including constituencies), and garnering legitimacy for new forms" (p 276).

Opportunity structures

Finally, social movement researchers have considered the relationship between what social movements are able to achieve and the political opportunity structures pertaining (for example, Lovenduski and Randall, 1993; Kreisi et al, 1995). Lovenduski and Randall's study of the feminist movement considers not only what the opportunities available to British feminists were in the context of developments within local government in the 1980s, during which many Labour authorities (in particular the Greater London Council) established women's committees, but also how a reliance on 'the local state' became a risky strategy in the Conservative backlash of the Thatcher years. More analytically, Melucci (1996) has addressed the question of how change is achieved in complex systems and what forms of mobilisation and representation ensure the greatest control over change processes. His analysis starts from an acknowledgement of the numerous institutions in which political decision making takes place, which creates a huge field within which movements can take action. He suggests that the multiple spaces in which people and interests can be represented increase the tension between "the structures of representation and the demands or interests of those represented" (Melucci, 1996, p 212). An empirical study of disabled people's and mental health service user organisations illustrated such tensions (Barnes, 1999a). Not only were user groups spread more thinly as the introduction of the internal market in health and social care created ever more spaces in which there were opportunities to take part; these developments also increased the tension between the representation of issues generated from within the groups themselves, and the demands from within service systems to respond to their agendas.

Nevertheless, the existence of groups that organise outside the 'invited spaces' (Cornwall, 2004) of participative governance increases the potential that both the agenda for and the rules of deliberation will be constructed jointly, rather than imposed by officials. In this context social movements play a key role in seeking to keep open the boundaries; they "push participation beyond the limits laid down by the political system, and they force it to change" (Melucci, 1996, p 214). Thus the importance of social movements in the contemporary system of complex and apparently open processes of governance is to constantly question the way in which the rules of the game are being determined and defined, in particular in relation to the rules governing the way in which those who are least powerful, or whose communication styles do not match official norms, are represented within such systems.

And finally Melucci himself provides a definitive statement of what democracy should mean in complex societies in which collective action plays a significant role in creating new democratic spaces:

Democracy in complex societies can only mean the creation of conditions which allow social actors to recognize themselves and be recognized for what they are or want to be; conditions, that is, which lend themselves to the creation of recognition and autonomy. In this sense, democracy means freedom to belong, or, freedom to construct spaces of recognition. Thus defined, democracy is also freedom of representation, freedom to express identity in systems of representation which preserve identity over time. (Melucci, 1996, pp 219-20)

Conclusion

Some of the case studies that we present in this book demonstrate that, empirically, it is sometimes hard to categorise specific examples of public participation as *either* exemplifying participative governance, *or* evidence of social movement action. Some case studies illustrate dialogue between public officials and social movement activists and others offer examples of public officials who are also social movement activists.

What we have argued in this chapter is that it is not sufficient to look at new forms of public participation solely from the perspective of the official discourses and aspirations evident within the ever-increasing initiatives coming from both national and local levels of government. The normative assumptions evident within the policy initiatives and schemes outlined in Chapter Two need to be tested by reference to the way in which power relationships shape the process of dialogue within deliberative forums, and in the light of the interaction between the new democratic spaces created by citizens themselves as well as those created within the official domain of governance systems (see also Fung, 2004; Cornwall and Coelho, 2006).

This analysis raises a number of questions that we will be considering in the detailed case studies presented in Chapters Five to Eight. We will be addressing the nature of the 'deliberation' that is evident in discursive arenas that are differently constituted and differently located in terms of their origins within or between the 'official' and 'community' spheres. We will also be looking at the way in which people come to take part in these different forums, at what motivates them to do so and whether there are similarities in routes towards and motivations for participation in officially constituted forums in comparison to evidence relating to social movement participation. Finally we will consider the internal dynamics of these forums, both in relation to the way in which they may be spaces within which collective identities may be articulated and formed, and in terms of the extent to which new discourses may be generated.

Note
[1] See Leach et al (2005) for examples of citizen engagement on issues of science and technology around the world.

FOUR

Shaping public participation: public bodies and their publics

Much of the literature on public participation is highly normative; the emphasis is on how new ways of engaging with the public can empower citizens, open up new forms of consumerism and choice, involve the public as stakeholders in communities or in the improvement of public services, or induce more responsible attitudes and behaviours. This normative emphasis stems in part from the policy climate discussed in Chapter Two, where public participation is viewed as a means of improving public services and delivering more effective outcomes; but it has also been generated by some of the academic work discussed in Chapter Three, where deliberative democracy is viewed as a means of democratic renewal. Here our emphasis is rather different; that is, we set out to understand the extent to which, and in what ways, the plethora of new initiatives might be able to produce fundamental shifts in relationships between state and citizens, public bodies and publics. To do so we draw on two different bodies of theory. New institutional analysis opens up questions about the influence of rules and norms about participation and deliberation. Such rules and norms shape the extent to which new relationships between public bodies and their publics, between officials and lay members of deliberative forums, might be possible. For example if the rules and norms of the council chamber or trades union are imported into what is intended to be a much more informal site of deliberation, the impact may be to constrain who feels entitled to speak and what contributions are viewed as legitimate. However, this body of theory can also illuminate the ways in which new rules and norms may emerge in the deliberative process itself. It can offer suggestive questions about how such rules and norms, and 'logics of appropriate action', may influence patterns of agency on the part of both officials and lay members of forums, and shape the depth of deliberation that occurs.

The second body of theory looks beyond institutions to problematise notions of 'the public' itself. The discussion in Chapter Two of the policy discourses that informed the rise of public participation initiatives under New Labour suggests that ideas about the public – whether it is to be empowered or responsibilised, conceptualised as consumers or stakeholders – may have profound consequences for the formation and conduct of deliberative forums. Here we draw on strands of social construction and post-structural theory to explore how ideas about the public in public participation are shaped and what their impact might be. This body of theory enables us to explore the ways in which particular conceptions of the public and of the public domain are produced – or constituted – through new participative discourses and practices; and how such conceptions may, rather than 'empowering' the public, be understood as drawing citizens and service users into new fields of power.

The chapter begins by outlining the kinds of public participation initiative that our research was concerned with, linking these back to the discourses discussed in Chapter Two and the social movement perspectives outlined in Chapter Three. The theoretical sections then suggest key questions and perspectives that underpin the analysis of the case studies in Chapters Five to Eight. We cannot hope to do justice to either body of theory here, but have selected those strands that seem most relevant to understanding the case study material.

Mapping public participation initiatives

A survey of public participation in two cities provided evidence of the wide range of public participation initiatives that were flowering in the first and second terms of the New Labour government in the UK. Survey responses indicated that participation initiatives were intended to involve the public from design through to implementation and evaluation. In both cities a number of modes of engagement were evident. Some were primarily about giving information to the public, either as a first step to wider participation or as an aim in itself. For example, early activity in primary care groups (PCGs) aimed to raise awareness about particular services or functions. Others were largely about consultation, an opportunity for the public to express their views about a particular service or issue within a framework set by the delivery organisation, for example establishing objectives in relation to services for mental health service users. However, some modes of involvement were more directly focused on creating opportunities for deliberation between organisations and the public in which communication was two-way and issues for discussion could be introduced by either party. Such initiatives focused on problem solving or identification. For example, the developing PCGs sought public participation in order to find out what services should be provided by a primary care organisation and which by other parts of the health service. Others focused on the contribution to local governance that could be made by a particular group such as older people. In both cases attempts were made to extend the influence of the public by securing their involvement in effecting changes to policies or services. The initiatives we studied can be loosely grouped into a number of different categories reflecting their purpose and origins:

- Initiatives that set out to address cross-cutting issues. These included a sustainability forum (environmental initiative established in response to Local Agenda 21), an action against poverty forum and a wider range of regeneration partnerships in both cities.
- Initiatives that sought to involve particular categories of the public in order to address questions of social difference. These included senior citizens' forums in both cities; a women's group; a lesbian and gay forum; a black and minority ethnic group council; and a social services project established to consult with disabled and other service users. Some were city wide, but these also included neighbourhood-based initiatives, such as an initiative designed to engage with young people as part of an area-based regeneration programme.
- Initiatives established by local authorities to involve the public and partners from other sectors in specific localities. These included an area forum initiative in one city and area committee programmes in the other.
- Advocacy initiatives stimulated by community or voluntary action to improve services or secure policy change. These might focus on a particular issue – such as a mental health consortium – or might have a locality focus, such as residents' or tenants' groups. These included issue-specific initiatives such as the redevelopment of a park and community action to prevent the closure of a health centre; a sustainability forum focusing on environmental issues; and a fuel poverty action group.
- Service-specific initiatives designed to involve service users. These included patients' forums/councils in hospitals in both cities; a women's information network for maternity services; Best Value consultations linked to different local government departments; tenant participation initiatives relating to housing; and PCG involvement activities.
- Area-specific initiatives including Education Action Zones (EAZs) (improving school attainment levels in targeted areas) and Sure Start (working with children aged 0-4) in both cities; a neighbourhood decentralisation scheme; and a community-led organisation.

We used this mapping exercise to help shape the selection of case studies for more detailed study. However, it will be evident that these categorisations are somewhat untidy; for example, 'locality' was an important basis for consultation and involvement in many service-based initiatives, not just in the area structures set up by local government, while social and political agency, most strongly highlighted in the advocacy and issue-based initiatives, informed the negotiations between public bodies and their publics in many other groupings. We return to these 'meta' themes in the conclusion in Chapter Nine. At this point we want to relate the mapping exercise to some of the themes developed in Chapters Two and Three. The initiatives reflected a mix of the policy discourses discussed in Chapter Two, although again simple mapping of each forum against a single discourse proved not to be possible. While the fit in some was fairly tight – for example the sustainability forum appeared to be most closely linked to a stakeholder perspective – most drew on a range of discourses. Although many of the service user-oriented initiatives (the patients' forum, the search team, Best Value consultations) were most closely linked to the 'consumerist' discourse, they also drew on other discourses (for example, the 'empowerment' of service user groups perceived to be disadvantaged or excluded). The area-specific initiatives tended to be associated with all four discourses, with 'empowerment' and 'responsiblising' discourses in uncomfortable coexistence in, for example, the Sure Start projects. Advocacy initiatives were strongly aligned with the empowerment discourse but the boundary between this and either the 'partnership' or 'responsibilising' discourse could become blurred.

Differences within the range of initiatives mapped here can also be understood in terms of the perspectives offered by the social movement literature discussed in Chapter Three. Some had their origins in autonomous groups formed out of some of the social movements that presented challenges to public policy and to the organisations that deliver it. The women's centre, for example, had its roots in both feminist politics and community activism, while the senior citizens' forums had strong links with political movements such as the National Pensioners' Convention and trades unions, from which many of the members were drawn, as well as voluntary campaigning groups such as Age Concern. Other initiatives were originated by public bodies in an attempt to engage more closely with various publics; or were linked to decentralisation initiatives in local government. As we will argue in later chapters, these different origins could have important consequences; however, the distinction between autonomous groups and officially sponsored initiatives became more blurred as officials and publics engaged in dialogue, and as a result of institutional processes that brought initially autonomous groups into new fields of power.

Finally the initiatives can be mapped in terms of their relationship to the different policy objectives (see Table 2.1, p 23). The objective of 'improving services' underpinned several initiatives that we group together in Chapter Five. Here the focus was on establishing dialogue with service users as consumers and/or as stakeholders, both in order to render services more responsive and to engage service users more fully in the process of service delivery through strategies of 'empowerment'. Other initiatives focused on 'engaging communities' through new strategies of community and neighbourhood governance, a theme we develop in Chapter Six. Here the emphasis was on opening up institutions by bringing them 'in touch with the people' (as the subtitle of a key government text on modernising local government expressed it: see DETR, 1998).

But as well as securing the legitimacy of public institutions, the emphasis here was also on building community capacity and developing new civic virtues. This chimes with the communitarian emphasis in many New Labour policies, an emphasis that has been widely critiqued (Hughes and Mooney, 1998; Newman, 2001). Social capital was not explicitly mentioned as an objective among the responses to the mapping exercise from either city. However, there was some evidence that building a collective capacity within specific communities informed the design of some initiatives. This was most explicit in one city where the responses revealed a focus on 'developmental capacity', that is, improving the process of engagement and interaction, as a purpose of public participation. This developmental capacity had two emphases. The first concentrated on building the capacity of groups and institutions to relate to each other. Activity was targeted at improving the understanding between communities and institutions and finding better ways to relate. Here black and minority ethnic communities were most frequently identified as target groups. The second emphasis of this developmental concern related to building the capacity of individuals, providing opportunities for them to associate with each other as well as with officials, to exchange information, to share personal experiences and to build personal relationships.

So cutting across the themes of improving services and engaging communities were more fundamental objectives concerned with delivering policy outcomes such as social inclusion and social cohesion. It is here that a third theme became evident: that of engaging particular communities (often called 'communities of identity') in order to reach specific categories of public – young people, black and ethnic minority communities, mental health service users and other groups. These were linked to particular problems of inclusion that presented challenges to government and to public service organisations. Finally we can trace ways in which public officials were, in some initiatives, working with issue-based groups to bring about change. In trying to assess the interaction between public bodies and the publics they seek to – or are obliged to – interact more closely with, the following sections develop the analytical frameworks that we draw on when discussing individual initiatives in subsequent chapters. Our emphasis here is on drawing out a number of questions from two different bodies of theory, beginning with 'new institutional theory'.

Remaking state–citizen relationships

Shaping the rules and norms of deliberation

The starting point of new institutional theory is that human actions and interactions produce rules (that regulate activity) and norms (that set out expectations of appropriate behaviour). This section asks how rules and norms come to shape the nature and content of public participation initiatives: who makes the rules, how norms of legitimate conduct develop and with what consequences. Even in the simplest encounters rules and norms – how people should greet each other, how they should conduct conversations, how they should position themselves in space in relationship to each other, whether they should stand or sit – all serve to guide behaviour. It is through the operation of rules and norms that actors interpret and respond to any given situation – they provide actors with clarity, predictability and reliability in their environment. Institutions are found in a range of contexts from interpersonal relationships to global governance frameworks. They simultaneously facilitate the behaviour of individuals, groups and organisations (by reducing the complexity of the environment) and constrain their behaviour (because of the power of existing norms and rules). Such norms are of course culturally specific: that is, different social groups may hold different values, and their experiences (perhaps of community action, or as service users) may have produced different normative templates. The focus of new institutional theory is on how some rules and norms become embedded and solidified. They are communicated and perpetuated through a range of mechanisms to produce stability, such that social action may be guided by norms that may no longer be relevant to a new context, or may be viewed as irrelevant or damaging in the eyes of some social actors. Institutions are, then, not static but are dynamic features of social life. That is, they are open to forms of social agency that mean that they change over time.

How institutions are made, and how social agency can influence their making and breaking, is understood differently in different disciplinary strands of new institutional theory, including those based in politics, economics, organisational sociology and cultural theory (Lowndes, 2001; Scott, 2001). Rather than describing these differences here, we draw on Scott's wide-ranging review of institutions to define them as "multifaceted, durable social structures, made up of symbolic elements, social activities, and material resources" (2001, p 49). His synthesis of institutional analyses explores the contribution of, and relationship between, rules and norms through the identification of three interlinked 'pillars of institutions':

- Regulative – a system of rules that frames and monitors action;
- Normative – prescriptions for appropriate behaviour in a given value set;
- Cultural–cognitive – a common construction of meaning producing templates of 'the way we do things'. (2001, pp 52-8)

Acting in concert these pillars can engender a powerful, stable institutional environment.

How might this body of theory help us to conceptualise public participation? We want to highlight three important questions that have informed our analysis. The first is, *how might the rules and norms associated with the institutions of representative democracy shape the practices of deliberation, and with what consequences?* Public participation – especially in its deliberative forms – is understood as overcoming some of the disbenefits of representative democracy by enabling governments and policy makers to respond to the development of a more differentiated, dynamic and plural polity. That is, elections, while providing the public with a crucial means of bestowing legitimacy on a government (national or local) or for dismissing it and electing an alternative, do little to enable them to channel their views on questions of detail or to make any real input into the policy process. Mass political parties are unable to reflect the diversity of interests and needs in complex societies; and notions of representation itself fail to address the changing relationships and identities that have made formal politics irrelevant to many citizens, especially the young. Deliberative democracy, as we argued in Chapter Three, is concerned with a set of claims associated with enhancing communication between citizen and government, between service user and service provider, and so on. However, representative democracy is associated with very strongly embedded norms and rules: those of parliamentary (or council chamber) debate, of voting as a form of decision making, and of the importance of representation as both status and as a claim to legitimacy. How far can deliberative forums be sites in which alternative rules and norms might be generated, or might those associated with representative democracy be imported – either as a common-sense way of doing business, or as a means of strengthening the legitimacy of the forum itself?

A second question arising from the use of new institutional theory is, *how do the rules and norms embedded in public organisations shape the nature of public participation initiatives, and with what consequences for the development of dialogue and partnership between statutory bodies and citizens?* Here we are concerned less with the kinds of constitutional rules associated with representative democracy than with the power of organisational, professional and managerial logics of appropriate action. The limited capacity of statutory bodies to develop partnership relationships with citizens in the UK is well known (Anastacio et al, 2000; Sullivan and Skelcher, 2002; see also the evaluation studies mentioned in Chapter Two). Part of the reason for this limited capacity lies in the way in which existing institutional arrangements serve to perpetuate prevailing state–citizen relationships. North (1991) specifies different roles for organisations: those of rule making, rule implementation, rule enforcement and rule advocacy. The ways in which local organisations pursue these roles in relation to setting up public participation initiatives are very influential, ranging from norms about who should be involved, how and where deliberation should take place, rules of representation and decision making, and so on. These are likely to be supplemented by more informal norms that officials and experts bring to the deliberative process: for example, what kinds of speech acts are to be expected and valued, and which to be silenced. Such rules and norms may reproduce existing hierarchies and decision-making mechanisms, but public organisations may also work with lay actors or social movement activists to develop frameworks that support alternative ways of working. The distinction reported by Scott (2001, p 64) between regulative rules (those that influence existing activities) and constitutive rules (those that create the possibility of certain activities) is helpful here as it draws attention to the need to adapt, change or reformulate institutions to allow new possibilities to emerge. For example Fourniau's (2001) study of the National Commission of Public Debate established four deliberative rules of procedure that created the possibility for a "contradictory, pluralistic and egalitarian dialogue to take place" among participants (2001, p 441).

A third question that arises from our use of new institutional theory concerns power and agency; that is, *how do the rules and norms of deliberation get shaped and how might they be re-negotiated?* For DiMaggio (1991) the issue of agency is more significant at the point of the creation of institutions rather than their application. This reflects the fact that once established, institutions and the routines that sustain them operate independently of individual actors (March and Olsen, 1989). The mechanisms used to sustain institutions are termed 'carriers' by Scott, and include culture, role systems, routinised practices and objects. Carriers act to communicate beliefs and practices to new actors. Their capacity to do this depends in part on the embeddedness of existing institutions. These may in fact be sub-optimal – for example, as we saw above, the rules of deliberation associated with representative democracy may militate against a shift towards more participative forms of state–citizen engagement. Institutional resistance to change may be manifest in logics of appropriateness and success that privilege and preserve inappropriate rules. Confronted with a new situation, actors draw on their existing resources to interpret and respond to it, based on pre-existing rules and pre-established logics of appropriate behaviour.

However, existing institutions, while shaping thought and action, are not determining in their effects. 'Constitutive rules' (used here to mean rules that are deliberately established to facilitate new dialogic activities) set the parameters of possibility within a forum. In the case of public participation, such parameters may be influenced by the degree of involvement of the public in this rule making. But ideas of agency also relate to the possibility of conflict between different actors about what rules are viewed as appropriate. In heterogeneous environments "different actors learn different rules and concepts of appropriateness as members of different national cultures, sub-communities, professions, and formal organizations" (March and Olsen, 1989, p 37). The process of conflict resolution and the interaction of actors will frequently result in the reformulation or adaptation of rules and norms. It may also involve the co-existence of 'old' and 'new' rules over time, each governing different elements or levels of the system (Lowndes, 1999). Variance between rules, norms and frames of meaning will produce tension that can induce "social and political instability" (North, 1993, p 20). Such instability creates the possibility of agency, including that of challenges to existing rules or norms.

So 'officials' rarely have a monopoly of power in the rule making process. And several studies suggest that the wider the involvement of stakeholders in rule formulation the better the subsequent rules (Vari and Kisgyorgy, 1998; Cattaui, 2001), and that without such involvement the results are likely to be the production of sub-optimal and unenforceable rules (Konur, 2000). As well as considering the extent of citizen involvement in rule making, questions arise about the extent to which citizen participants accept the prevailing norms, or negotiate with officials to establish norms developed through their own experiences and expectations. But such negotiations are notoriously problematic. Key here is the issue of trust in experts. March and Olsen (1989) point to the need for expertise to be reliable; that is, for it to be congruent with the values of specific groups. The trust of politically important groups (most conspicuously lower-status groups and non-establishment social movements) is particularly difficult to win, and where it breaks down will be difficult to re-establish, especially where loss of trust is reinforced by experience of neglect or the hi-jacking of successful community initiatives.

The final question concerns the *symbolic power of institutions.* Here we highlight the role of 'myths' or 'symbols' present in the wider institutional environment in shaping organisational structures and cultures. These are drawn from a range of sources – including cultural norms, political ideologies and public policy discourses – and combine to form institutional templates that organisations adopt in developing their own strategies and practices, whether or not these are appropriate or effective in specific contexts (Meyer and Rowan, 1991; Powell and DiMaggio, 1991). The legitimacy afforded to organisations that adapt to the dominant 'templates' is accompanied by access to greater resources, or by enhanced reputation and legitimacy among their peers or competitors.

In relation to our research, public participation can be understood as a key element of the prevailing institutional environment. Demonstrating a commitment to public participation is vital if public agencies are to retain their legitimacy with government. It also affects the level of resources made available to public agencies, with some government programmes such as the National Strategy for Neighbourhood Renewal awarding resources on the basis of expressed commitment to public involvement. The penetration of public participation into the design and operation of local organisations is evidenced formally in the requirements of key policies such as Best Value and the revised configurations of local service organisations, together with the expectation that community members will have a role to play in their governance. However, the adherence of public organisations to such strategies may be largely symbolic; their policies may be 'loosely coupled' to day-to-day operational practices. More attention may be paid, for example, to launching high profile initiatives than to managing their interface with mainstream organisational decision-making processes. This makes the kind of empirical work we have been engaged in important; rather than simply highlighting the extent of public participation initiatives, there is a need to pay attention to the extent to which formal policy and organisational acknowledgements are supported by real change and new forms of social action.

The work on institutions as 'myth and symbol', and on understanding the significance of templates and frameworks that bestow legitimacy on organisations in an increasingly competitive field, takes us close to a more cultural set of perspectives on public participation. In the next section we develop this by drawing on social constructionist and post-structuralist perspectives, but here our focus shifts to the analysis of 'the public' of public participation.

Constituting publics

The previous sections referred to the 'public' in an unproblematic way: as a pre-given entity that public bodies can engage with. Here we open up this concept to critical scrutiny, drawing on social constructivist and post-structural perspectives that suggest ways in which the new practices of public participation may serve to produce – or constitute – their publics (Barnes et al, 2003). The assumption here is that groups or individuals do not arrive with a neatly bundled set of needs or interests that can be expressed in a rational process of debate. While needs and interests may have a strong material base (in poverty, disability, social exclusion and so on), people's understanding of them, and of the legitimate ways in which they can be expressed, are formed through social practices, including dialogues with others sharing similar experiences, and/or dialogues with professionals and other public officials. In what follows we outline two frameworks through which such social practice might be analysed; we then go on to suggest the questions these frameworks open up for the analysis of case studies.

First, concepts such as the 'public', the 'community' or the 'citizen-consumer' can be understood as *social constructions*, formed out of a range of discourses and ideologies that are historically embedded in institutional practice (Burr, 1995). This framework draws on a long tradition of analysing the social construction of social problems. When, for example, people in a particular neighbourhood come together and demand that the council 'do something' about, say, anti-social behaviour, they are engaged in a process of translating private concerns into a public issue that requires a public response. The social construction of social problems is an active process of defining and redefining an issue in ways that shape it as a matter for public concern (Clarke and Cochrane, 1998). The term 'anti-social behaviour' itself is part of a fairly recent political discourse through which certain categories of behaviour, often linked to young people, come to be targeted for social intervention. In other times such groups might have been viewed through other discourses – for example, gangs or hoodlums, or even just teenagers 'letting off steam'. These stigmatised the person rather than the behaviour. As such, unless disruptive young people engaged in specifically criminal behaviour, they were viewed as a social problem about which little could be done. The term 'anti-social behaviour' is, then, a social construct that renders a troubling phenomenon more readily available for public action. It has also provided lay people with a new bit of language to learn in order to be able to voice their concerns in the public domain. Imagine, for example, a residents' meeting in which one voice speaking the language of 'black troublemakers' is silenced while another speaking the language of 'anti-social behaviour' is allowed to speak and be heard.

One of the benefits of a social constructionist perspective is that it allows us to unpick the idea of policy making as a rational process in which policy formation is clearly distinct from the administrative mechanisms through which policy is delivered. The conceptual distinction between policy making and policy delivery has been subject to a range of different critiques, and has become even more difficult to sustain in the context of new understandings of the importance of 'policy networks' that cut across the policy/delivery divide (Marsh and Rhodes, 1992). This reminds us that policy is a social process that draws on a wide range of actors – including many of those contributing to the participative processes described in this book. As Chapter Three argued, social movements have played an important role in both challenging existing policy and in opening up alternative policy agendas. Much of the literature on policy networks, however, views their dynamics in terms of processes of resource bargaining and negotiation between different interests. Social constructionism adds something different to our understanding of these dynamics, noting how social interactions within networks may help shape how people come to define their interests, rather than viewing networks as just the place in which such interests are negotiated.

This has wider implications for how we understand the political process. Rational models of the public sphere draw on particular assumptions of human identity and agency, notably the assumption that citizens can be understood as rational actors weighing and assessing arguments and putting forward their objective interests to policy makers and/or politicians. This ignores "the role of language, discourse, rhetorical argument, and stories in framing both policy questions and the contextual contours of argumentation, particularly the ways normative presuppositions operate below the surface to structure basic policy definitions and understandings" (Fischer, 2003, p 14). Finally the idea of social construction also allows us to highlight ways in which the 'public' itself is understood by policy makers and public service staff. Here we turn from a focus on social construction to the discursive constitution of publics.

As we noted at the beginning of this chapter, much of the literature on public participation – both academic and policy – is highly normative, couched in the language of improving public services, empowering service users, renewing civil society and so on. However, the post-structuralist critiques of these developments argue that the initiatives associated with public participation might be conceptualised not as 'empowering' the citizen, community or service user but as drawing them into new fields of governmental power (Rose, 1999). New forms of citizen participation may not just *reflect* external changes in the public realm and the public itself but may be *constitutive* in their effects.

Such perspectives develop the Foucauldian concept of 'governmentality'. This denotes the flow of power beyond the state, drawing attention to ways in which multiple organisations, groups and individuals have become implicated in the process of governing (Foucault, 1991). "Political forces seek to give effect to their strategies, not only through the utilisation of laws, bureaucracies, funding regimes and authoritative state agencies and agents, but through utilising and instrumentalising forms of authority other than the State in order to govern ... 'at a distance'" (Rose, 1996, p 46). Such processes of governing take place through technologies of power based on knowledge and expertise. These encompass the expertise of the state professional (defining the problem on which an agency wishes to consult its public), the expertise of the state official (designing a consultation strategy or setting out the seating plan for a public meeting) and the expertise of an 'expert citizen' (voicing the claims of a particular group in a way that can be heard by the relevant officials). The technologies of power include the 'know-how' of state officials who go on training programmes or read guidebooks on how to conduct a participation exercise. They are transmitted through consultancy organisations advising officials on how to go about engaging the public, and by voluntary organisations advising community actors on how best to engage with state officials.

A post-structuralist perspective turns the normative emphasis on the benefits of public participation on its head. In particular, the work of Rose (1996, 1999) highlights how apparently 'free' actors are subject to new discursive practices that seek to constitute governable subjects. The use of the term 'discourse' here implies more than language. It is a way of speaking and acting that draws its authority from a particular source of expertise and power that produces new ways of knowing the self and others. It is important to note that the use of the term discourse in post-structural theory is rather different from the focus on discourse as communicative acts in Habermas's work. Although language is implicated in each, Foucault's work highlights the ways in which language and communication are anchored in social processes – discursive practices – through which knowledge is produced and practiced. This implies that conceptions of interests – whether self-interest or a wider conception of a public interest – are formed in a discursive domain. This does not mean that people are (necessarily) manipulated by governments; more that discourse may set the limits of what it is possible to think, and thus understandings of the choices that can be made or the interests that can be legitimately expressed. As Fischer comments, "It is not that institutions cause political action; rather, it is their discursive practices that shape the behaviours of actors who do" (2003, p 28).

These frameworks of analysis open up important questions that will inform our analysis of the case studies discussed in the following chapters. One set of questions focuses on *the categories of public that are produced for the purposes of participation*. This asks how particular publics targeted for specific initiatives are defined by both officials and citizens, and how such definitions inform the practices of participation. It is through discursive practices that identities are bestowed on particular forms of social subject: consider, for example, the possible implications of discourses that constitute groups or individuals as the socially excluded, disabled people and children with special needs. Each of these has been 'normalised' in current policy discourse; but their unacceptable antecedents – 'beggars', the 'handicapped', the 'retarded' – give a clue not only to the constitutive power of discourse, but also to the ways in which they are open to forms of contestation and challenge by the kinds of social movements discussed in Chapter Three.

Discursive forms of power may well have consequences for how both staff and users understand themselves and their relationship. It is through discourse that particular conceptions of the public realm are enacted and through which the public – in its many forms – is constituted as a governable entity.

A second set of questions focuses on *how questions of difference are accommodated*. The emergence of new forms of participation creates more differentiated forms of engagement between state and citizen, and between citizens. But how are questions of difference to be accommodated? One of the difficulties facing both officials and lay members of deliberative forums is how to constitute the public into a differentiated entity so that citizens or service users can be selected from appropriate categories. There are at least three possible approaches to this. One is based on the principle of openness. For example, neighbourhood or area forums tend to be viewed as open to the public as a whole. Here the problem of differentiation appears to be avoided, but of course access issues – the timing of a meeting, the place where it is held, the design of the building and so on – may well limit who can attend. The second draws on ideas of representativeness. Here there is an attempt to ensure that different interests and identities are represented in a specific forum, so that it includes, say, an appropriate mix of male and female, young and old, and so on. For example, the kinds of 'citizen panel' that have been established by both central and local government have been scrupulous in trying to ensure representative samples of different population groups. The third approach targets those whose voices it is deemed important to hear, either by inviting particular identity or interest groups to attend or by going out to them. These different approaches have important consequences not only for the inclusion and exclusion of particular individuals or groups, but also for what kinds of collective voices and interests can be heard.

Public participation and deliberative practices are viewed as more capable of accommodating questions of difference and diversity than representative democracy (Benhabib, 1996). While the latter takes account of individual preferences, the aggregative process of elections and the ambiguity of how elected representatives might 'represent' their constituency tend to squeeze out subtle differences of interest and identity. Of particular importance in the context of our study is the meaning of 'community'. As argued earlier in Chapter Two, community may designate an imaginary domain of social relationships based on mutuality and reciprocity, or it may designate a spatialised concept of locality. These may of course be conflated. And other, more identity-based concepts may be found, as in categorisations such as the 'black and minority ethnic community' or the 'gay and lesbian community'.

The final set of questions derived from the frameworks discussed here concern *how notions of 'representation' and 'representativeness' are constructed and negotiated*. A key characteristic of the deliberative forums we studied is their divergence from formal notions of representation enshrined in parliament or the local council chamber. Traditionally, citizens elect someone to represent their interests (although of course this is mediated by political parties). This form of representative democracy is a relatively blunt instrument that cannot adequately address the problems of representation in a heterogeneous and plural society. However, it is enshrined in the cultures of many nation states and gives rise to many of the assumptions about how deliberation should be conducted (see the discussion of norms and rules above). Notions of representation and representativeness – who can speak for whom, and on what basis – are, then, likely to be used in the shaping of new forms of interaction between public bodies and publics. However, they must be understood as social constructions whose meaning may shift as the context of interaction diverges from the classic model of representative democracy.

Such constructions necessarily bring into question issues of identity. Attempts to categorise the public into mutually exclusive groups assumes a stable, fixed and singular identity, a conception that the post-structural approaches described here would contest. And if identity is fluid and unstable, then the idea of one individual 'representing' others with a presumed similar identity is highly problematic. As Saward (2005) argues, the process of representation itself is one that is constitutive of those who are deemed to be represented; that is, the person who takes on the task of representing others has to imagine – or construct – an image of those they represent. And the idea of publics as constituted entities "... turns the theories of politics upside down: the established thinking focuses on the issue of how to represent a (given) community.... Here we see how policymaking leads to the creation of communities that for themselves have to determine what constitutes a legitimate decision in a particular instance.... Politics is about defining what is a legitimate political institution. This is what governance in the network society is also about" (Hajer, 2003, pp 96-7).

Conclusion

This chapter has introduced a number of questions that inform the analysis of specific case studies of public participation that are discussed in Chapters Five to Eight. Underpinning each are issues of power; however, the understanding of power is approached rather differently in the different theoretical perspectives on which we have drawn. In new institutional theory the emphasis is on the power of existing institutions – rules and norms of social action – to limit the possibility of new forms of social agency. Institutions play a significant role in the shaping and functioning of public policy. In relation to public participation, institutional capacity can be utilised to facilitate dialogue with communities in a number of ways, including the development by local statutory players of a range of sites and processes where official and citizen participants can interact as partners, and the extension of local governance networks to include 'self-organised' groups in addition to those sponsored by statutory bodies. Government can also change the 'rules of the game' by introducing new incentives and can offer new symbols that create an enhanced climate of legitimacy for public involvement. However, institutions can also act to constrain dialogue by imposing particular templates of decision making; by failing to assign sufficient resources to sites and processes to enable them to function effectively; and by persisting in questioning the legitimacy and validity of citizen groups and forums.

The interaction of these facilitating and constraining factors may not be uniform, with some forums sponsored by the same organisation operating in entirely different ways. This suggests the possibility of separate and distinct logics of appropriate action in operation in different parts of the same organisation and across different communities. A number of factors contribute to the development of logics of appropriate action including the definition and association of 'expertise' by officials and citizens. Once again, we can only understand the complex interplay of different factors – and so understand some of the power dynamics involved – by studying the interplay of new and old rules, facilitating and constraining norms, in specific case study sites.

In opening up questions about how the 'public' of public participation is socially constructed and discursively constituted, the chapter has also highlighted the importance of post-structuralist understandings of power. The practices of public participation, while appearing to be empowering, may be a new form of domination. However, as Foucault comments, new discourses and strategies may also produce new sites of social agency. "Discourse can be both an instrument and effect of power, but also a hindrance, a stumbling block, a point of resistance and a starting point for an opposing strategy" (Foucault, 1991, p 101). It is in the small, everyday acts of generating meanings, appropriating and reworking discourses and shaping new patterns of allegiance that such possibilities arise. Involving individuals and groups in deliberations about the forms and practices of state services inevitably draws them into new fields of state power, opening them up to new forms of disciplinary practice and professional or bureaucratic domination. But it also fosters citizen engagement in the public sphere, producing the possibility of new forms of voice and even dissent. The case study chapters that follow, by studying the micro-politics of participation in specific sites, will enable us to explore this tension between participation as a new form of governance and as a source of social agency.

FIVE

Re-forming services

For many citizens, their relationship with the state is experienced primarily through their experiences of using services provided by or through government. The potential of increased public participation will be judged by many participants by its capacity to generate services that are of better quality, more responsive, culturally appropriate and designed in ways that reflect their lives and circumstances rather than the preferences and interests of service providers. The significance of public services to the lives of most citizens, particularly at times and in circumstances when personal resources may be low, or when they have no option other than to receive services, accounts for the power of the consumerist discourse and its expression in the Thatcherite 'reforms' of the public sector during the late 1980s and 1990s. But the way in which people use public services also explains many of the inadequacies of consumerist developments in terms of 'empowering' individual service users or generating services that are collectively experienced as more responsive to the needs and circumstances of their users (see, for example, Barnes and Prior, 1995; Barnes and Walker, 1996).

In this chapter we consider five initiatives, which, in different ways, illustrate how citizens and service users are taking part in action intended to shape and change public services. They demonstrate ways in which a consumerist ideology is inadequate in accounting for why people get involved in such initiatives, or in understanding the relationship between citizens and officials and the nature of the dialogue that develops between them. We reflect on such motivations and relationships as well as locating the initiatives more precisely within the policy discourses discussed in Chapter Two. The five examples are:

- a community health forum involved in developing a community-run health centre;
- a social services user group seeking to influence the design and delivery of social care services for adults;
- a patient participation group in a GP surgery;

- a group aiming to secure the free provision of religious circumcision services for Muslim men by the NHS;
- a multi-ethnic group convened by an NHS trust to contribute to ensuring the provision of more appropriate services sensitive to the needs of different ethnic groups within the city.

We provide a brief description of each before discussing what these case studies have to say about the questions raised in Chapters Two to Four.

Community health forum

This forum was established in an area of City B, which was the subject of a number of regeneration initiatives. There was also a strong tradition of community activism, much of which was based around very local areas. The forum was unusual in that it covered two areas that had usually been the focus for separate action. The forum originated in a community-led research project organised as part of a campaign to resist closure of a local health centre. The campaign was successful: the health authority agreed to keep the health centre open and a new GP was recruited to work there. Residents decided to continue working to improve health services in the area because the health centre was in a poor condition and they thought that local people deserved better.

Our research took place six years after the success of the campaign to save the health centre. The group was uncertain about its future and frustrated about the lack of support from health service officials. However, they had decided to bid to the New Opportunities Fund (NOF) to establish a community-run healthy living centre (HLC). In order to qualify to bid to NOF the group had to reconstitute themselves and they became a health forum, with some members taking on the role of trustees holding formal responsibility for financial affairs. At the time of our research, members were preparing the NOF funding bid. They were also looking for other sources of funding, and trying to work with the health service to negotiate what services would be provided within the centre.

The group included people working for the NHS and other local agencies as well as local residents. Among the members were people who had direct experience of low incomes, joblessness, poor health and disability. Collectively members could draw on a range of experiences of activism, including within trades unions, service user and disabled people's organisations, religious groups, voluntary and direct action. Some were identified by other local people as a source of information and advice about a range of issues including housing and benefit problems, health and transport issues. While the constitution required that trustees had formal responsibilities, the forum was open to anyone living in the area. But there were few active members and it was not easy to encourage people to come to meetings. One interviewee estimated that there were about eight active members. Although only a small number of people were actively involved, many people in the area knew what was going on and regularly asked forum members about progress. There was a view that there was such a level of expectation within the area about the planned centre that it would have to be built – local people would not accept failure.

Observations of meetings revealed that discussions were highly task-focused and the language often quite technical. Much was concerned with the criteria for funding and what the group needed to do to meet these criteria, the information sources they could draw on, issues relating to planning permission, the charges that could be levied for space to be used by GPs and so on. A consultant (paid for by the Primary Care Group [PCG]) had been brought in to advise and support forum members in the preparation of the NOF bid. Many of these issues were followed up by the chair, secretary and treasurer outside the meetings and they reported back to other forum members.

Social services user group

A social services user group was established in City A in the late 1980s as part of a wide-ranging initiative to develop user-centred community care services. The group was intended to act as a watchdog to ensure that the user focus did not disappear once the special initiative came to an end. It was a broad coalition of service users, carers, voluntary organisations (groups *for* as well as *of* disabled people) and also some interested service providers. Originally supported within the central executive department of the council in order to reflect the corporate commitment to community care that had been an important aspect of the special initiative, by the time we were researching the group support was provided from within the social services department user and carers' unit. It worked closely with a local carers' forum that also had its origins in the community care initiative.

The group had three levels of membership: officers, a steering group comprising officers plus 10 elected members, and open meetings, ostensibly open to anyone sharing the objectives of the group, but in fact usually attended by 30-40 people: primarily disabled people and carers. Some representatives of mental health and learning disabilities groups attended, but in the early days of the group there had been a schism and many mental health services users had decided their interests were best served by a separate organisation focused on health services. The group had two sub-groups: an older people's forum and a black community care forum. The groups also hosted occasional conferences on specific themes. Attendees at open meetings were ethnically diverse, broadly reflecting the ethnic mix of the city.

The agenda for debate was discussed among officers and within the steering group, but was strongly influenced by requests for users' responses to proposals emanating from within the council. The volume of such requests and the short timescale given for responses meant it was very difficult for such issues to be discussed by the full membership. On a number of occasions council officers, invited to meet with the group, had declined, citing pressures on their diaries. During the research period the issue of engagement between the user group and council officers became a theme for debate in its own right, prompted in part by the group seeking an official response to a conference hosted by the group on a new consultation and commissioning structure, and in part by an inspection report that had commended the authority on its consultation structure, but criticised it for the absence of mechanisms for action in response to consultation. A new model for consultation was in the process of being developed at the end of the research period. This included proposals for separate reference groups to mirror the commissioning process within the social services department, that is, there would be a separate reference group for older people's services, although the group as a whole would maintain its overall 'watchdog' function. Some group members were optimistic and others cynical about the potential of these proposals to enhance service user/city council engagement.

Primary care patients' participation group

This group came about because of the commitment to patient participation of the senior partner in a GP practice. He was also the chair of a PCG board in City B and had been an advocate for patient participation within the board. He was supported in developing a practice-based group by the practice manager, although initially not by other doctors in the practice.

A leaflet left in the surgery invited patients to apply to become members of the group and this prompted 25 applications. From this, 12 people were selected by partners, although the criteria for selection were not made explicit. It was suggested that selection was intended to weed out those who might use the group as an opportunity to air long-standing grievances. However, when vacancies arose following the original selection, replacements were found by contacting those who had initially expressed their interest. Existing patient members declined the invitation to take part in the process of recruiting replacements. At the time of the research 10 of the 12 patient members were women, most of whom had experience of working in the health service or elsewhere in the public sector. Some concern was expressed about the absence of young people among the membership. The only formal staff representative was the senior GP partner; however, other disciplines within the practice usually sent a staff member to meetings. The PCG participation coordinator also attended and was eventually given a regular slot at meetings.

The agenda was largely set by staff and based on issues on which they wanted to consult patients. Meetings were chaired by the senior partner who often adopted a 'steering' role in discussions. The decision-making body of the practice remained the partnership and thus suggestions from the patients' participation group (PPG) had to be referred to partners for ratification. One positive example cited by all interviewees was the PPG suggestion that a separate telephone line should be provided to enable patients needing to cancel appointments to leave an answerphone message to this effect. In contrast, partners had rejected the proposal that a new practice leaflet and newsletter should be produced.

Patient members of the forum were concerned about the legitimacy of their status as 'patient representatives' and proposed two methods of enhancing their legitimacy. One was to provide a suggestion box in the surgery that would enable any patient to raise issues to be taken up by the group; another was to carry out a questionnaire survey of all practice patients. Partners were reluctant to support such a survey. Patient members also spoke of the difficulty of meeting together without staff being present. The presence of staff in PPG meetings meant there was some discomfort about expressing criticism, although there was also evidence of strong views being expressed in meetings. Contributions to discussions drew on members' own patient experiences, their perceived affinity with a particular 'type' of patient, information supplied by other patients and their own work experience.

Muslim male circumcision group

This example differs from others in the specificity of its original focus. A PCG in City A was approached by a local Muslim organisation with a request for religious circumcision to be made freely available on the NHS. The organisation noted the availability of this service elsewhere in the region. The PCG responded that while it was not possible to provide this service immediately, they were happy to facilitate talks with the health authority in return for broadening the focus for discussion to wider health issues relevant to the Muslim community, such as relatively high rates of coronary heart disease and smoking. Regular meetings were established as a result of this, with the first action being to draw up clinical guidelines for the practice of religious male circumcision.

The core membership of the discussion forum was small: a PCG representative, a health authority representative and two (male) representatives of the Muslim community. However, the consultation process involved broader contacts, through, in the first instance, umbrella organisations for mosques and, subsequently, selected individual mosques.

There were tensions throughout the period of discussion between the Muslim community and NHS representatives. These derived from the initial compromise over the focus for negotiation, and were exacerbated by the negative approach often taken by the health authority representative. The issue of NHS funding was not resolved during the research period and this, together with the change in internal NHS structure and subsequent move of the PCG representative to a high level post where he could no longer take direct responsibility for these discussions, meant that the sustainability of dialogue was uncertain.

Minority ethnic group council

Our final example in this chapter is also an instance in which issues of ethnic identity coalesce with those of re-forming services. The origins of the minority ethnic group council (MEGC) were in the recognition by a community health trust in City A that there was a need for information about health services to be available in different community languages. Further investigations led to a recognition of the importance of input from the range of minority ethnic groups in the city on this issue, and indeed on wider issues concerning the way in which services were designed, staffed, resourced and delivered, particularly in view of acknowledged health inequalities experienced by these groups. This led to the establishment of the MEGC comprising trust senior executives and members of local minority ethnic community organisations. The MEGC established a number of sub-groups, one of which, the human resources group, was the focus for our study. This was set up in 1999 and was selected for study both because it was one of the most active of the sub-groups and because it addressed an area – employment policy – about which public authorities have traditionally been very protective. The principal aim of all the groups was "working together to propose actions to address identified needs and shortfalls in service provision accessed by minority ethnic communities".

There were nine community members on this group, all of whom were members of groups represented on the full MEGC, a council intended to represent the diverse minority ethnic communities in the city. Other organisations that were not members of the MEGC were invited to give presentations on particular issues and this led in one instance to a request for continuing membership of the group. A debate about the issue of 'representation' ended with the woman concerned being invited to attend as an observer and contributor, but without offering her voting status. The group's support officer from the trust attended regularly and kept the minutes, the senior officer responsible for human resources attended less regularly and other officers were invited to attend to discuss particular agenda items.

The main discussion took place at bi-monthly evening meetings, although most members also represented their organisations at MEGC meetings and ad hoc meetings also took place on specific issues – one observed during the research focused on the ethnic monitoring of recruitment. Meetings followed a formal agenda and included reports back from non-group members and broader discussion items. There was often considerable debate and some quite sophisticated argumentation. The group initiated its own projects – such as a Jobs Fair – as well as responding to organisational and administrative issues from within the trust. There was some evidence of officials appearing somewhat apprehensive in the face of questioning by group members. The support worker can be seen to have fulfilled a dual role: both as trust representative to the sub-group and the sub-group's representative to the trust. Her work was seen as important in bridging the gap between a strong commitment at the very top of the trust to the MEGC, and operational managers and staff who appeared less committed and from whom there was fear of a potential backlash.

These brief descriptions illustrate the very different origins and histories of these initiatives. Only two were established solely as a result of initiatives from within service provider agencies: the PPG and the MEGC. In the case of the PPG this was influenced by the local PCG, which, in common with others, saw encouraging patient participation as part of its remit. In the words of the practice manager, the *NHS Plan* (DH, 2000) created a situation in which "we have no option in delivering these issues". The case of the MEGC was similar in being developed within a broad context within the NHS in which patient and public involvement was starting to be encouraged from the centre, but where there were key local actors who also drove its development: the chair of the community trust board and the trust chief executive. It was not just NHS policies relating to involvement that were significant, but also New Labour's highlighting of health inequalities in the context of the social inclusion agenda. The chief executive was described as "really pushing social inclusion".

In the other three cases there was pressure 'from below' that led to the establishment of these initiatives. Nevertheless, each was shaped by the evolving policy context in which they were operating.

The religious circumcision group was also helped by an NHS environment supportive of public involvement and in which the possibility of action to reduce health inequalities was opening up (see Barnes et al, 2005). The PCG representative on this group spoke of the issue of:

> "... clinical safety and quality of care. Almost from a citizens' rights point of view. That even if it's not an NHS treatment, a citizen should have a right not to be inappropriately mutilated by poor aftercare, by ignorance about hygiene...."

At the same time, what could be achieved was constrained by being raised just at the point at which PCGs were taking over from health authorities the responsibility of commissioning services. Moving resources from elsewhere to pay for circumcisions provided to meet religious requirements was considered to be a contentious issue in this context.

The particular strategy adopted by the community health forum to take forward its objectives to secure improved health services in a disadvantaged area was enabled by the introduction of the national policy to create HLCs, in which community and voluntary sector involvement was a key dimension. This policy was also influenced by the comparative priority being given to action to address health inequalities, a factor that also influenced citizen motivations to take part in this initiative. At a local level, the health authority commitment to community development was being passed on to PCGs and thus there was (at least in principle) support and encouragement for a community-led HLC bid from local health service organisations.

When it was first established around 1990, the social services user group was an innovative development, created in the context of early initiatives within social services departments to involve service users that can be located in the consumerist developments of the 1980s (for example, Barnes et al, 1990). As it developed, it became less unusual and increasingly had to respond to the impact of a range of policy initiatives that required social services departments (and other agencies) to consult with or involve their users: "... the Department has got to take service users' views into account more than they did before.... They are actually saying 'we need service users'" (user group chair). The key national policy initiatives that were identified were: Best Value, the National Services Frameworks and Joint Investment Plans. The group was seen from within the social services department as providing the potential to create a mechanism by which the various different consultative processes required by these developments could fit together and to act as a check on the 'quality of the machinery for consultation'. A joint inspection review of the department had praised it for the existence of consultation mechanisms, but criticised it for the absence of systems to respond to such consultation. This reflected the experiences of service users who hoped that the inspection report would make a difference in this respect.

Purposes and discourses

In the introduction to this chapter we suggested that consumerism was too narrow a concept to account for or understand these initiatives. If we look at the ways in which both citizens and officials spoke about their nature and purpose we can reflect on the dominant discourses that constructed the ways in which participation took place and was experienced. In addition to notions of consumerism, the public as stakeholders or responsible citizens, and an appeal to empowerment, these case studies illustrate the significance of contemporary policy discourses of partnership and community. As we will see, these two concepts are often interwoven.

Partnerships for progress?

The concept of partnership was employed both to claim such initiatives as examples of partnership between citizens and officials, and to illustrate the unequal relationships evident within them. Thus, for example, the PCG representative working with the religious circumcision group said they were "happy to partner with" the Muslim community representatives in order to develop clinical guidelines for the practice of religious circumcision and to explore ways of achieving changes that might reduce levels of diabetes and coronary heart disease among the Asian population. One of the Muslim community representatives explicitly contrasted the experience of trying to secure funding for the procedure with other examples of 'partnership' on public health issues that had been determined to be priorities by the NHS. The trust support officer working with the MEGC talked of "the benefits of working in partnership with communities". The chair of the social services user group noted that the social services department should realise that their relationship with the group needed to be an equal partnership, but that it was not. And similar points were made in the context of the relationship between the community health forum and local health officials.

Thus while the concept of partnership was used in the context of relationships between officials, service users and citizens, this can be considered to be more of an aspiration of officials than an expression of the reality of the relationship as experienced by lay participants (see also Barnes et al, 1999). It is not surprising that few spoke of the purpose of these initiatives in terms of 'empowerment'. With the exception of the community health forum, neither officials nor citizens spoke in a way that suggests that the 'empowered public' discourse was significant in framing the way in which these examples of participation were designed or conducted. Whether the initiatives were the result of action by officials, citizens or some combination of the two, the objectives were focused on securing services that were better quality, culturally appropriate, and more user-centred, and ensuring that all who could benefit from services knew about them and their entitlements to use them. Objectives were not focused on 'empowering' service users, either individually or collectively (although the social services user group took on a very limited advocacy role in some cases). The only outcome objective that focused on users (or 'community members') rather than services was the potential for such services to reduce health inequalities in the long term.

The community health forum was different. The chief executive of the local PCG located this in the context of a broader commitment within the PCG, not only to "be out there listening to people and hearing and then trying to come back and take action on what's been heard", but also "dealing with the community development side of things as well.... We're working a bit more upstream I suppose and looking at community development and working with people who might in the longer term have a health forum but don't have it yet".

She spoke of being "privileged" that there were so many active community health groups in the area. But she also saw the primary purpose of community involvement as "to influence service development" and the PCG representative who became a trustee of the group also linked her involvement in the group with her role in terms of service development for the PCG. She also said "... the whole purpose of it is to have the ... healthy living centre built. That's its sole purpose". Community members of this forum saw things rather differently. They shared the objective of creating a HLC, but located this within an 'empowered public' discourse that was not evident from the NHS officials. One aspect of that was to bring "the community and the professionals together, because it had never been done before. The professionals for some reason were nervous of the community and the community were nervous of the professionals. Neither trusted each other, basically."

But community members saw the purpose of the forum not only to get the health centre built, but also for this to be a community-owned and community-run centre, providing a range of resources designed specifically with and for residents who understand what it is like, for example, to try to follow a healthy diet in an area with few shops and considerable poverty.

In the context of the four discourses introduced in Chapter Two, the way in which both citizens and officials spoke about these initiatives revealed the dominance of the 'consuming public' and 'stakeholder public' discourses. With the exception of the community health forum, these case studies were seen predominantly as spaces in which there could be a dialogue between citizens and officials about the design and delivery of services, and factors (such as recruitment policies and the make-up of the staff group) that affect this. The community health forum was different in that it was focused on the development of a service that did not exist. However, we can also trace a rather different discourse emerging: that of the 'expert user' (a discourse that is explicit in the 'Expert Patients' programme within the NHS, for example, www.expertpatients.nhs.uk). The legitimacy and value of citizen input comes from their identities as service users, as stakeholders and, in some instances, as having a particular expertise on which officials can draw.

Power and agency

The PPG was the most circumscribed of these four examples in terms of the control exercised over it by officials. The practice manager talked of the practice management wanting to keep a grip on the process in order to "make it realistic", while from the perspective of 'patients', another factor constraining dialogue was the doctor/patient relationship. This woman compared contexts such as restaurants and holidays where there may be a need to complain about the service with the GP surgery context: "But when you are actually in a relationship where someone – you need to be able to go to someone with the most sensitive and delicate and urgent things that affect your life...", indicating important limitations in consumerist notions of participation (see also Barnes and Prior, 1995; Newman and Vidler, 2006). In this context it is unsurprising (if somewhat depressing) that the focus of discussions was limited to issues such as the attitudes of reception staff, systems for making and cancelling appointments, and the wording of letters to patients. From the practice manager's perspective the group was a 'sounding board', while one of the patient representatives described it as "a little committee, tagged on to management". He also went on to say that there was a feeling of being "unqualified" to raise certain issues, while another patient member said "we don't have any authority as patients". Thus, while they were able to point to some successes, most notably a new system for cancelling appointments, there was no sense that this forum went beyond the consumerist notion that service providers should invite feedback from their users.

The social services user group can be contrasted with this, much less well-established, patient group in part because of the acknowledgment from within the social services department of the expert knowledge that service users can claim. The support officer for the group also identified them as "stakeholders in community care services because of their need to use them". However, the use of service users' expertise was itself a source of frustration for one group member because, having accessed this expert knowledge at no cost, there was little indication that it was used:

> "Why should I go to a meeting and let people suck my brains of all the knowledge I have got for them to just do nothing with it? They want to know about A, B and C, then pay me a consultant's fee and I will come and do a presentation."

This comment was made in the context of broader criticisms of the way in which the group operated. This woman had extensive experience of action within the disability movement and saw the user group as not having progressed beyond providing a space in which people gave voice to complaints about services without linking these to a broader analysis of disabled people's oppression. She saw little evidence of the group exercising real influence. Similar concerns were expressed by the group's chair: "I feel that the Department will use us when it wants to use us and won't when it doesn't". However, others were rather more positive about the opportunity for voice that this forum represented.

The MEGC sub-group also evidenced the power of the stakeholder discourse, although the focus of their activity on human resource activity was unusual. The trust support officer described the purpose of the forum as to examine whether the policies and practices of the trust reflected equality of opportunity for all. In this context the minority ethnic communities that were the focus of the group's attention were viewed as stakeholders with a right to hold the trust to account and to expect that trust services would reflect their cultural as well as health needs, and that this would, in turn, contribute to achieving equality in relation to their health status. The discourse is not that of consumerism – the members of the group were not there because of their identities (actual or potential) as 'consumers' of the trust's services, but as representatives of minority ethnic communities. We discuss the significance of this in more detail below when we address the issue of who is involved and how they become involved.

Stakeholder communities

The relationship between 'stakeholders' and 'community' is evident here. Because of the size of the minority ethnic population in City A, participation discourses and practices were strongly focused on community in terms of identity as well as locality. Thus the many references to 'community' or 'communities' in relation to the MEGC referred to groups of people, who may or may not be service users, rather than to places. Such groups could have very different cultural, social and health circumstances, but are all entitled to expect that services would be appropriate to and for them. In setting up the MECG and its sub-groups health service officials were inviting people to take part on the basis of categorical identities and their public involvement in groups advocating for specific minorities.

The assumption here was that both factors conferred legitimacy on the basis of experiential knowledge. This was articulated by one sub-group member who said that because "we are from the communities" they had the understanding necessary to develop culturally aware practices, and others expressed similar views about the expertise they could bring. But this was contested by another sub-group member (himself a doctor) who was dismissive of such experiential knowledge. For him, relevant 'knowledge' derived from research, and he saw the dynamics of the group as including "battling against lay people, of their own perception". He said: "I do not think that the members of MEGC can give them [the trust] any information, any additional information which will be useful for the community trust to change its policies".

In the religious circumcision group the link between communities and stakeholders was also evident. Muslims were identified as stakeholders, a particular cultural community seeking health services responsive to their needs. One of the Muslim representatives appeared to recognise the importance of making an argument that acknowledged potentially competing stakeholder interests. He suggested there was an economic argument in favour of providing this service freely because this would reduce the need for health service input should complications arise from botched procedures. However, the health service perspective that shaped the field within which this group could operate expressed the broader stakeholder issue very differently:

> "… it's not just a decision affecting the Muslim community, because it could be that the money comes out of alcohol services, in which case we'd need to talk to the families and the carers and patients within alcohol misuse. And the doctors and nurses who want to keep their jobs and keep their clinics going, because they believe in them with a passion. And the local politicians."

In the case of the community health forum people living in the area were stakeholders because of their immediate interest in ensuring good quality health services capable of addressing the relationship between poverty and poor health in the area. They were also experts, drawing on personal experience of the difficulties faced by local people, on experience of advocating, campaigning and developing other alternative services (such as credit unions, and a 'baby barrow' – a service to enable single parents to buy baby equipment at minimal cost), and, in some instances, experience of working in health, local government and other public services. But the discourse of forum members also reflected their perception of themselves as 'empowered citizens' identifying themselves with 'community' in terms of the people in the local area. The following quote from one woman member acknowledges the fragility of this position:

> "Well, the overall purpose has always been the aim of the community to have their own healthy living centre.... Because we always say that the community is the front-runner. They are the most important people that you work for and you fight for.... My only fear is that the medical staff, the so-called professionals, will try to take over."

Motivations and identities

In discussing the discourses within which these participation initiatives were framed, we have started to identify ways in which those taking part might be conceptualised. Here we consider how people became involved and why, and the relationship between action within these forums and the construction of collective identities. Our focus is not just on the citizen members of these participation forums, but also the officials with whom citizens were in dialogue. We consider these forums as constitutive of identities as well as forums within which officials (and citizens) seek the representation of particular publics.

Elsewhere (Barnes et al, 2006) we have identified different types of 'commitments' that motivate people to take part in such initiatives, commitments to:

- an area
- religious values
- a cause or causes concerned with social justice
- a people, and
- commitments deriving from personal experiences.

We can identify each of these commitments among participants involved in initiatives to seek service improvements, but they are often interrelated. As a comparatively affluent member of the community health forum in City B commented:

> "What originally got me involved was living in the area, being part of the church in the area and feeling that I wanted to be involved in the community. Because my background is nursing and because we've got a disabled child, health was the sort of forum I slipped into really."

These different types of commitment interact dynamically with the particular opportunity context to shape people's involvement. Thus, for example, one woman who became involved in the social services user group found out about this by accident (she happened to see the group meeting in a disability resource centre), but talked about her involvement by reference to a strong identity as a disabled person committed to action:

> "I used to describe myself as a disability activist which I suppose underneath I still am.... It is part of my life. I am a disabled person. My mum has got this impairment, so I was very much aware of it as I grew up. I have brothers who have got it. My son has got an impairment. I live very much in a disability world. So I am just a natural fighter I think. It is naturally part of who I am. That is why I say I am a disability activist."

In contrast, patients invited to take part in the PPG identified reasons why they thought it was worthwhile to respond positively to this invitation, but without locating this within a strong sense of personal or social identity. One woman related this to her own experience trying to get feedback from service users in the context of her work for Connexions, while a male member of the group referred to the shock of having to receive treatment for a major health problem and wanting to "give something back" as a result. In other cases involvement in the *particular* participation initiative was perhaps less significant than the fact that citizen members could point to wide-ranging involvement in community activities, and that this had led to invitations and opportunities to take part in the context of these case studies. This was evident to a varying extent in all groups apart from the PPG.

Many of the officials involved in these initiatives shared not only quite similar social identities to the lay members, but also expressed similar motivations for their involvement to those expressed by community members. For example, the trust support officer working with the MEGC talked not only about her commitment to working with communities in both paid and unpaid capacities, such as membership of a local Hindu council and her role as chair of a Hindu women's network, but also of the origins of these commitments in both her family origins and her faith:

> "... we believe in purification of the soul and you've got this life and you make the best use of this life and we can

do that by helping others ... to give a bit of yourself to the society which is looking after you and that's where we come from, what we believe in."

The PCG chief executive who was working with the religious male circumcision group did not share a social identity with the Muslim representatives, but did declare a strong professional commitment to minority ethnic health issues and located this within a social justice frame motivated by anger at social exclusion and racism.

Some participants struggled with their identities as 'official' or 'community' members. A woman who worked for Sure Start, but who was involved in the community health forum, was uneasy about us identifying her because when she first became involved in the campaign to keep the health centre open she was working within the NHS. She could claim legitimate membership of the forum because she was a local resident, but because she also worked locally in roles that placed her within the official sphere she struggled to hold back from playing a leading role in the forum, drawing on her professional knowledge and official contacts in the process. She also talked of not wanting to "go native", which, when asked, she defined as: "Become a member of the community and lose my skill". In contrast, the doctor who was a 'community' representative on the MEGC distanced himself both from 'the community' and the trust managers. He described the purpose of the group as:

> "... doing some research, and then motivating the community at one extreme to take responsibility of their health into their own hands. But on the other side also trying to get statutory bodies to change their methods of service delivery...."

Here he positions himself as a clinician appealing to research evidence as the basis on which decisions should be made and questioning the capacity of community members (other than himself and another doctor) to make a real contribution to service development or health improvement.

In the case of those whose involvement primarily resulted from 'doing their job' these tensions between 'official' and 'citizen' identities were usually resolved in favour of the official identity. The MEGC trust support officer was clear about this: "I'm biased. I'm the XXX trust, I'm not a community member and that has to be very clear in my head. And that's the only way I can do this kind of work or the boundaries will get fudged, and I can't let that fudge my thinking process because then I'd become judgemental as well in how I work with the communities and so a line has got to go up" (the interaction between lay and official forum members is explored further in Chapters Seven and Eight). This is important in considering the extent to which these forums can be considered spaces within which collective identities were being constructed.

Collective identity building: among citizens, between citizens and officials

A key factor in the selection of forums for study was that they were spaces within which there was dialogue between citizens and officials. This distinguishes them from social movement organisations (SMOs) that deliberately operate outside the official sphere in order to oppose and challenge. However, as we and others (for example, Taylor, 2003) have argued, it is hard to draw firm categorical distinctions between SMOs and many of the hybrid participation initiatives that have developed out of the contexts we have discussed in Chapters Two and Three. We need to look more closely at the dynamics of particular initiatives in order to consider the extent to which these forums are spaces in which the collective identity building that Melucci claims sustains action is evident, and to reflect on whether such collective identities are forged among community members or between community members and officials.

We can see very different types of relationship between citizens and officials in these five case studies. As we have argued above, the notion of 'partnership' is highly problematic as a means of characterising these relationships, but simply to point to an inequality in the power relationships involved is insufficient. Once again the PPG stands out as the clearest example of the difficulty of developing a collective identity among patients in a situation in which the forum was controlled by doctors and other practice staff. This difficulty was practical: the problems experienced in trying to enable patients to meet together without practice staff, constrained by an unwillingness to be seen to be "doing anything underhand ... splinter group, you know, ummm rebel patients" in the context of the doctor/patient relationship, and inhibited by the apparent unwillingness of practice staff to support the capacity of patient representatives to build their links with the patient population as a whole.

Lay members of the religious male circumcision group were highly focused on the specific objective of securing a service paid for by the

NHS and there was little evidence that this particular forum was seen as a space within which enduring identifications might be grown. Rather it was a space within which negotiations between two distinct 'sides' could be carried out, with sufficient common purpose to sustain largely amicable relationships.

The other three examples offer rather more complex pictures. Both the social services user group and the MEGC sub-group deliberately sought to build alliances among different community groups – with varying success. The early days of the MEGC were described by a number of participants as difficult in terms of the relationships between different minority ethnic communities represented. From one perspective this was a distinction between an African Caribbean focus on 'race' and racial discrimination in jobs, and a focus among at least some Asian representatives on the need to understand the diverse health needs within different Asian communities. Another described the early dynamics as "haggling", and offered the following explanation: "Because most community groups, because while they are involved in something new the natural communities that help secure your territory are making their mark". While most of those interviewed considered that these early difficulties had been overcome (not least because of the successful intervention of an African woman appointed as the first chair of the group), the position of the doctor quoted above suggests that the notion of a collective 'we' among community representatives was still somewhat fragile. His urging of the importance of distinguishing among different ethnic, cultural and class grouping within Asian communities was reflected by the concern of an African member that representation should distinguish African from African Caribbean communities. And the doctor's identification with another doctor member, and his personal distancing from lay members he felt had little to offer the forum, constituted a further axis of difference.

The social services user group was comparatively unusual in seeking to bring together all users of community care services (disabled people, older people, people with mental health problems and people with learning difficulties) with carers and anyone else who was interested in the development of community care services. Among its sub-groups it included a black community care forum in recognition of the distinctive needs and circumstances of black service users. However, one member of this sub-group who was interviewed stressed his commitment to the value of collective action across lines of racial or ethnic difference: "... they all need to be under one umbrella, and therefore if everybody can do this they get things done. It doesn't mean you lose your identity". In practice there was very little direct involvement of people with mental health problems, and group members recognised they needed to do more to ensure issues relating to mental health service users and people with learning difficulties were better represented. But beyond this questioning of the group's capacity to encompass the range of interests of all service users, there was another, perhaps more fundamental, questioning of the extent to which the group could claim to have developed a collective identity. The purpose of the group was described as enabling a voice for users of social care services. Members contested whether voice should be understood as individual advocacy, personal testimony or collective action with specific change objectives. Some spoke of the importance of the forum as a site in which experiential knowledge, expressed in personal accounts, could be exchanged. Others saw this as inadequate as a basis for achieving change, and there was little evidence of testimony informing more general campaigns. Thus there was a tension between different perceptions of the group and the extent to which this required a stronger collective identity, or whether the group's objectives could be achieved either by representing individual issues, or by acting as a support group. This can be contrasted with, for example, autonomous disabled people's organisations whose action is framed within an explicit ideological position (the social model of disability) and which has created a movement based within a strong shared identity as disabled people (Campbell and Oliver, 1996).

In neither case, despite supportive officials who might be considered 'allies' of the groups, was there evidence of collective identities being forged between citizens and officials. In these case studies, as in others, the dominant discourse was that of citizens and officials as occupying different spaces, but seeking to find a way of maximising the points at which similar objectives could be achieved by working together. Shared interests and shared social identities were more often cited as a source of tension than as an opportunity for collective identification. In the social services user group there had been discussion about whether employees of the local authority would be allowed to become members. The current chair of the group reflected on the debates there had been about this:

> "They aren't at the moment, but there is kind of two groups. One is saying 'no, they shouldn't', but another is saying 'well, what about home care assistants? And what about gardeners and stuff who may be carers?'."

In noting the potential for officials also to be service users, it is perhaps significant that such identifications were located among frontline workers rather than managers. This suggests that it is easier for service users to imagine a collective 'we' that involves comparatively powerless officials than powerful officials.

From her hybrid perspective the Sure Start worker involved in the community health forum recognised the significance of the emotional engagement of community members in the group in securing its objectives:

> "I'm very aware that this is a community-driven initiative and the community have got to be allowed to drive it, and if mistakes are made, well that's fine, and I'm quite happy to stand alongside them to do that. I will ask pertinent questions, but also they're very emotionally involved in the development as well and that's quite difficult."

This was reflected in the fears of community members that professionals (by which they usually meant medical staff) would try to take over control of the HLC once it had been established because they saw control of such a resource by local people as a threat. Even though there were differences among group members deriving from class positions, gender, professional backgrounds and political views, the framing of their objectives in relation to injustices to be overcome by community control of the centre provided a stronger sense of a collective 'we' than was evident in others of these case studies. This was also related to the strong identification with the area and the people living there and the often-lengthy history of activism on a range of issues in which key members had been involved. Some health service professionals were identified as genuine allies in this process, while others were unhelpful or actively hostile.

Representations and connections

The issue of 'representation' is seen to be at the heart of the legitimacy of such participation forums as spaces within which new relationships between public bodies and their publics can be built (Barnes et al, 2003). Both citizens and officials were concerned about issues of representation, although the significance of formal or semi-formal processes by which groups might be represented within these forums was very different.

Within the community health forum it was considered to be much less significant than in other cases. Here the legitimacy of those involved in the forum was seen, rather unproblematically, to derive from their connections with the area and their willingness to take on the task of securing funding and negotiating with planners, service providers and other officials in order to create a resource from which the whole community would benefit. The problem of securing a wider level of activism was noted and the drop in level of input from the time when they were campaigning to keep the health centre open, to the point at which the research took place, was a particular issue:

> "They'd be going out cold winters' nights canvassing to preserve the clinic. But once everything's up and running, they got a nice house, they got a nice garden and everything, they say 'that's it, why should I bother going to the meetings anymore?'."

But this was not seen to undermine the legitimacy of those who were involved. Indeed, the fact that participants were known as activists who were in regular contact with other community members in a number of both individual and collective campaigning contexts, suggested that it was almost expected that the participants would take on a leadership role in securing the HLC.

The origins of the social services user group also meant that participation derived primarily from interest and willingness to get involved rather than any more formal notion of representation or representativeness. Positions on the steering group were filled by nomination and voting, but the open meetings could be attended by anyone with an interest in community care. The officer supporting the group considered that "Its validity depends on it having a main core of people who actually do have an interest. They are stakeholders in community care services because of their need to use them!". He also talked of members bringing both contact with broader 'constituencies' and their own personal knowledge; however, he also considered that "it does have some representative structure but again it needs a lot more development". This suggested a wish to formalise the membership in order to link the group much more closely to the decision-making structures of the Department. Thus, at the time of the research, discussions were taking place about linking group members to specific commissioning groups (which themselves were organised by reference to distinct user groups). This suggests that the notion of an all-encompassing, open grouping was starting to be considered incompatible with the process of influencing service decision making. The ambiguity of the group's position is perhaps best expressed by one disabled member of the group: "It's an independent body, run by the city council".

The complaint that lay members had insufficient time and resources to enable effective communication between themselves and their constituencies was a common one. But the resistance of GP partners to enabling PPG members to survey other patients is perhaps the only example of a deliberate attempt to prevent connections that might add to the legitimacy and perhaps power of citizens vis-à-vis officials. In other instances the legitimacy of representatives was questioned: "are they really the true representatives of the community or not?... we are asking that question because some of them are just sitting there because they want to sit there, it's quite high profile" (trust support officer, MEGC). This comment is especially pertinent in the context of an initiative that did have quite a formal process of representation. The trust identified a number of community groups that were invited to send representatives to sit on the umbrella group and it was only those groups that could be represented on the sub-groups (including the human resources group that was the focus of our study).

Rules, norms and institutional practices

Here we consider the way in which deliberation within the forums was shaped by the institutional context and the way in which behaviour and responses (both of officials and the public) were guided/influenced by the rules and norms that operated within those contexts.

One aspect concerns the way in which membership was constituted and the extent to which this was defined by official definitions of what constitute legitimate publics for the purposes of public participation. As we have discussed elsewhere (Barnes et al, 2003) much of that centres around ways in which notions of representativeness are constructed. In the case of the MEGC this was determined by the health trust's identification of (ethnic) community groups in the city and invitations to organisations based around those ethnic identities to send representatives to the full group. In turn, membership of the human resources sub-group depended on representation on the full group. Things were very different in relation to the PPG in the GP surgery. Although there was a notional attempt to ensure inclusion of patients in a range of different circumstances (young parents as well as older patients, for example) the primary factor guiding selection from those volunteering to take part in this group was the senior partners' assessment of whether they were 'genuine' or whether volunteers were likely to use the group for their own purposes. The practice manager commented: "sometimes people have different agendas as to why they want to be there".

There was much less control by officials in relation to membership in the other three cases although, as we have seen, things were likely to change as social services officials were suggesting that more formal representative structures should be introduced. The difference was that neither the community health forum, nor the social services user group, nor the religious circumcision group had been established as a result of initiatives solely within the official sphere. To a greater or lesser extent, these were initiatives coming from within 'the community' and thus it was harder for officials to impose their view of what constituted legitimate membership.

But in all cases there was substantial evidence of institutional factors constraining both the way in which dialogue developed and what it was possible to achieve. This was more overt in some cases than others. Thus in the PPG control was exercised: (1) by the unwillingness of patient representatives to be seen as 'rebel patients' in the context of the need to sustain their confidence that they would continue to be treated properly by doctors; (2) by the unwillingness of patients to be critical of staff when they were present within the forum; and (3) by patients' sense of their lack of knowledge about the details of the NHS context, as well as by the overt decision of the practice staff that they needed to set up the forum in such a way as to ensure that "we had to keep ownership of it".

In the community health forum, where there was in principle considerably more autonomy for community members to decide how to run the process, the necessity to focus their activities on meeting the criteria to get funding for the HLC, and to negotiate with the PCG in relation to health facilities to be located in the centre, resulted in a very task-focused way of engaging. It also had the effect of relegating issues that community members wished to pursue (such as interest in developing ways in which fresh vegetables may be grown and made more widely available in the area), but which were not *as* high priority in terms of achieving the main objective.

The pressure to be seen as 'reasonable' was a powerful one shaping the practices of many community members involved in these initiatives. It was particularly evident in the MEGC where it was referred to in a number of different ways. The current chair spoke about the group adopting a "softly, softly approach, but to show that we mean what we say". Another community member spoke about not saying "anything which was unreasonable" and asserted that "we don't demand anything that is not deliverable". The assessment of what was and was not deliverable was based on their understanding of the constraints operating within the trust. Although they might be very frustrated about aspects of this, for example, the decentralisation of recruitment processes to individual directorates within the trust, their attempts to challenge this were based on reasoned argument in the context of good-humoured relationships between community representatives and officials. The chair explicitly commented on his unwillingness to embarrass any manager who came to meetings of the group: "I rarely ask a question that will be seen as being critical. I tend to do my homework in advance...". A similar sense of needing to understand the constraints each side was working under was evident in the relationship between the PCG representative and the community lead on the religious circumcision group. The PCG representative understood the community lead's position as a high status member of his community who needed to be able to point to achievements to reassure his community that he was not being hoodwinked by white managers. For his part the community representative talked of the way in which the PCG manager "showed us the way we could walk hand in hand", and acknowledged his position having to make decisions about what was and what was not going to be funded by the PCG.

Not all community members were comfortable with this dominant sense that they should mould their approaches and demands to an understanding of what was likely to be acceptable to the officials they were dealing with. One of the social services user group members was critical of the fact that, as she saw it, agendas were largely set by the social services department and the group were insufficiently demanding. She compared one of the group's successes – getting changes in the design of Orange badges (for disabled car users) – with their failure to achieve a change in criteria for accessing occupational therapy services: "we can have a say on the orange badges, because they're only little, it doesn't affect everybody: OT [occupational therapy] services – oh no...".

In most cases there was little explicit discussion of the rules of the game as far as the way in which dialogue should be conducted. Some negotiation of rules for membership did take place, but this also was more a question of working things out as they went along rather than a very explicit process of negotiation. In this context the form of dialogue usually followed fairly traditional meeting processes, with little sense that innovative methods were being developed to ensure the inclusion of people unfamiliar with both formal and informal meeting rules.

Overall, what was possible in terms of service outcomes in each case was largely determined by what service providers could accept without either incurring significant costs or making significant change to policies or procedures. The institutional context in each case was largely supportive of consultation with service users, but also created counter pressures, often explained as budgetary pressures, which, it was argued, placed definite boundaries around the extent to which they could respond to such consultations. In some cases other constraints were recognised. The social services official who supported the user group both referred to the need for cultural change to convince some officials that they should not only listen but also take action, and highlighted the bureaucracy and inertia that get in the way of change. The outcome of the community health forum's activities was uncertain when the research ended, and because their focus was on the development of a new service for which new funds were being sought, the stakes were higher as well as being more uncertain. In this case key officials were largely supportive of the group's objectives, not least because these did not require them to change their own services or to fund new ones.

Conclusion

In each of these cases citizens took part because they wanted to see changes in the services that they, their families and/or other members of their communities needed to use. Evidence of significant service change resulting from these activities was slight, but those who remained involved did so because they continued to hope for change and thought it important to continue to have a voice. The officials with whom these citizens engaged in dialogue supported the idea of user-prompted improvements, but either saw themselves as unable or were unwilling to question fundamentally what is possible in terms of service change. In some cases these messages were too effectively communicated to citizen participants who modified or restricted their claims on the basis of what was possible rather than desirable. These dynamics were less evident in the more autonomous community health forum, but here the demands of negotiating with planning and funding bureaucracies tended to have a similar restraining impact.

'Having a voice' was important in itself in the early days of the development of 'user involvement', in particular for people often denied a voice because they were considered too frail, incompetent or 'lacking in insight' to express their views about services. Being taken seriously was often cited as a valuable outcome per se. But it is uncertain how sustainable such initiatives will continue to be in the absence of real change. These examples do not suggest that a shift from a consumerist to a partnership discourse represents real change in the power relationships operating in these forums. Shared social identities, either among citizen participants, or between citizen and official participants, do not necessarily generate a strong sense of collective identities, and alliances may operate along rather different lines, as well as creating tensions that can be difficult to manage for individuals and groups.

In Chapters Six and Seven we consider how these dynamics operate in the context of initiatives focused around place and identity.

SIX

Neighbourhood and community governance

The 'neighbourhood' is receiving increasing attention from politicians and policy makers at all levels throughout Europe (Allen and Cars, 2002). Targeted neighbourhoods are subject to major 'revitalisation' programmes, stimulated by government and frequently undertaken in partnership. Neighbourhoods have also proved attractive as spaces for community governance in which the complexity, fragmentation and remoteness from the public of the prevailing system may be overcome by combining network organisation and a citizen orientation (Sullivan, 2001b, 2002; McLaverty, 2002). Intertwined with these ambitions is an aspiration that neighbourhoods might also contribute to renewing democracy through the development of new pathways for public participation in decision making offered by devolved institutions (Pratchett, 2004; Sullivan and Howard, 2005).

Attention on the neighbourhood has coincided with the emergence of new governance arrangements in many western democracies characterised by: an up-scaling of authority to global institutions and a down-scaling of responsibilities to the sub-national level (Brenner, 2004, p 3); technological advances and moves to privatisation and partnership that create options for more responsive and particularised forms of service delivery; and a 'new politics' that utilises new kinds of political agency and organisation to connect international concerns with their impact on local communities. Lowndes and Sullivan argue that, in combination the elements of the new governance "combine to create space for the emergence of neighbourhoods as an important institution in the multi-level and multi actor environment" (2007: forthcoming).

In England, policy makers have been drawn to the neighbourhood as a space for policy action since the 1960s, although definitions of 'the neighbourhood' have always been rather ambiguous (Lowndes and Sullivan, 2007: forthcoming). While New Labour has demonstrated particular enthusiasm for the neighbourhood as a source of economic, social and democratic renewal, each of these ambitions had antecedents in the policies of other postwar governments.

Perhaps foremost among these ambitions is the attempt to alleviate poverty and stimulate economic regeneration through targeted neighbourhood action. This was a key claim of the architects of programmes in both Conservative and Labour administrations from the 1970s. Criticised for failing to take sufficient account of the fact that the root causes of disadvantage may lie in wider processes of economic and social change beyond the neighbourhood (Bradford and Robson, 1995), governments persisted with these programmes because of a fluctuating awareness that persistent inequality in neighbourhoods may be due in part to the actions of unresponsive and uncoordinated public service organisations (Sullivan and Skelcher, 2002).

Consequently some targeted neighbourhood programmes sought to make an immediate impact via their economic, social and physical interventions, but also had longer-term objectives about reorienting the mainstream patterns of service delivery among key providers. One of the case studies in this chapter focuses on the experience of a group of residents involved in a Conservative government-initiated regeneration programme with these objectives. Prompted by dissatisfaction with the quality of the regeneration work under way in their neighbourhood, and with what they saw as the failure of the existing community representatives to do their job, a small group of residents established their own residents' group to represent their interests to decision makers and service delivery bodies on the estate.

Another fluctuating feature of neighbourhood policies and programmes is the emphasis placed on local communities' contribution to the success of the initiative. Evident in the Conservative government's SRB programme of the 1990s, it found its strongest expression in New Labour's NSNR, which identified the neighbourhood as the source of local intelligence, community motivation and momentum for renewal (SEU, 2000). The discourses operating in these programmes expressed a concern with empowering (usually poor) communities to enable the lay expertise and energy contained within them to be released, coupled with an emphasis on the role of neighbourhood communities as responsible citizens, charged with taking advantage of the opportunities provided by government interventions, for example by taking up training opportunities to improve their skills and chances of employability, and with contributing to the good governance of the neighbourhood through community organisation and action.

Two of the case studies in this chapter illustrate the way in which these dual discourses found expression in New Labour's Sure Start programme. Supporters of the programme emphasise its potential to empower (mainly women) participants by increasing their confidence through an appreciation and development of their parenting skills, while critics focus on the way in which the programme supports the discourse of the 'responsible' public by specifying particular ways in which parenting should be undertaken (Toynbee and Walker, 2005; Hey and Bradford, 2006). Our case studies examine the experiences of officials and parents in two different areas, exploring the purchase these official discourses have on local participants and their impact on the practices of each local programme.

Bringing decision-making processes closer to the neighbourhood and opening them up to influence by the public in the hope of stimulating democratic renewal is another ambition of neighbourhood policy. Initiatives tend to be universal in their application rather than targeted on particular communities and they are more likely to be initiated locally than nationally. English local authorities have considerable experience of experimenting with decentralisation schemes for a variety of purposes, usually including increased and enhanced public participation in local decision making (see Chapter Two, this volume, and Burns et al, 1994; Hambleton et al, 1996; Carley et al, 2000; Sullivan et al, 2001). At the same time grass-roots organisations have also made use of neighbourhood-based approaches. For example the Neighbourhood Councils movement of the late 1960s and 1970s argued for urban parish councils in metropolitan areas as a means of bringing government closer to communities (Cockburn, 1977).

In its third term, New Labour emphasised the potential of the neighbourhood as a space within which to develop more 'joined-up' and responsive local services for all, not just those in 'deprived' communities (ODPM/HO, 2005), with individuals and communities able to exercise greater 'choice and voice' in the context of a wider programme of devolution from central to local government and beyond to the neighbourhood (ODPM, 2006). Reflecting the significance of local initiatives in shaping this policy agenda, two of the case studies in this chapter examine local authority-sponsored area committees or area forums. For the sponsors, these area-based governance structures were operationalising a stakeholder discourse in which the public and local public, voluntary and community bodies were invited to participate as agents with a legitimate interest in decision making about issues that affected the neighbourhoods within which they lived and/or worked. The case studies explore the extent to which this stakeholder discourse was either recognised and/or realised in these local initiatives.

Given the level of attention paid to the neighbourhood by policy makers, this chapter considers the importance of a sense of attachment to the neighbourhood as a motivator for officials' and public participants' involvement in our five cases. Four of the cases were 'officially sponsored' initiatives so we explore the influence of existing institutional rules and norms on these emergent neighbourhood bodies, considering the extent to which they were adopted, resisted and/or replaced, and the impact of these institutional influences on the nature and quality of the resultant participation. Finally the chapter takes the opportunity provided by this new material to revisit some key arguments in the decentralisation debate: the interaction between representative democracy and participative approaches, the capacity of place-based activity to reflect diversity, and the impact of small-scale deliberation on wider political engagement (Dahl and Tufte, 1973; Newton, 1989).

A summary of each of the cases is presented below as a basis for the subsequent analysis and discussion.

Residents' group

The residents' group came into being to represent the interests of people living in a small part of an estate managed by the Housing Action Trust (HAT), a nationally funded 10-year regeneration scheme voted for by the residents in 1993. The resident population of the estate was largely white European, in sharp contrast to the city's overall population. The success of a small group of residents in getting together to press for gates to be placed on the back alleys to their properties, so as to avoid young people congregating there and causing a nuisance, led to the formation of a permanent residents' group. With the encouragement of the HAT participation workers, the group adopted a constitution enabling them to be recognised formally by the HAT. This required the group to have an elected committee and a 'code of conduct' to guide its operation. The relationship between the residents' group and the HAT was fractious as the group saw the HAT as another organisation that had come on to the estate, divided the residents through the participation structures it had established, and pursued its own goals with the contractors, rather than those of the residents.

Membership of the group was determined by residence in a specific part of the estate consisting of 300-400 houses. Those elected to the group committee had a range of backgrounds. Some had considerable experience of committee activity, either as trades union officials, in relation to other interests or hobbies or as part of their employment. Some were members of other voluntary groups on the estate. Others had no past experience and had got involved in the residents' group because they were concerned about their local area. The members of the residents' group interacted in three key ways: with other residents to identify concerns and feed back the results of representations to the HAT; with each other in committee meetings to decide on key issues to pursue or formulate courses of action; and with representatives of the HAT, contractors or other relevant bodies to pursue particular enquiries. The group was supported in its work by the HAT participation workers, who provided data and other resource materials, organised meetings and helped identify who might be the 'right people' to speak to in any given circumstance.

Sure Start in City A

The origins of this Sure Start lay with the development of a successful under-5s project by a local voluntary organisation and the emergence of a multiagency city-wide 'family support strategy' led by the health authority. In 1999 the health authority asked the voluntary organisation if it would be prepared to host the bid for a Sure Start scheme. The project was based within a socially mixed suburb, with a majority white European population, although the percentage of minority ethnic groups was much higher in the birth-to-five age group. Sure Start funding was used in two ways. Capital was invested in developing and extending a pre-existing local authority-owned centre home to a voluntary organisation working with pre-school children that was the focus for developing the Sure Start programme. Revenue funding was used to support outreach and home visiting services to parents and carers in the catchment area (of 1,200 parents and 800 children). A small Sure Start core team managed the programme and delivered the outreach services, and statutory and voluntary organisations were drawn in to provide additional services to the area.

The Sure Start governance arrangements were devolved to an interim advisory board (IAB) with the health authority retaining responsibility as the accountable body for funding purposes. Our research was undertaken at the point when the governance arrangements for Sure Start were becoming established. The IAB was made up of representatives from all the key sectors involved in the Sure Start initiative including health, local government and voluntary sectors. Eight seats on the board were reserved for parent representatives. The board was responsible for overseeing the implementation of the Sure Start programme, holding the programme manager to account and addressing issues of practice and policy where necessary.

The vast majority of the IAB members were female, spread across a wide age range (30s–60s). A majority of the participants were white European although key senior managers within the Sure Start team were from minority ethnic communities. Common among participants was a specific interest in children and families, either through the direct experience of being a parent or carer and/or through professional experience. A number of participants also had quite considerable experience of voluntary work in relation to children and families. Deliberation was primarily concentrated within the work of the IAB. However, other mechanisms were used to encourage dialogue between parents and carers and the Sure Start project. Some of these were 'one-offs' (organising a 'fun day', conducting a service audit of local parents' needs), while others were more regularised (task groups to develop a local newsletter and a parents' forum to secure wider engagement).

Sure Start in City B

This Sure Start project was based in one of the most deprived estates in the city. It was established through the work of a consortium of local bodies led by the local regeneration partnership. The consortium spent considerable time engaging parents and consulting with them in a variety of ways (open days, focus groups, free phone lines) to determine the key areas of activity for Sure Start in the locality. This process of consultation brought a number of parents onto the Sure Start board. The Sure Start project was one of a number in City B all linked together through a city-wide Sure Start strategic partnership group.

The Sure Start board was the key decision-making body for the project. At the time of the research the Sure Start project was chaired by a local parent. There were 14 board members, six local parents/grandparents, a small number of Sure Start staff and representatives from local statutory and voluntary organisations that provided services through the Sure Start project (including the local authority, housing association and health organisations). Some of these bodies were local but most had a city-wide or even regional remit. Originally the city council was the accountable body for the project but dissatisfaction with the service provided and the amount charged meant that the board was considering becoming a limited company responsible for their own funds at the time of the research. Board meetings were held bi-monthly. Considerable activity was devolved to task groups (for example, capital projects, childcare planning and teenage pregnancy) as it was felt that local parents would be more likely to get involved in smaller, purpose-specific forums. In addition the project had regular 'away days' where particular issues were explored in more depth and also organised 'fun events', for example, Christmas parties, as a way of engaging local residents more informally with the activities of the project.

At the time of the research the Sure Start board was experiencing considerable conflict in its meetings: a combination of very powerful personalities and some contentious issues. Managing this conflict was a key challenge for the chair and the Sure Start coordinator.

Area advisory board in City A

Area advisory boards were the local authority's 'flagship' policy for increasing citizen participation in local decision making and facilitating neighbourhood renewal. The boards were established in the mid-1990s following many years of experiments with decentralisation. They operated at ward level in parallel with city council ward sub-committees, were supported by council officers and had links with more localised and resident-led neighbourhood forums. Each board was encouraged to bring together local residents and service deliverers outside the council to advise on local issues, help develop future plans for the locality and determine the allocation of discretionary 'community grant' funding that was channelled through the boards by the local authority. Guidance on how the boards should operate was issued by the council's central policy team. Selection to the boards was based on two core criteria, that individuals should live or work in the area and that they should be representatives of an organisation.

The area advisory board studied in the research was established in 1997 in a suburban ward made up of interwar owner-occupied housing and postwar council development. The population was mainly white European, older and less deprived than the city averages. At the time of the research the board had approximately 40 regular members, the majority from local community and voluntary groups, with local elected members and officials from the local authority and other service providers also regular attendees. The majority of members were white European and middle aged or retired.

Deliberation within the area advisory board was based on an agreed agenda of items, which emerged in part from the deliberations of previous advisory board meetings. In addition, the meetings had a number of common agenda items including: applications for community grants, community safety issues and health issues. The applications for grants dominated the meetings for some time and were the source of considerable debate between board members. The role of the board in facilitating dialogue outside of the bids process was less easy to describe. Health and police representatives brought information to the board and responded to questions about new developments or specific problems, but the board was not involved in discussions about local policing plans or health service priorities. The area board created a network of informed participants that could 'do business' outside the meetings of the area board.

Area committee in City B

In 1999 a new council administration sought to fulfil its manifesto pledge to devolve power to communities by establishing 11 area committees in the city. The council's primary aim for the committees was to give local people an opportunity to take part in the decision-making process and to hold local councillors to account for the performance of the council and other public service bodies. As committees of the council they were subject to the rules and conditions that regulated council conduct. The area committee that formed part of our research covered three wards, which although adjacent were very different in terms of their demography and socioeconomic conditions. Two of the wards were relatively affluent while the other experienced considerable disadvantage and had a more diverse population.

The area committee had four different forms of membership. Elected councillors from each of the three wards that comprised the area committee were full members with voting rights. Lay advisory members were individuals selected through open recruitment and selection processes to serve as members but with no voting rights. Membership was also extended to representatives of key public organisations, for example, the police and key partnerships, with no voting rights, and to individuals who may be co-opted onto focus or task groups of the committee because of their particular expertise, again with no voting rights. In addition, the area committee recognised three stakeholder groups as participants in the workings of the committee. These were members of the public, representatives of local community/voluntary organisations and officers of the local council. The vast majority of members and participants were white European. Councillors were mainly middle- and older-aged men; advisory members were more diverse, younger and with a greater proportion of women to men; and members of the public tended to be white, middle- to older-aged men and women. The absence of young people was a concern and attempts were being made to engage more regularly with local young people in a range of ways including through the establishment of a youth forum.

The area committee meetings tended to be very formal, not least because they were framed by the rules and practices governing council committees. They followed a common format including: updates from councillors and partners on matters of local relevance, presentations from external speakers about identified issues of key concern or future service/policy developments and public 'question time', the point in the meeting where local people could raise their issues. The chair of the committee was very conscious of the formality inherent in the operation of council committees and regularly tried to lighten the tone and find new ways of communicating/interacting.

The diverse origins and contexts of the five cases shaped their development and their character. Consequently, initiatives with similar aspirations operated very differently. The residents' group modelled itself on a trades union or lobbying group, setting itself in opposition to the estate contractors and having a clear demarcation between itself and the HAT (to avoid 'conflicts of interest'). It was formal in its organisation and had a clear set of rules and expectations of members. The Sure Start scheme in City A was much softer by comparison, with an emphasis on informality and relationship building. Rather more battle scarred in City B, the Sure Start initiative was deliberately inclusive in its dealings with parents, but had a much tougher edge that it displayed to statutory bodies and professionals. A similar distinction can be drawn between the area advisory board and the area committee. In City A the area board was generally considered 'a safe space' in which members felt comfortable and at ease, although there were clear protocols that guided the meetings. In City B, by contrast, the area committee was an antagonistic space, dominated by council rules and personalities and generating heated reaction from those outside the power base.

Purposes and discourses

In the introduction to this chapter we identified neighbourhoods as being considered particularly appropriate sites for the achievement of urban revitalisation, the development of 'joined-up' policy making and service delivery, and the renewal of democracy. The summaries of the five cases that form the basis for this chapter echo these ambitions albeit to different degrees. However, underlying these formal ambitions were rather different, although no less important, purposes that also manifested themselves differently across the five cases.

New forms of accountability

Securing accountability in a public policy environment with a large number of actors and very complex chains of decisions is both vitally important but also hugely difficult (Sullivan, 2003). One response has been to focus on smaller, more localised units of governance as potential sites for improved accountability. The rationale behind this is that by bringing decision makers, providers and the public together in more intimate spaces, the knots in the chain of accountability can be more clearly identified and worked at. The accountability purpose was evident in all of our five cases, although it was most strongly articulated in the residents' group. Here accountability was considered both as holding service providers to account and seeking redress where appropriate, and also as resident group members being prepared to give an account of their actions to the wider group and the residents they represented. Four kinds of accountability were articulated by resident group members: accountability of themselves to the group and their residents, accountability of the estate contractors to the group for their performance, accountability of the HAT to the group for its actions, and accountability of residents themselves for their own actions. A key manifestation of the focus on accountability was the way in which names and contact details of anyone expressing a view were recorded. This included resident group representatives at meetings, statutory bodies and contractors in their exchanges with group members, and residents themselves who were making complaints that they wanted the group to address on their behalves. For the chair of the group this was important in terms of fairness and transparency:

> "I say to people who attend the meetings, 'say what you want to say, but remember what you've said will be written down, and will come back at you'. This is why with our complaints form, it's always name, address and telephone number, in black and white. People tend to forget that once it's on file, there's no comeback, no argument. It's being fair both ways then. You can't say you haven't said so-and-so if you have. They can't either. So everything's out in the open, nobody has anything to hide."

In the area advisory board the emphasis was on the board acting as a space in which local residents could hold service providers (for example, local authority, police, health bodies) to account with the support of their local councillors. There was another dimension to the accountability purpose that related to the allocation of community grants by the area board in response to local bids. While technically it was the local councillors who were accountable for the decisions, in practice they left it up to the resident and community members to make the decisions, debating with them when they disagreed but being prepared to acquiesce to residents'/community views rather than enforce their own. This was important evidence for public participants that the local authority was serious about devolving power, as one respondent indicated,

> "The thing that's sometimes clearer than others is the dynamic between the advisory board and the councillors. Obviously the advisory board is there purely to advise the councillors in constitutional terms, and yet the councillors are pretty happy to let the advisory board make most decisions over grant giving and that sort of thing, it certainly feels as though the advisory board is actually making the decision ... I'm always aware that the councillors could say 'thank you very much for your advice but as the ward committee we'll actually be doing something different'. But I can't think of that having arisen."

Resident and community members were themselves aware of their accountability to others in this context and expressed views about wishing to see 'fair play' and 'justice' in terms of how the funding was allocated. The fact that they had to make these decisions with the applicants in the room was recognised as an added pressure and responsibility.

In the area committee, accountability was understood rather more conventionally, the area committee being one way of the council being accountable to the public, and also of local councillors holding other service providers to account in a public forum. However, in practice there was very little sense that either the public or the councillors got much satisfaction from the area committee in this respect. This was partly because of the language used by officials, which some members of the public experienced as alienating,

> "It's open but it's not yet transparent ... unless you actually understand the jargon it's not transparent."

It was also linked to the substance of the area committee meetings and by implications the limited power or influence that the area committee exercised. This was summarised by one IAB member as follows,

> "Okay we all need our bins emptied ... [but] the key issue is policing which is dealt with elsewhere, health decisions by the PCT, transport decisions taken by [the travel body].... And that's what they haven't cottoned on to."

Challenging professionals

Operating at the neighbourhood level exposed important blockages and barriers between the public and professionals and between professionals themselves. Across our five cases there were different levels of recognition that achieving programme goals required significant changes in how things were done and how people related to each other, and different levels of success in taking action to make these changes. Central to success in making change appeared to be the preparedness to *listen* to others and the capacity to *learn* from others.

For the residents' group not being listened to was a long-standing problem and one that was supposed to have been addressed by the introduction of the HAT but, according to one respondent, it "didn't start off very well with communications ... very very poor. They did try to improve ... and we've kicked their arses about communication. They are getting their act together".

In the Sure Start schemes the emphasis was on listening to parents to find out what their needs were and to develop appropriate services. For one Sure Start coordinator this required service providers to adopt a completely different approach, one based on community development principles. However, this learning from others outside the profession was a difficult message to sell to her colleagues as the following quote reveals.

> "It's always been my aspiration to support community development empowerment schemes. I've learnt quite a lot about management but I've also felt extremely frustrated about people not fully understanding community development as a process of empowering people ... some staff do not capture that vision.... Perhaps it's years of

"experience working in a day nursery setting, where you're just looking at ensuring that staff arrive on time, the children-to-staff ratio is fine, the personal development's sorted and so on. This job isn't like that. It's about planning. You're involving parents in your plans, you're supporting your staff to deliver the plans with the people that live in the area."

The tensions that existed between different professional groups came to dominate both Sure Start cases during the period of our research. At one level this was about how the different organisations learned to work together in the Sure Start partnership and some time was spent in developing 'guidance notes' about operating alongside each other, and trying where possible to reconcile different policies and procedures. At a more fundamental level, the differences between professionals were about individuals working with 'people from different schools of thought'. Here, getting professionals to listen to different perspectives could be difficult as these often challenged the value bases of others. Nonetheless if new ways of working were to be developed and services redesigned so that they were accessible and appropriate to parents and children, the different professionals needed to be able to listen to and learn from each other. The capacity of Sure Start to meet these challenges was a key test of its efficacy for many of the participants. In City B, where Sure Start was simply the latest in a long line of 'partnership' initiatives to have come to the area, some respondents expressed considerable scepticism as to whether there was really 'anything new' about the scheme, or whether it was just another ABI. By contrast in City A where the Sure Start area had experienced much less in the way of external funding, there was more optimism that progress could be made. The fact that the Sure Start scheme was linked to a successful voluntary organisation was also seen as an advantage as there was already a history of innovation and 'joined-up' working that the Sure Start scheme could build on, and which would act as a bulwark against the health and local authorities' more traditional ways of doing things.

Examining the cases in relation to the four discourses identified in Chapter Two reveals some interesting tensions. Local perceptions of the Sure Start schemes fit relatively easily into the 'empowerment discourse', with most respondents (official and lay) in the cases articulating this without prompting. Officials emphasised the importance of the Sure Start schemes in involving those 'beyond the usual suspects' and they devoted considerable time and energy to their empowerment as parents and as active citizens, something that was also acknowledged by parents themselves. The view of Sure Start as illustrating a 'responsible' public discourse was not articulated locally, even in Sure Start in City B, where participants tended to be more politicised and relationships with state organisations more difficult.

The area board in City A was readily acknowledged as emanating from the 'stakeholder discourse', the stakes being based in participants living and/or working in the local area and having an interest in promoting the quality of life of the locality. However, it was much harder to locate the area committee in City B in the 'stakeholder discourse' because, although the above rationale should apply (and does in the minds of those who drafted the manifesto), the practice of the area committee served to devalue the contribution of most stakeholders, something that the stakeholders themselves were quick to identify.

Of most interest was the residents' group, as here it was possible to see some difference between the perception of participating officials and those of the residents themselves. For the residents the group was an expression of the 'stakeholder/responsible citizen' discourses; residents had a stake because they were residents and had valuable experiential knowledge (equivalent to the 'expert users' identified in Chapter Five) to bring to deliberation, but they were also required to do things for themselves without relying on others and to demonstrate a wider commitment to their neighbours through their own actions. Conversely the 'participation workers' attached to the residents' group viewed it in terms of the 'empowerment' discourse; a group of residents who were being supported by them to realise their objectives. The residents themselves would reject this as they rejected the offer of 'skills training', seeing the group as an expression of the capacity they already had and viewing the participation workers as conduit to the HAT. In fact both the participation workers and the residents saw 'empowerment' as most relevant to the workers themselves – it was they who had benefited from the experiences they had had, who had developed new skills and who now felt better equipped to fulfil their role.

Motivations, identities and constituted publics

Motivations

The idea of 'neighbourhood' or 'local patch' proved to be dominant motivators to involvement in our five cases. Citizen participants and officials reflected on the importance of 'doing something for the local area'. For some (both citizen participants and officials) this motivation was underpinned by a set of values that had always pushed them towards community or voluntary work, for others these values had found expression in vocational activity, for example, the church, education. A small number were motivated by a strong belief in devolution as the way to enhance democracy. However, for other citizen participants the opportunity to participate in local decision making coincided with a dissatisfaction with the way things were in the neighbourhood and a desire to 'fight back' against neglect, anti-social behaviour and/ or poor public services or to "make sure the council knows that we're onto them". This was expressed by some as a desire to 'recreate a sense of community' or 'neighbourliness' that had once existed.

Among officials, the participation initiatives provided an opportunity to engage more directly with local concerns and issues and often fitted with an emerging culture of public engagement and partnership working in their host organisation, such as the police or the primary care organisation, that they had championed and felt strongly connected to. In some cases, the opportunity for officials to engage in this way in a locality in which they had grown up and in which they still lived provided a powerful stimulus. For example, for one police officer,

> "I'm probably what we called years ago, the residential beat officer. That's somebody that lives on his area and works his area. I live not far from the 'Q' centre so I'm obviously there a lot and around the area all the time. I go the youth forum. I go to meetings when I'm not on duty. It's commitments I go to in my own time just to keep that continuing."

In practice not all of our cases were able to fulfil the aspirations that respondents associated with the idea of neighbourhood. For example the area committee was dismissed by one participant as not being local enough (it covered three wards) and also for not having sufficient power to do anything about the issues raised:

> "I went along, hoping to represent what was going on in [my neighbourhood]. I thought initially that these meetings would carry some weight. Now I realise, that they are only a paper exercise, a complete waste of time.... I think that underlying their intention was a good idea in the fact that they could get the citizens around. But for instance [we're

covered by area committee K], we are not at all interested
in what's happening in that meeting tonight. But we are
interested in what's happening around here in [my
neighbourhood]....The meeting covers too big an area."

The idea of 'neighbourhood' was mediated in some cases by other
motivations, specifically the motivation to act to promote the interests
of a particular group; the interests of women, parents and children
were strong motivating factors in both of the Sure Start areas, while
the rehabilitation of the image of 'local youth' and a desire to improve
the services and opportunities available to them was a strong motivating
factor for one worker involved in the area committee:

> "I don't think the community actually gives young people
> the chance to get involved in anything. So, then there's the
> fear factor. If they see a group of young people hanging
> around outside the bus stop, might not be doing anything
> wrong, but they look intimidating.... But there's nothing
> for them to do and this is something the area committee
> should be looking into."

While motivations were largely shared, the ways in which people got
involved in these different initiatives varied. For some officials
involvement was an expected part of their job, as councillors or local
service providers (statutory and voluntary sector). For others it *was*
the job, for example, participation workers, area forum coordinators.
Some citizen participants were invited to participate because of their
position in a local community group, some saw an advertisement in
the local paper and applied for and were appointed to a position, some
were aware of the initiative because of their involvement with a related
voluntary organisation and then got elected to positions on the
governing board of the initiative, and some responded to public notices
and leaflets and 'turned up' to meetings to see what was going on. The
parent chair of the Sure Start board in City B got involved as a result
of a visit to the library:

> "I saw leaflets, I said yes I would like a bit more
> information....Then they said they would arrange a crèche
> and everything.... And I ended up being the worker, to
> look after the children. And as we had no children turning
> up, I thought oh, I might as well sit in on the meeting....
> So then we was invited after listening to what they was

going to do for the area, people who were actually at the meeting was invited to come along to the board.

And I decided well, I wanted to go, 'cause I thought, from my own experiences as a parent, there wasn't much information and advice like what I needed at the time. And I thought parents shouldn't have to through that. It's hard enough bringing up children without going to this department and that department. And they were saying we will have one-stop-shop information. And I thought well that's really good and we can get involved.... We need this for the area."

Identities and roles

Matters of identity became important for both officials and citizen participants in these case studies. These were often expressed in terms of the development of new roles, the balancing of a number of roles or challenges to existing roles. For parents taking up the role of 'board member' in the Sure Start scheme, the fact that their value to the board was vested in their identity and experience as parents was often something that took a while for them to become convinced of. Initially, parents often expressed anxiety about interacting with professionals on an equal basis, saying that they were 'afraid' of them and uncertain about the role they were meant to play. However, this anxiety tended not to last long and parents quickly gained confidence:

> J: "It was a little daunting at first, 'cause as I say sit around this table with all these professional people and you think – I hope they aren't going to listen to me. You know – I'm just a mother."

> Interviewer: "And how long did that feeling last?"

> J: "Oh I think after the first couple of meetings it was really dispelled and now you know I think nothing of giving an input.... And I think the other parents that are there we have all sort of grown together. 'Cause at first I think we were all quite nervous and used to stick together. The bunch in the corner and now when we go to a meeting, I could be sitting next to a councillor of somebody you know, other professionals and it doesn't faze me."

In some cases officials saw the need to play a number of different roles in the initiative, to 'wear different hats' as the occasion demanded. This proved to be more challenging for those officials who lived and worked in a locality and had roles as both community activists and paid workers in that locality. Those officials with paid employment as 'participation workers' often found themselves having to manage boundaries with their host organisation as well as with the community groups they supported. Describing themselves as 'ambassadors' or 'go-betweens' they inhabited a difficult space, part of a large organisation but often considered 'other' by that organisation.

Elected members appeared to be most challenged by the new roles they were being asked to play. In City A the fact that the area board was a 'new space' appeared to help the councillors and the other participants to develop an understanding of what role they might place. However, in the area committee in City B, the strong identification of the 'space' as that of 'the council' appeared to render the councillors unable to act in new ways and the public and other officials unable to see them in new ways.

Constituted publics

The development of a collective identity was a specific objective of one group in our case studies. In the residents' group, part of the frustration felt by the original members of the group was the way in which they perceived the HAT as trying to 'split' the residents by insisting on dealing with them on the basis of their tenure type. So residents were regularly referred to as tenants, leaseholders or owner-occupiers. This was partly a consequence of the legal framework within which the HAT was working and, partly as a consequence of real differences of view between these groups as to what should/could be done on the estate. However, the residents involved in our case study felt that there was more to be gained by residents insisting that they be dealt with as residents whatever their tenure, and they saw the establishment of their group as one way of breaking down the boundaries between tenure types.

It was also clear from the views expressed by the participation workers that they felt a strong affinity with the group, although they remained aware of their role within the group and in relation to the HAT:

> "I would say I'm still an activist even though I'm employed by the [HAT].... I think that's how we've gelled with the resident groups, it's because we're perceived as being as

much an activist as they are, because we will question things.... I think my voluntary role helps me because I can see both sides. I can see the officer role – what I need to be doing as an officer ... but I can also see the impact of that on the other side. One of the things I'm trying to do as an officer is to make my life easier as a volunteer...."

Elsewhere, shared perspectives were developing among members of our case studies. Sometimes this was a consequence of confusion and adversity. So in the area committee the uncertainty about the lay advisor role, the conflictual nature of the area committee proceedings and the underlying commitment of some of the members to the idea of devolution had led them to begin to think about meeting together as a group to try and develop a common view about how and whether they could best support the chair of the group (a local councillor) in making the initiative work.

Rules, norms and institutional practices

Three dominant experiences of institutions were apparent in our case studies: institutions as sources of support, institutions as sites of challenge and opportunity and institutions as prisons. Each is explored below with reference to a number of common factors: access and membership, agenda setting, rule making, challenge and change.

Institutions as sources of support

The residents' group provided the best example among our cases of the way in which the institutional framework could be shaped so as to offer support and safety to participants. Central to the emergence of this supportive framework was the genesis of the residents' group: it came from the 'bottom up' and was led by individuals with considerable experience of working with a range of interests and with confidence in their own capacity to act and influence. This meant that in negotiations with the HAT about becoming a formally constituted and recognised group, the resident leaders were aware that they had choices – they could work with the HAT and develop a constitution and set of rules that suited both parties, or they could opt out of the negotiation and continue to press for change on their own terms. They were helped in the negotiation process by the fact that the HAT was aware that its life span was limited and that part of its role was to foster participative processes that could be self-sustaining once the regeneration programme came to an end.

The residents' group was also helped by the fact that its remit was simple and clear – to represent the interests of residents in the neighbourhood to the relevant bodies, most obviously the HAT. Access to the group was through attending the meetings, and membership was automatic for residents, who could put items on the agenda by speaking to one of the committee members or turning up at a meeting. The group was not responsible for the management of large funds or the delivery of a programme and as a result the constitution it agreed to with the HAT was also relatively simple. There was a 'code of conduct' that identified unacceptable forms of behaviour (for example, use of racist language) and a requirement that the group appoint a chair, secretary and treasurer.

In practice it was the way in which the individual residents operationalised these conditions that rendered the residents' group a safe space. The chair, vice chairs and secretary drew on their own experiences as trades union representatives, committee members in voluntary organisations and their work experiences to develop a set of rules that governed their activities in a way that they believed provided them with considerable legitimacy as a group and that also maintained a clear separation between themselves and their sponsoring body, the HAT. They did this in the following ways: by ensuring that resident group committee members interacted regularly with local residents to identify key areas of concern and to record and report them; by requiring resident committee members to attend all meetings and to have a limit on the number of meetings missed before losing their position; by ensuring that they were well informed technically as well as in terms of residents' lived experiences before making their case to the contractors or the regeneration body (this often meant spending a long time at meetings exploring plans and specifications); and by not getting too involved in the internal workings of the HAT. For example, the chair of the group would not stand for election as a resident board member of the HAT, nor would he consider getting too closely involved with the estate-wide residents' forum (the umbrella body for voluntary and community groups) as he considered the fact that they were paid activists to be a source of weakness.

Institutions as sites of challenge and opportunity

The bulk of our cases fell into this category, although there were important differences in the extent to which each could meet the challenges presented and realise the opportunities on offer.

An important feature of Sure Start in our two cases was that most participants, wherever they were from and whatever their background, were partially outside of their 'comfort zones', as professionals, experienced activists, regeneration managers and parent participants. Therefore there was some scope for participants to develop the operating rules together. For example, as indicated earlier, the 'newness' of Sure Start meant that different participating organisations had to develop common 'guidance notes' that would direct how they contributed to Sure Start and how they worked together. This produced some interesting tensions in practice, particularly in relation to ways of working (social workers would only make home visits in pairs, voluntary sector workers were used to going alone) and the relationship of different professional groups to the board (some saw the role of the staff representative on the board to represent the views of the staff, others saw it as a means of ensuring regular communication with the board about the progress of particular initiatives). For all the talk of relishing multidisciplinary working, it was clear that at some points Sure Start became the battle ground for the dominance of different professional values and cultures. One programme manager described her experience in community development as causing friction with some of the health and social care professionals:

> Interviewer: "What do you think will affect your continued involvement in Sure Start?"
>
> B: "Calculated manipulation by staff.... I think it is a sad fact that if staff lack an understanding in community development, it's sad for them and it's sad for the programme manager. I think that is really what's going to hold the programme back, if it does. I might just have to be really thick skinned, take it all and just keep beating against the brick walls and kicking the bricks down one by one."

A fundamental challenge for Sure Start was to find a way of engaging parents/grandparents in the initiative, and getting them to stand for election to the governing board. In City B considerable effort was put into demystifying the Sure Start scheme to the local community by engaging with them through video, fun days and one-off consultation events for some time prior to the initiation of the programme. Information about the scheme was placed in sites that parents would use and presented in such a way as to encourage interest and involvement.

Most participants were strongly aware of the potential for the programme management element of Sure Start to both dominate the deliberations at the Sure Start board and set the tone for the way in which business would be done. Consequently, both Sure Start schemes went to some lengths to try and set a different, more inclusive tone to proceedings (this is reminiscent of the approach adopted by the women's group in Chapter Seven). This took a number of forms including: ensuring that there was always time for refreshments before and after the meetings so as to encourage informal chatting; organising the meeting in such a way as to encourage discussion and involvement, for example, round tables, splitting up into smaller groups for some items, limiting the amount of paper reports and ensuring that the contents were presented in an accessible way, challenging anyone who used impenetrable jargon, and providing a suggestion board where participants could record comments for how to run future meetings; always providing a crèche in an adjacent room for parents to leave their children during the meeting; and doing as much business as possible in smaller sub-groups, which could involve other parents as well as those on the committee.

These efforts were not always entirely successful. In some early Sure Start meetings in City A, too-crowded agendas meant that meetings overran so that the parent representatives had to leave to collect their children from the crèche. In addition a number of the parents who had become board members subsequently got jobs with the programme that meant they could no longer sit on the board. In City B the poor relationships between some professionals and activists generated a tense meeting environment that limited the participation of those parent participants not privy to the shared history of these individuals.

An important concern among Sure Start participants was that of avoiding the scheme becoming colonised by the ways of working of one of the big partners, either the local authority or the health authority. This concern was felt perhaps more keenly by participants in the area board. Here the core challenge was how to develop an inclusive forum for deliberation under the auspices of the local authority. The solution arrived at by the local authority, following consultation with local people, was to establish a new space for deliberation between local authority councillors, local partners and the public outside of existing ward level local authority committees. Membership was easy to obtain and, as in Sure Start, attempts were made in the area board to conduct deliberation differently using one-off events, annual conferences and fairs as well as the regular meetings of the forum. What mitigated against this was the fact that the local authority resourced the forums from within its organisation and set the rules for participation centrally (for example, how community grants were to be allocated). This meant that inevitably the local authority style infiltrated the area forums and in some cases rendered them indistinguishable from the existing ward committees. What appeared to make the difference in terms of rescuing the forums from the hand of the local authority was the skill of the chair of the forum in opening up dialogue and debate rather than closing it down. This was illustrated in the following exchange:

> R: "[The area forum] needs to be an environment that people feel comfortable in, and where people feel listened to. Some members are obviously better at this than others."

> Interviewer: "How does it work in [area Q]?"

> R: "We've got a very good chair. I think he chairs the meetings very well and he does notice when people want to speak. That's part of why I think it works so well."

> Interviewer: "Does he actually involve people who haven't contributed to see if they want to say anything?"

> R: "Yes he has, he's addressed someone and said 'what do you think?', and he puts things out to the whole meeting for them. He's very skilled at what he does. Obviously if there was a change of chair, that situation could change altogether."

This was contrasted to the experience at an adjacent area forum by a public sector representative who attended both.

> A: "I think there's more, I would say, an informal approach in [area Q] than for example in [area H]. I think, to that end, people do come forward and feel they can speak.... At [area H] if you call the chairman the wrong name, i.e. if you don't call him chairman and you accidentally say 'chair', you're publicly humiliated. The first time I went I was

warned 'watch you say "chairman"', because you often say 'chair' particularly now with women and men, there's this thing about how archaic the word 'chairman' is. In [area H], his normal procedure if anyone dares to call him 'chair', he stands up and he says, 'I am not a piece of furniture, do not call me a piece of furniture, you address me as "chairman", or if there is a woman here, "chairwoman".' The poor person that gets it. These are usually city council officials that get it, or some poor person representing a voluntary organisation. There isn't this ridiculous ritual in [area Q]."

Institutions as prisons

The area committee was a clear manifestation of a rule set and a way of operating that effectively imprisoned all participants, officials and the public alike. Designed as a means of opening up the local authority to public scrutiny and increased engagement, the initiative appeared to be directed in practice by an underlying dynamic that no one could counter. The local authority faced the same dilemma as that in City A, how to develop a scheme sponsored by the council that was not dominated by the council culture and way of doing things to the detriment of the involvement of others. The local authority's strategy was to try and introduce new rules into existing council institutions as a way of prompting wider change among the officer and member ranks as well as creating a new relationship with the public. Consequently, while the area committee was constituted as a committee of the council, it was subject to certain innovations including the involvement of a body of 'lay advisory members' appointed by the local authority, the operation of 'question time' during the meeting when members of the public could enter into exchanges with the councillors and the officials over particular issues, and the development of more deliberative parts of the meeting stimulated by a presentation on a topic of local concern. In addition, the majority of the councillors on the area committee were senior councillors, skilled at dealing with a range of people and situations, the chair of the committee was generally acknowledged to be both skilful and adept at managing the meetings effectively and the advisory members were experienced activists, voluntary organisation representatives or community leaders.

In practice, the area committee failed to function, generating tension and frustration among councillors, other members and the public alike and usually resulting in open conflict between and within different groups. One incident observed as part of the research serves to illustrate the point. We quote this at length because it reveals the way in which newly established formal rules can be comprehensively undone by long-established norms of behaviour, in this case the behaviour of politicians, professionals *and* the public.

> E: "Well what happened at the meeting last week a sort of series of events that started I think with the school hall not being heated. It was absolutely freezing and I don't think people's tempers improve when they are kept in the cold.... Prior to the meeting I had gone through the usual preparation in terms of having an agenda setting meeting with all the council officers before the agenda went out, and this time I insisted that they all turn up.... During that meeting I had a discussion with the lead officer about the presentation on the older persons strategy. Because we had a quite difficult situation about residential homes coming up in the council.... He said he would speak to V [person giving the presentation]....
>
> So the matter of it being cold. I'm faced with a choice – do I cancel the meeting or go ahead? Well I just felt it was pointless to cancel it ... and I was optimistic that we were organised and prepared ... so we went ahead....
>
> We had the presentation from V, which I thought was appalling. She claimed that she wasn't quite sure what the brief was. Then the lead officer claimed that he had told her how to pitch the presentation and the committee clerk backed him.... Anyway she's a senior officer. I would have thought she'd have looked at her audience and thought well I've got some very elderly people and some approaching elderly and yes I can do a presentation on the older persons strategy that will make sense to them. I mean she should have been able to do it off the top of her head.... But you were there. You know I had to constantly de-jargon things and I think we were all bored to be honest...."

This first excerpt identifies a problem with the setting (the 'cold' school hall). It also reveals how the chair of the committee regularly experienced resistance from officers in her attempts to make preparations for the area committee meetings (having to insist they all turned up to a pre-meeting, the failure to brief the speaker, and/or the failure of the speaker to prepare properly).

> E: "So then we had ward reports ... and I felt that the C ward report had gone right off theme. Not to criticise colleagues, but the point of the reports is for councillors to show people what is being done, not to say 'I want this and I want that but we've been told we can't have it'. Well frankly when you are in control politically you are scoring an own goal doing that....
>
> Then we moved to advisory members' questions, didn't we, and that was it. It was J's question about transport that put Cllr S into an absolute paddy.... Now it just so happens that three of our advisory members are Labour Party members. Now I don't have a problem with that. If it was a Labour council and I wanted to take part in scrutinising it, I would do exactly the same thing. But there is resentment among some of my colleagues that these three people are there.... But I think they're perfectly entitled to ask a question that scrutinises a decision that's been made ... and J has got woolly answers and he's an intelligent man. He asked a question about transport and Cllr S just went off at the deep end then. It was apparent that he had been challenged by something and so he went off at a tangent, and what did he do? He said 'I think the agenda should be ripped up. We never have time to discuss these things properly and the public aren't interested. We're constantly being hurried on by the chair...'."

This excerpt illustrates how the elected members of the committee ignore the rules governing the meeting (using ward reports to score political points rather than give information), react badly to public challenge from an individual appointed to sit on the committee (denying the legitimacy of the speaker because of their political party affiliation) and then try to blame the chairperson for the way the meeting is going (even though they are operating to rules agreed by the ruling group).

> E: "I was completely taken aback by that. I was also annoyed because we have [preparatory] sessions at which we discuss what issues we should raise at the area committee and if he

knew how much work went in to getting items on to the agenda in an appropriate way ... but unfortunately he's never been to a development session, neither has Cllr C or Cllr T. It's only really me and Cllr E that go....

So I fired back at Cllr S and said, 'look you can't just rip up the agenda, they're set in [preparatory] sessions', and anyway it was him that wanted ward reports on the agenda and now I felt he was publicly blaming me for this. So I thought I am not letting officers and members of the public think that this is all my fault. So I fired back at him. Parts of it too sharply, I don't know. Which is when Cllr C gets up and decided in his former Lord Mayor style, that he would be as pompous as he could possibly get and tell me basically that he thought [preparatory] sessions were a waste of time. And I was lost for words and I looked over at the public who has just completely blanked over, and one of the officers said, 'look you've got to move this on'."

This final excerpt illustrates how quickly matters deteriorate and how elected members engage in self-promotion as a way of distancing themselves from the initiative, while at the same time attacking their colleague, reinforcing the view that whatever has gone wrong is her fault.

There were a number of reasons why this apparently innovative initiative failed to generate the formally desired outcome. The rules governing the operation of the area committee were arrived at by the local authority with no consultation with the public about either the size of the committees (at least three wards) or the added value of appointing lay advisory members onto the committee (most people did not know what they were for and their presence was never explained). The meetings of the area committee were organised in such a way as to perpetuate the divide between councillors and the public. Councillors sat at the 'top table', lay members below and the public in the well of the hall. Councillors were always invited to speak first, then advisory members, then the public. Debate was not encouraged and usually the agenda was so full that there was no time for it. There was a mismatch between public expectations and the role of the area committee. The committee had no power to take executive decisions but local people attended with demands for "something to be done about ...". The combination of this mismatch in expectations and the failure of the council to rectify small problems in relation to rats and rubbish rapidly reduced the public's commitment to the initiative. Although the case study committee was populated by powerful and senior councillors, not all were supportive of the initiative. It was not uncommon for these councillors to use the meetings to make speeches and to demonstrate their lack of interest in proceedings by doing paperwork, jingling keys, talking to colleagues and leaving the meeting early. However, even those that were instrumental in driving the initiative seemed unable to change their behaviour in the meetings (evidenced by the above example), often engaging in furious arguments with those they perceived to be their political opponents among the lay members or dismissing the interventions of members of the public who breached the rules in an effort to make their voices heard.

Representation, diversity and capacity building for citizenship

Three issues will be explored in this section. The first concerns the capacity of a representative political system to accommodate developments that promote participatory approaches. This is of particular interest in relation to those 'neighbourhood initiatives' sponsored by local government, as here the assumption might be that the interaction between a representative system and participative approaches has been anticipated and will be welcomed. The second issue is the impact of 'neighbourhood-based' initiatives on diversity. One argument is that sub-local or neighbourhood-based initiatives enable the diverse needs of the public to be identified and responded to as a much wider range of public participants are able to shape decision making at this level. An equally powerful contrary argument is that sub-local or neighbourhood-based initiatives in fact suppress the expression of diversity, 'crowding out' minority views and articulating instead only the views of the dominant group in the neighbourhood. This is a vital debate given the diverse populations that share spaces in many English neighbourhoods and the government's desire for public participation to contribute to community cohesion. Finally, there is the argument that small-scale involvement by the public can provide a 'training ground' for political engagement more widely, acting as a source of capacity-building for the expression of citizenship. We are interested in this argument, both in terms of how public participants experience engagement but also in terms of how this kind of engagement can, in turn, enhance the capacity of officials to engage with the public.

Representation

Matters of representation were dealt with differently in our case studies. The most common form of representation understood all participants to be representatives of organisations with a specific interest. This applied to both officials and citizen participants. It took effect in two ways. In the area board all of the members of the forum were directly linked to a residents' group, community organisation, voluntary body or service provider. In some cases, individuals who had been approached to join the forum were subsequently linked to other organisations so that they fulfilled the criteria for membership, as this interview reveals:

> "I went to a couple of ward meetings because I was interested to find out what went on locally. After the second one I spoke to Cllr H. She sort of nobbled me and I did say 'look I'm quite interested to go on one of the local governing bodies' to which she said, 'you look like a keen committed person, would you like to come on the area forum?'. To which I said 'yes' and about three days later I got the note saying 'you've been appointed to the governing body of 'W' school as an LEA [local education authority] rep'."

While this was a condition of membership it acted more as a way of legitimising the participants' presence rather than requiring them to necessarily represent that organisation's perspective in the forums' deliberations. On occasion, individuals would make clear they were speaking on behalf of their organisation, for example, in discussions about crime or anti-social behaviour, where citizen participants would articulate the concerns of their residents' group and the neighbourhood police officer would respond by outlining the activities of their organisation to deal with those concerns. However, on other occasions, for example, when discussing the allocation of community grants, participants would deliberate as individuals without reference back to their organisations.

The other dominant form of representation was evident in the Sure Start schemes. Here, while official participants were present at the board as representatives of their organisations, each of which had some involvement with the Sure Start programme, parent representatives did not have an organisational basis and, while most of them had been through a process of election to get on to the board, they did not perceive themselves and were not perceived by others to be representing a specific organised constituency. Instead their presence on the board was in order that they could represent 'the parent's perspective', which would invariably have been informed by their interaction with other local parents but was not contingent on it.

This approach was echoed in the area committee through the appointment of lay advisory members. These were expected to draw on their local expertise and experience to further the work of the committee, but not to make the case for any particular organisation that they were involved with. As indicated earlier in this chapter, it was not entirely clear either to the lay members themselves or the wider public that this role was understood or appreciated and some individuals were anxious about their role being misconstrued by members of the public in particular, as one interviewee explained,

> "I said I didn't want to be called a representative. 'Cause I didn't want to upset anybody. I am not involved in any neighbourhood stuff around here. So I couldn't bring anybody else's views.... 'Cause sometimes it's quite frightening really, you know people questioning what you do. And no one has ever said it yet, but you think sometimes a resident's going to say it, you know, 'what are you doing, you don't represent me'."

The interaction between public representatives and elected councillors occurred in all our case studies, as elected councillors sat alongside the public representatives on boards governing the different initiatives (with the exception of the residents' group, which was separate from the governing body of the HAT). In the Sure Starts, elected councillors were one among many board members, all of whom had a different basis for representation (parents, an organisation, a locality). An elected councillor's impact as a board member was linked to their reputation as a councillor, most particularly the extent to which they were perceived to be an effective local representative and community champion. In the area committee and area forum the context was rather different as these forums were local authority creations built around local authority councillors. Here the likelihood of conflict between different kinds of 'representative' seemed inherent in the design of the area bodies. As our previous discussion has revealed, this tension emerged very clearly in the area committee in City B where a hierarchy of membership coupled with other rules that privileged the role of the elected councillor proved to alienate and exclude public participants. This tension was less evident in the area forum in City A, partly because the design of the area forums did not put elected councillors and other kinds of representative in such direct tension with each other and partly because of the way in which the elected councillors in the area forum chose to act.

Diversity

Addressing diversity was a factor in all of the case studies, although more obviously an issue at the time of the research in the area committee and forum, than the Sure Start schemes. Both the area committee and forum were keen to find ways of engaging young people in their activities, the committee having a sub-committee to look at this and the forum targeting some of the community grants' funding to youth activities and trying to secure a space for young people to air their views at its annual conference. As the case summaries in the introduction to this chapter indicate, most of our cases were situated among populations that were predominantly white European. The one exception to this was the area committee, where one of the constituent wards comprised a number of minority ethnic groups. Participation in the area committee from people in this ward was much lower than from the other wards and the chair of the committee was conscious of this and had determined to try and do something about it,

> "In the new year I've arranged a meeting with ... our equal opportunities bloke. And we were going to go and talk to some people from ethnic minorities about the area committee, what would they want. But I'm nervous to do that if I can't actually deliver something."

Awareness of 'race' equality was not, however, restricted to localities with diverse populations. In the area forum, deliberation among participants about an application for funding helped to generate a shared perspective among the participants that reflected the diverse ethnicity of the city, if not the ward, as one respondent explained,

> "It was a bid for someone to translate a youth directory – she wanted some help with the funding and it was to be translated into 12 recognised community languages. It was for some piece of research that she was doing.... The councillors, looking for value for money, were minded as a group to say 'look we'd like to be realistic about the number

of people involved with these community languages who would actually use the project – maybe we could restrict it to three, because obviously it's very expensive'. I felt, and several other people did as well, that it wasn't very fair. Then quite a lot of people then, instead of nodding it through, said, 'no, no, no, we agree, we must publish it in all the required languages'. I think the councillors were quite surprised."

This need to think beyond the immediate interest was reflected in another way in the workings of the residents' group. A key figure in the group was clear that the group needed to be able to recognise that there were some issues about which it was important to have an estate-wide view and that barriers between residents' groups needed to be challenged and overcome if they got in the way of the expression of this 'estate voice'.

"I think that's good, it's healthy to get to know one another.... Because at the end of the day it's not just your area, this patch, it's all over the estate. I don't think the [regeneration body] comes round and says 'oh we'll just do T's place', they do the whole lot, and we've got to do that. Although we're residents of this part, I think we should be more global, more estate minded...."

Capacity-building for citizenship

As many of the participants in our case studies had experience of civic engagement prior to their involvement in the initiatives we were studying, it was very difficult to determine what kind of impact involvement had on them. This was as true of the officials as it was of the public participants and while there was some evidence that engagement in the different case initiatives generated new thinking within the initiatives about how to work together better, there was little evidence that this led to any significant change in the way in which officials went about their business. Sure Start was perhaps the exception as here it was possible to identify parents for whom Sure Start represented their first taste of participatory activity. The managers of the Sure Start programmes were aware that they had only limited time to impact on individual parents, who would only be directly connected to the scheme until their children started school. Consequently the ambition of empowering women to realise their potential in any way they wanted required the Sure Start scheme to make a big difference in women's lives in the short time they interacted with the scheme. In general the experiences we recorded were positive, with parents quickly overcoming their inhibitions at being part of 'the process' and taking on roles as chairs of task groups and organisers of activities. However, while the experience had generated a stronger sense of 'community' among participants, it did not necessarily translate into them feeling more able or likely to participate in other initiatives in the future.

Conclusion

The extent to which 'community governance', that is, governance that is 'joined up' among local providers and driven by very local publics, is realised in our case studies is questionable. Certainly it is possible to identify points at which some of these initiatives were able to express a clear public will – the decision making about 'community grants', for example. It is also possible to focus on the work of the Sure Start initiatives as clear examples of attempts to 'join up' the range of services available to local parents and to increase the influence of local parents over the design of those services. However, overall the impact that each of these initiatives was having on mainstream service providers appeared limited. To a very large extent this is an issue of power, specifically the amount of power vested in each of the case study initiatives, which was very little. In general, the initiatives operated in the hope that they might be able to exercise influence over the service and policy decisions of others, rather than in the expectation that they could change those decisions to suit their own circumstances. In practice, it appeared that the area committee and the residents' group were able to wield similar (that is, limited) amounts of power, regardless of the fact that the area committee was a formal committee of the council run by senior elected members and officials. To some extent it could be argued that the residents' group was in a more advantageous position than the area committee: it covered a much smaller geographical area than the area committee and so was better able to relate directly and frequently with the residents that it represented.

This then raises the issue of what constitutes a 'neighbourhood' and whether there is an optimum size. Clearly an area committee covering three wards (upwards of 45,000 people) has much less purchase on 'neighbourhood' than a Sure Start initiative (8,000-10,000 people) or a residents' group (200 people). The trade-off that large units are more administratively efficient and so are likely to attract devolved resources and decision-making power seems not to have been the case in the example that we studied. Recent academic and policy literature has argued persuasively that neighbourhoods come in many shapes and sizes and that individuals may be members of multiple neighbourhoods (Kearns and Parkinson, 2001; ODPM/HO, 2005). There is a risk that this approach conflates ideas about 'neighbourhood' with those of 'community', rendering both relatively empty terms. However, there is good evidence for understanding neighbourhoods as both subjective and dynamic. Consequently there may be no optimum size but, as our case studies demonstrate, individuals do need to feel some connection between the scale of the initiative and their sense of 'neighbourhood'.

The significant role played by institutions in the shaping and functioning of public policy is evident from the case studies. Institutional capacity was utilised to facilitate dialogue with communities in a number of ways, including the development by local statutory players of a range of sites and processes at the 'sub-local' or 'neighbourhood' level (a move incentivised by central government's use of 'neighbourhood' as an important symbol of the 'new governance'). Powerful institutions such as local government and NHS bodies, with long-embedded rules and ways of doing things, found it very difficult to resist applying those rules and norms in 'new' deliberative settings. In some cases, the creation of an entirely separate deliberative space, where all participants were outside their 'comfort zones', and where rules and norms were negotiated as part of the deliberative process, provided sufficient scope for changed relationships between the public and the state to begin to emerge. However, in other cases none of the actors appeared to be able to resist the pressure of the dominant institutional environment, with the consequence that dialogue was constrained and existing relationships hardened.

Post-structuralist insights have helped to illustrate how practices of public participation, while presented as empowering, may be a new form of domination. However, the case studies also point to evidence of where new discourses and strategies may also produce new sites of social agency. Some of the interactions recorded in the case studies provide indications of resistance, as citizens take decisions about how they will engage with officials and on what terms, something that was most plainly evidenced in the residents' group. It is also possible to identify the roots of dissent in what appeared to be the weakest participation initiative, the area committee. Here the refusal of the public to 'play the game', for example by continuing to raise issues that mattered to them regardless of what was on the agenda, and also by failing to acknowledge the different categories of 'public' determined by the officials, namely the distinction between 'ordinary' public participants and 'lay advisory members', denied the rules and norms created by officials and challenged the very basis of the initiative.

This chapter has focused on public participation in initiatives that are built around a sense of identity associated with a particular geographical area. In the next chapter, we explore the other ways in which people's sense of identity can be sources of energy for participation in different initiatives.

SEVEN

Responding to a
differentiated public

In contrast to the case studies considered in the previous two chapters, where forums were established in order to improve services, or were linked to new models of neighbourhood and community governance, the cases we consider here all had their origins in the voluntary sector and/or in social movements. Each focused on a particular category of public, differentiated from others in terms of presumed commonalities of interest or identity; that is, they required people to claim a particular social identity based on age, gender, sexuality or other characteristic. In this chapter we consider five case studies: two senior citizens' forums, a women's centre, a youth forum and a lesbian and gay forum.

Our interest lies in what happens when groups whose roots lie in voluntary, political or community activity, and who claim independence from statutory bodies, are brought into dialogue with such bodies. The imperative to involve communities as part of shaping policy and delivering services, discussed in Chapter Two, creates a climate in which nominally autonomous or independent groups move closer to official bodies. However, in their interaction with such bodies, questions have been raised about the possibility of incorporation. We are concerned then, with how far the capacity of groups constituted around presumed commonalities of identity to act as 'counter publics', opening up new agendas, acting as advocates, challenging the status quo, developing new or sustaining alternative political discourses, comes to be limited or contained by their closer engagement with institutional and governmental power (Craig and Taylor, 2002; Newman et al, 2004; Newman, 2005b; see also Chapter Four of this volume). Our case studies in this chapter demonstrate different degrees of embeddedness in state institutions. Two of them – the senior citizens' forums in each city – were established through close interaction between the statutory sector (local authorities, health authorities), the voluntary sector (Age Concern) and campaigning organisations (the National Pensioners Convention). Two had their origins in new social movements (the women's centre, the lesbian and gay forum) but were increasingly interacting with official bodies, and, to a greater or lesser degree, dependent on their financial support. The fifth – the youth forum –

was, during the course of our research, confronting the constraints of closer engagement with official support and funding for the first time, a confrontation that produced high levels of conflict and that led to the eventual withdrawal of their engagement.

This makes the issue of institutional rules and norms, discussed in Chapter Four, particularly significant. Membership of groups constituted around notions of identity may be fluid, producing particular challenges to norms of representation and representativeness. There is also likely to be a strong ethos of inclusion and empowerment in such groups, and they may (or may not) offer alternative conceptions of democratic practice to the conventions of the formal meeting. Each of these means that interaction with official bodies is likely to be problematic, not least since officials tend to want those with whom they consult or interact to be somehow 'representative' of a wider public, and because lay members of such forums may be less willing to conform to, or may be less skilled in handling, the institutional practices of state agencies. Again, our case studies offer contrasting data on the ways in which such groups work to achieve their aims, and on the experiences that members bring to their encounters with each other and with public officials.

The *senior citizens' forums* were part of a strong tradition of organisation around issues of importance to older people, including the retired members' sections of trades unions, the National Pensioners Convention and organisations such as Age Concern. At a local level, a number of senior citizens' forums have come to provide a focus for dialogue between local policy makers and older people. While these were autonomous bodies, their development was shaped by negotiations between the local authority, the National Pensioners Convention and Age Concern. In City A the local authority had had considerable influence over the founding of the initiative and provided support in terms of an officer to undertake administrative tasks and free accommodation in the council house. In City B the impetus and support was provided by Age Concern and the forum was much more strongly oriented towards consultation and negotiation with the health authority rather than the city council, in part because of the reluctance of the latter to engage with it. The substance of discussion among members reflected the purpose of challenging the government in relation to issues that discriminate or disadvantage older people – such as the reduction in pensions during hospital stays, and attempts to get an Age Discrimination Act passed, as well as issues of local service quality within the NHS, local transport and road safety issues, and the closure of residential homes.

The *women's centre* was formed in the 1980s in the context of the then thriving women's movement. It was initially set up as a collective women's centre, but later, in order to secure funding, narrowed its aims to focus on the provision of advice and information to women in City A. Its dual purposes were described as 'empowerment' (including that of its own volunteer workers) and 'promoting a gender perspective' in relevant policy forums. It was viewed by the coordinator as "an arena in which some women have the space to shape and articulate a collective voice based on their experience". Funding came from the local authority and a variety of charitable sources, but tended to be piecemeal and insecure. However, at the time of the research the centre had recently expanded and had moved to new, larger premises. It had no formal membership, but a network of volunteers who staffed the telephones and developed outreach services. A climate of optimism and expansion influenced the ways in which the group was perceived by both workers and volunteers. A core activity was the development and management of a training programme for volunteers. Issues that surfaced during the period of the research included an attempt to secure European Social Funding for work on social inclusion and women's poverty; questions of 'race' in inter-agency work on domestic violence; and campaigning on behalf of a Pakistani woman threatened with deportation following the breakdown of her marriage.

The *lesbian and gay forum* emerged from work between members of the local lesbian and gay community and the city council as part of City B's equalities strategy. This had led to the negotiation of a proposed lesbian and gay equalities manager. However, at the time – the late 1980s – the city council had been experiencing a financial crisis, and in a climate of cut-backs councillors had failed to support this move. Instead it had supported the establishment of a lesbian and gay community forum. Initially, this was very active in exchanges with the local authority, with regular meetings. But work with the local authority had dwindled and attention switched to attempts to influence the police service on issues such as hate crime. This had, members argued, met with a much better response, including better resourced meetings. The forum had a formal membership of police officers, voluntary workers and members of the gay and lesbian community. It met in closed session three times a year, but drew on, and was supported by, a much larger network of contacts. Police officers were in the minority on the forum (only 'out' police officers were directly involved as members) and membership mainly comprised gay men rather than lesbians. In contrast to the women's centre the focus of activity was policy involvement alone rather than advice or support to individuals.

The purpose was to inform police policy by acting as a channel of communication between the police and the 'gay community'. Issues arising during the research included hate crime and the policing of public space.

The *youth forum* had been founded independently of the City A's youth service by a young Muslim man with a long history of street-based work among the local Kashmiri-Pakistani youth in the area. All of the officers and members of this forum lived locally and demonstrated a high level of commitment to the young people with whom they worked, both by getting them involved in sports and other activities and by supporting them in representing their interests to official bodies. Its independence from the youth service presented difficulties when the local authority, as part of a regeneration initiative for the local area, held a ward conference (one of the ways in which it engaged with local publics), and a decision was taken to set up a planning group to work towards a future youth conference. Officials argued that this would be an opportunity to portray a 'positive image' of young people, that it would contribute to confidence building among young people and that they would be enabled to offer 'positive criticism' of the council. During the course of the research the attempts to establish this conference produced conflict with the existing youth forum over issues of who could best represent the interests of young people in the area, resulting in their withdrawal from the official planning group.

Each of the case studies, then, can be understood in terms of the social movements discussed in Chapter Three of this volume, although their forms and practices were mediated – in different ways and to different extents – by strong elements of official sponsorship, with local councils, health authorities or police services influencing their development, providing funding or other forms of support, and – at least in part – shaping the rules and norms of engagement with public bodies. The extent and nature of official support was strongly influenced by the dominant policy discourses on participation described in Chapter Two. We discuss this further in the next section, then go on to focus on questions of the 'publics' they represent through their membership and their institutional practices: the rules and norms of deliberation. We conclude by developing the theme of 'new spaces, new voices', reviewing our data to assess what happens in the interaction between publics who have their roots in social movements and the state institutions seeking to support, consult or engage with them. These issues are developed further in Chapter Eight, where the focus shifts to forums in which officials engaged with more explicitly campaigning movements.

Policies and discourses

While consumerism was a strong theme in the service-based forums discussed in Chapter Five, it was less significant in the majority of the case studies we consider here, with one exception – the senior citizens' forums. Indeed the senior citizens' forum in City B was partly formed from a number of previously existing 'consumer councils' set up by the local Age Concern organisation. The senior citizens' forums tended to be viewed by statutory bodies as a means of consulting with a 'representative' body of older people on service-related issues. However, one limitation was that the majority of forum members were not in fact 'consumers' of many of the services about which they were invited to express their views: for example, of residential care services for older people. Indeed in City A the assumption was made that the users of residential care services might not be competent to speak on their own behalf.

However, it is important to note that the consumerist discourse here is inflected with collective, rather than individual, norms of identity and action. The citizenship-based notion of 'representation', in which representatives act on behalf of others and seek to express the interests of a wider collectivity, sits uneasily with the consumerist notion of individual interests expressed through choice in the marketplace. And in the senior citizens' forum we can trace ways in which their campaigning roles intersected with their positioning by statutory bodies as an easy means of seeking consumer views. Not least was the critical stance of the terms in which consultation was conducted. As one facilitator commented,

> "I think city councillors are a little bit frightened of us because the council has this policy of questionnaire consultation … [but] it's not the consultation that this group actually want…. They think it's just going to be a bang of the drum, and we'll do as they tell us…. But older people vote. We can understand 'no' if we are given a reason why. And [as a result of experience in the past] … the senior citizens' forum will not undertake consultation unless they are actually given feedback."

The consumer role was not the only function that the senior citizens' forum in City B performed in relation to the city council and the health authority. As we noted in Chapter Two, public policy has increasingly tended, since the 1990s, to view publics as *stakeholders* in governmental decision-making processes; and to place greater emphasis on the need for citizens to take greater *responsibility* for their own self-governance. These two discourses intersected where statutory bodies sought to extend the role of the senior citizens' forums beyond consumer-oriented forms of participation by inviting them to deliberate on local policy developments. An example during the course of the research related to the requirement, on local authorities and the health service, to develop new National Service Frameworks for the delivery of health and social services to older people. One member was invited to represent the forum on the local implementation team set up to ensure the delivery of the new National Service Framework for Older People. At the same time the group was asked to take on a monitoring role in relation to the delivery of this initiative on behalf of the local Community Health Trust. A suggested questionnaire to be used for monitoring purposes was given to the group by the Trust. Here we can see a slippery slope in which 'participation' in policy or service developments slides towards 'acting as an agent of' government itself. This has potential consequences for who people think they are and how they understand their role in balancing the forum's stated aims as a 'consultation' group and a 'campaigning' organisation.

Similar processes of progressively closer engagement can be traced in the women's centre and in the lesbian and gay forum. The coordinator of the women's centre sat on a range of policy and service committees, and was a crucial part of a network of women's organisations set up by the gender equalities manager of the city council. However, the attempt to develop gender-sensitive policies was, in this period, difficult, in part because of the increasing attention to 'race' as an issue following the McPherson Enquiry[1] and the attempts by public bodies, especially in City A, to enhance their legitimacy with black and minority ethnic groups. Progressive marginalisation was also faced by the lesbian and gay forum in relation to the city council of City B, and its inclusion as a stakeholder in policing. This is somewhat surprising since this forum relates to a form of public that has only latterly been identified as a specific 'community' in policy discourse. And it presents particular problems because of the history of legal impediments to its acknowledgement by public bodies[2]. Describing the communication and marketing group of a police service's survey of 'hard to reach' groups, a respondent noted how the service had overcome barriers to reaching young people, travellers and other groups, but not the gay and lesbian community "because, you know, it's just people won't be identified". Nevertheless, gay and lesbian issues surfaced as a matter for public concern as part of the equal opportunity policy agendas of the 1980s. Rather than 'empowerment', the forum was viewed by both members and the officials with which it interacted as a stakeholder in police policy, and as a partner in problem solving around policing issues:

> "We can sort of advise the police. If for example the police in a particular area are having a problem they contact us, we can also say right these are the people you need to contact. These are the things that have been done elsewhere."

As such, the forum can be characterised in terms of an attempt to develop a *partnership* model of relationship between the gay 'community' and the police.

The example of the youth forum suggests that a shift towards a partnership/stakeholder model was not a universal trend, despite attempts by officials to draw groups into closer forms of collaboration. However, this case study suggests ways in which the 'empowerment' of young people through a youth conference proposed as part of a regeneration initiative was heavily circumscribed by practices enshrined in local authority ways of working, a theme we develop further below.

Constituting publics: identities, roles and relationships

In this section we explore the ways in which identity-based 'publics' are constituted as actors in the public sphere. To do so, we explore the membership basis of the forums concerned, and how roles and relationships were established. Our concern is with how questions of difference are accommodated, and how notions of 'representation' and 'representativeness' are constructed and negotiated.

As noted earlier, membership of the *senior citizens' forums* was initially composed of those already involved in established older people's organisations. The older people that formed the committee of 'insiders' who interacted with city and health officials tended to be well organised and articulate; outside the bounds of what might be termed the 'socially excluded'. Management committee members in City A were, by and large, people who had been involved in some type of political, trades union, church or welfare activity at different stages of their lives. Of the 13 committee members, 10 had been – or continued to be – engaged in other voluntary activities, five were active in a religious organisation, eight in community groups and three in sports or social clubs. Six were members of a political party, five of trades unions, four of self-help groups, three of advocacy or user groups, and two of disabled people's organisations. For most, then, involvement in the forum was a logical extension of activity that had been an important part of their lives, whether in trades unions or political parties or in voluntary welfare activity, often through churches. For example the facilitator in City B had had experience as a community activist in the Preschool Playgroups Association, in a successful campaign to prevent the local council selling off land for development, then in Age Concern. She said of herself: "I am quite argumentative, have a lot of views and opinions on lots and lots of things".

In both senior citizens' forums there was a clear distinction between overall membership (open to all senior citizens within the city) and membership of the management committee (formed from those representing organised groups and agencies). This concept of representation was acknowledged to be problematic – in interviews, members expressed concern about the legitimacy of their representative role and some recognised that few older people were likely to know that the forum was speaking on their behalf. Nevertheless, when the forum in City A formulated its response to the closure of residential homes, it did so without consulting with residents of such homes.

There was a strong group ethos, with frequent references in interviews to the friendliness, respect, tolerance and humour, and their desire to help others:

> "I think possibly we are all very tolerant people. And we are all in it to help each other. You know we are taking sides and if I can help Ali or Fred or Maisie or Elsie, well that's it. That's what I'm here for. Help groups, help anybody we can. And this is the ethos that we have got now, and we have been together for over two years. So we've got that ease with each other. We can say anything to each other."

But this degree of comfort and familiarity tended to occlude questions of difference and to act as a barrier to wider participation. In City A there had been attempts to broaden the membership, especially to Afro-Caribbean and 'Asian' groups, but, despite a positive response from some black-led churches, this was viewed as not having been effective. In City B, despite smaller black and minority ethnic populations, there had been a stronger attempt to engage with them. However, there were also inherent difficulties in seeking a broader membership base in that the aim of the forum was to express a collective

– and consistent – view to official bodies. Token 'others' could be incorporated and tolerance espoused. For example in a discussion about whether a lesbian and gay group should be represented within the forum, this proposal was initially opposed by one member who referred to the 'extremist tactics' of such groups, but this view was not condoned. And when an African member of the group had been subjected to racist abuse at an annual general meeting, the person who had made the abusive comment was ejected from the meeting and a letter of apology was sent to the person concerned. Nevertheless the committee members of senior citizens' forums enjoyed a relatively strong shared culture, consolidated through jokes and anecdotes before and after the formal business. And as some interviews show, this shared culture was not easy for new people to find a place in.

In the *women's centre*, in contrast, diversity was a more explicit issue for the group. Membership included older and younger women, women from working- as well as middle-class groups, and a number of women from minority ethnic groups (although issues of sexuality and disability were less well represented in the membership at the time of the research). In contrast to the senior citizens' forums, there was no requirement that its members were there as representatives of other organisations. Some women had previous experience of voluntary or community work, but many became involved through having been a user of the advice service. A few went on to view their voluntary work for the group as a means of gaining experience to enable them to qualify for education or employment opportunities. Although there were attempts to build a shared culture through extensive strategies of participation and inclusion, there was also an explicit recognition of the need to deal with issues of difference, with 'diversity' an important component of the training programme for volunteers. Transport, childcare and other issues were carefully addressed, and support offered to women who may have lacked the financial resources to participate. Personal experiences narrated by the women directly involved in the forum provided a way of affirming membership and connecting individuals to each other. There were deliberate attempts to make connections across lines of difference between women, and interviews with women involved suggested this had a transformative impact – not simply on women's opinions, but a deeper transformation of their sense of self:

> "It's made me look at people quite differently – because I'm from an older generation, I had set ideas – working here has challenged those."

The full-time coordinator was paid through a grant from a Trust with a brief of bringing about change, and hers was the role that was most significant in terms of participation in formal policy forums. Rather than seeking to represent the voice of women in the city in general, the concern was to use issues raised in the work of the group to inform policy debate and decision making. This is a very different model of representation from that of the senior citizens' forums, who sought to speak for older people in general by including 'representatives' from a range of organisations and groups. Indeed the terms 'voice' or 'influence', rather than representation, tended to pervade the interview transcripts of women in the women's centre.

The lesbian and gay forum comprised community liaison staff from the police, voluntary workers and individuals from the gay and lesbian 'community'. As with other case studies those who were active lay members of the forum tended to have been active participants in other groups or movements. One commented, "I have always been involved, though. I am a political addict, basically", listing a long history of involvement in party politics, campaigning groups, anti-apartheid groups, and the peace movement. He talked about his "enjoyment" of the process. In contrast one of the police officer forum members described her motivation as trying to make things better for new recruits to the service in the light of the discrimination and bullying she had experienced herself (she had only come out after 25 years as a police constable). Her involvement in the lesbian and gay forum was part of her role as a community liaison officer, but her status as an 'out' gay officer had had a particular impact:

> "And then when all this gay stuff started to circulate ... because of diversity projects and the Stephen Lawrence [McPherson] inquiry etc, all of a sudden I was getting phone calls from inspectors ... 'you're gay, aren't you?'. 'Yes.' And then it's really going up and up. Every other day now [I'm] getting contacted because I am gay, rather than because of what I'm doing."

Membership of this forum opens up issues of representation in at least two senses. One is how far it 'represented' the wider lesbian and gay population of the area. As a lay member of the forum commented,

> "I am very reluctant to use the word representative. Because I don't think anyone really is representative as such. We are self-selecting; we are the people who actually choose to

get involved.... So, given that that's the case, no, I don't think we are representative. I think what we can do though is perhaps give voice to experience. And I mean quite a lot of the people are not only talking about their own experience, they are talking from the knowledge that they have and the fact that they talk to others. And then those issues can be brought forward."

The second was the extent to which non-gay forum members could represent the views of the gay 'community'. Negotiations between the lesbian and gay forum and the police were mediated through a formal contact:

"It's her job to take the stuff back to the police. It's not really my job as part of the committee. [Name] is not gay, and sometimes the gay community, being the sort of community it is, sometimes issues are brought up, and I can say no, hang on, this is [what this issue is about]. In the police we deal with things that way and it's a clash between the gay lifestyle and the police culture. Whereas [name] is not in a position to do that."

In other words, the messages from the gay community to the police service needed to be mediated and interpreted by someone with insider roles in each. Our respondent argued forcefully that it is difficult to understand the lesbian and gay community without being part of it: "It doesn't matter how many gay friends you have, unless you are gay yourself you don't understand. And I think being on the working party I can put both sides in respect of the police".

This insider/outsider duality constructed here created an image of a relatively undifferentiated gay and lesbian 'community', packaging it as an entity that fitted within the increasing salience of community perspectives in both local authority and police services. Some concern had been expressed within the forum that too much attention had been focused on the lesbian and gay 'scene', while other issues were not as carefully addressed, especially those relating to older gay men or lesbians. And one member acknowledged that, rather than representing the whole gay community, the forum was only effective in giving voice to a 'particular perspective'. Of course this is the case with all of the groups we consider here, but was most explicitly recognised by some members of this forum.

The issue of how far a forum represents the whole community (in relation to a particular category of identity), and the processes of inclusion and exclusion that surround this, was most sharply evidenced in the youth forum. Here membership was explicitly not on the basis of the 'representativeness' of different youth groups and organisations in the area. Its origin as a group of concerned local Kashmiri-Pakistani young people – predominantly male – produced a very strong group identity. The individual who had been formative in founding the forum emphasised that the purpose was about achieving real change in the area.

> "I have been working in this area for about eight years with young people.... The thing is we have got a couple of [youth] organisations in this area [named]. I noticed they weren't targeting the young people they were supposed to be. Because I have quite a bit of influence over the younger people in the area, I decided to set up my own youth forum."

Tensions around the planning of the youth conference arose between the youth forum and the official planning group set up by local youth workers. But on the basis of seeking openness, inclusion and 'representativeness', this planning group was open to all youth organisations, and youth workers used their networks to seek members:

> "... so it's just a question really of saying to various adults can you identify some young people, preferably young men and women who live in the area and who you think might be happy to be involved in this particular project."

Youth forum members worked actively towards the establishment of the conference but felt that their contribution was not sufficiently recognised, and disagreed with some of the activities proposed; they eventually left the official planning group. Their attempts to continue organising the conference independently failed despite enthusiasm, partly as a result of problems in securing funding and premises and partly due to conflict with officials around notions of legitimacy and recognition. The attempt to establish young people's participation cut across different definitions of legitimacy, principally between an inclusive perspective (the conference planning group needing to be inclusive and representative of different groups) and an identity-based perspective (the conference should reflect the strong identity of those viewing themselves as representing the voice of Kashmiri-Pakistani youth). This was played out in terms of a struggle between different community 'leaders' (councillors, youth workers and the lay leader of the youth forum) about who could best represent the voice of young people and the interests of the area. This produced frustration and a certain amount of hostility between the members of the youth forum and the professional youth workers. This was articulated by youth forum members in terms of identity with place (youth forum members being part of the area, youth workers living elsewhere), questions of pay ('they' are getting paid and 'we' are doing it for free) and issues of having the contribution of forum members recognised.

The roles and relationships explored in this section, however, are not simply a product of the individual preferences, motivations and experiences that individuals brought to the forums; they shaped, and were shaped by, the institutional norms that developed within each group around the process of deliberation itself.

Process of deliberation: institutional rules and norms

In this section we focus on how the rules and norms of deliberation get shaped; and in what ways these rules and norms influence the actions of officials and lay members. We again begin with the senior citizens' forums, where the background and experiences that members brought to their deliberations, coupled with their desire to secure legitimacy as 'non-political' and independent bodies, had a profound impact on the conduct of the forums themselves. Each had a formal constitution, and meetings had formal agendas and an annual general meeting (AGM) to which motions could be submitted. In City A this took place in the local authority council chamber, a highly formalised deliberative space in which officers sat on a raised platform with members in a tiered hemisphere of seats with microphones that had to be switched on in order to make a contribution. The meeting began with officers' reports, followed by consideration of motions and the formal election of the next management committee. This formal structure was reflected in the nature of the contributions made, consisting in the main of questions or points directed to speakers on the platform rather than exchange between members on the floor of the council chamber. Time was often given over to input from speakers, usually local authority or health officials describing new policy initiatives or, in one example, presenting the need for budget cuts. While the format of meetings and the physical space of the venue meant that the emphasis was on information giving, discussion – in the form of what our observer termed 'polite debate' – also took place, with officers agreeing to 'take back' comments for appropriate officers to respond to.

This formal structure did not prevent conflict and disagreement – the style of deliberation was described as 'polite but robust' – but it did tend to militate against differences of view being fully explored among the committee and tended to limit the nature of contributions, with expressive or emotional discourse subordinated to the less personal norms of rational argumentation. Indeed the senior citizens' forums were strongly rules-based. Much work in City B had gone into getting the terms of reference for the forum right. As the facilitator commented,

> "We wanted to make sure everything was spot on.... Although I put the terms of reference together, I was not sure whether or not legally it would actually be binding. So we went to the Council for Voluntary Services, for them to come in and advise us. Just different ways to get the pedantics right, you know."

And 'pedantic' niceties sometimes arose in meetings: for example, there was a discussion about whether one member's role on the committee of an organisation called Communities Against Poverty was in the capacity of an authorised 'official' representative of the forum or simply in a personal capacity; and another member was criticised for writing a letter from the senior citizens' forum to the local paper without the prior approval of the committee. A debate about a challenge that had arisen in relation to the treatment (or not) of lesbian and gay issues within the forum had been resolved by 'reverting back to the terms of reference' that meant that issues of sexuality and racial origin could not be a bar to membership.

The forum also sought to be 'businesslike'. The committee comprised a diversity of individuals but people with professional or business backgrounds tended to hold the key roles and to dominate discussions. The facilitator was herself taking a business qualification and had extensive organisational experience as an employee of Age Concern. And at one meeting the committee was introduced by her to the technique of SWOT analysis (identifying the strengths and weaknesses of the group, and identifying opportunities and threats), and asked to use it to undertake a review of their activities. Here forum members appeared to be uncomfortable with the exercise, and it was not viewed as a success. This was in part since each was challenged to recount what they had done for the forum over the previous month, but also since the organisational development norms underpinning such exercises seemed to fit uneasily with the outward facing and political orientation of the group – an external, rather than internal, focus was the norm, and attention to process was limited. This, it was argued by the female facilitator of one of the forums, was in part because the group was strongly male dominated, having lost some of its key female members.

In contrast there was a strong concern with getting the process right in the women's centre. This had formal structures in order to meet the requirements of funders: a management committee with officers that met monthly, and an AGM. However, the deliberative style, both in these and in everyday meetings, differed markedly from that of the senior citizens' forums, not least because experience was highly valued and there was a strong climate of affirmation that enabled women to speak about their lives, bringing their 'private' experience into a safe public forum.

The AGM involved music and food and the 'business' agenda was dealt with in an inclusive and participative way, with women sitting in a circle and being invited to contribute to discussion. The key decision making took place at an annual review and planning meeting that was facilitated (usually by someone invited in from outside the membership) and which used techniques to maximise participation. There was also a real attempt to overcome power imbalances between full-time staff and volunteers. The result was a strong sense of attachment and involvement: "It's the first place I've been where I feel on an equal with paid workers"; "There is no sense of being judged here"; "We are all involved in every area [of decision making] so we feel very committed and engaged". Affective discourse was common – even at an AGM when those attending were asked to introduce themselves, most spoke in terms of their feelings about their involvement in the work of the group, using words such as 'joy', 'pleasure' and 'reward'.

The (paid) coordinator recognised that there were times when she took a much more directive role within debate. In the example that follows it is evident that she limited argument because she felt she had access to knowledge that other members of the group did not share, and she was worried they would make what she considered to be the wrong decision:

> "I try not to be directive, but sometimes I have to be. For example, the debate about the city council funding recently. There were 12 people at the meeting. It took a lot of time for me to explain exactly what this means to [the group]. I put two scenarios to them. Basically if they want to effect

change they may not want this money. And they debated it for so long, there isn't really time to do that. Also, because we're a limited company, and because we're a registered charity, I have to explain sometimes what the limitations are in relation to their decisions. For example, those who are trustees have a responsibility under the charity law not to refuse any source of funding, really."

This suggests ways in which institutional norms and rules imposed by official bodies can influence the style of deliberation itself in groups who strive to maintain a different kind of participative space. A rather different perspective on the process of influence is offered by the lesbian and gay forum. The forum comprised regular monthly meetings that were limited to official members. However, the forum was situated in a wider network of links with groups and individuals, and had an extensive mailing list that supported informal communications. This loose network structure was deliberate, and there was no desire to become a more formal group – indeed it was felt that this would constrain their activities. As one commented, "it's pretty loose really. I mean as an organisation it hardly exists". Although initially there was the idea of having elections, this fell by the wayside and "It's more of a network really. It's a network to hang things on".

Nevertheless deliberations within the forum itself were relatively structured, with agendas and report backs from previous issues raised, and with regular invited speakers. Confrontation between the forum and visiting police, health or social services officials sometimes arose, often to the discomfort of the official. For example forum members identified a social services official as 'complacent' on a matter with which they were deeply concerned:

> I think he said something like I am not used to people having this sort of emotional reaction. I said, well you ought to recognise that these are issues that affect us personally … you know, we are going to say what we think here. I said that these are issues that are affecting people and I don't think he could cope with that at all. I don't think he could cope with that at all, actually.

This question of the capacity of officials to deal with expressive or affective interventions is a theme reflected in the social movement literature we discussed in Chapter Three.

Because it covered a large geographical area, and because some of the police officers lived outside the area, members tended not to know each other informally: "you don't tend to sort of go to a pub and bump into one another as you do in the gay community generally speaking", and some efforts had been made to arrange social events such as a Christmas meal to which partners were invited. Identity as gay formed the main link between police offers and other members of the forum, and many did not necessarily identify with the area: "Not being funny, those of us with money and transport socialise in [neighbouring city name]. I wouldn't go into a gay club or pub in [name of city in which forum was based]".

This latter comment suggests the need to consider ways in which concepts of place and space intersect with the formation of identity-based publics that appear initially to cut across localities in an undifferentiated way. The youth forum condensed questions of space and identity in a particularly sharp way, being held together through a strong attachment to working with a particular category of young people (Kashmiri-Pakistani Muslims) in a particularly deprived – and multicultural – area of City A. Members of the youth forum based their work on forming relationships with young people at street level and many of the concerns that they sought to voice came from those encounters. However, unlike the experience of the women's centre, the informality of contact between members produced difficulties in engaging with officials. Those adults working with young people were very keen to elicit their views, but the young people themselves were often reticent. This reticence may be attributed in part to the formats in which they were invited to speak – for example the relatively large and formal ward conference – but also, our interviews suggest, may be because they had had bad experiences and perceived themselves to have been let down in the past. The nature of the deliberation itself was also problematic. Any initial statement made by a member of the youth forum or other youth organisation would be enthusiastically seized on by adults without leaving space for the young people to suggest other concerns they might have had, or to suggest where the concerns they did express came in their priorities. Rather than a fluid deliberation, a frustration built up on the part of the young people, which the adult workers appeared to either miss or underestimate, producing the potential for conflict. At the ward conference this conflict was sidestepped by the offer of the youth conference as a further space in which young people could express their views. However, in the planning process this space became confined and the promises were perceived not to have been met.

The norms of professional practice, evident in the behaviour of youth workers, aimed to elicit engagement through facilitation and support. But this tended to have a negative rather than positive impact, the youth work strategies being linked to control rather than empowerment:

> "I think the youth workers were there to facilitate the whole meeting, they were supposed to be there to support, but every time we went to the meetings it was 'we're doing this activity. You're splitting up into groups, you go there, you're discussing this'. That's how it was. Like I said, it was a youth conference for young people by young people, but it was never the young people who were putting the agenda together for the meetings, or taking the minutes of the meetings."

There was evidence that the officials believed they had knowledge that was unavailable to young people and that this should carry particular weight within the debate, that is, that it should not be subject to challenge:

> "The conference – the idea was always there among young people and among us, but to actually develop that you needed somebody. They don't understand that. They are not willing to understand that. One or two young people, they might have a bit of difficulty with it – they don't understand the city youth service, how it's working and the resources that they have…. Due to health and safety reasons I can't work outside on my own, I'm not allowed to go out on my own, I must have somebody with me. Young people don't understand that."

For this youth worker the institutional constraints on the way in which he worked were not open to challenge by himself, and thus he appeared unable to engage effectively with the young people concerned. Later in the interview he suggested that without his input they would ignore issues fundamental to the success of the venture:

> "I see my role as that, when they do something, I'd like to raise some issues with them – have they thought of this? This? This? It's not dictation. 'Yes we want to jump off the cliff.' 'Yes fine, but have you thought that you might break

your legs, how are you going to get the emergency services
to come and pick you up?'."

Youth workers expressed disappointment that their aspirations to
develop innovative forms of deliberation were frustrated by the apparent
intransigence of the young people involved. The official perspective
was that there was evidence of an inability on the part of young people
to move beyond the expression of challenges to achieve any sort of
transformation of ideas or approaches. From the young people's
perspective the problem was caused by officials' attempts to control
the process of deliberation:

> "… the youth officers tended to – not put ideas forward,
> but prompt people into saying what they wanted to say in
> a sense, what they would like to see, what the youth officers
> would want the conference to be about."

The young people's strong sense of injustice was related to the perceived
ineffectualness of the youth workers in securing resources. There was
evidence of considerable mistrust of workers who were perceived as
drawing a salary and as not having a real commitment to the area. The
young people contrasted this with their commitment that derived
from living in the area and having an expectation that they and their
children would continue to live there. In terms of the nature of the
discourse in which they were engaged, the young people were drawing
on their experiential knowledge of the area and their sense of injustice
because of the failure on the part of public agencies to invest in the
area. They saw such experiences and values as legitimising the positions
they took on issues. In contrast, the youth workers were seen to appeal
to institutional rules and procedures and to adopt a range of tactics to
neutralise what the young people were saying.

New spaces, new voices?

Here we consider the impact of the kinds of issues raised in the previous
three sections on the capacity of the forums we studied to challenge
the policies and practices of public bodies. As noted above, the
backgrounds of members of the senior citizens' forums meant that
they saw their role as campaigning on issues relevant to the lives of
older people, not simply as a consultative group. The formal style of
the forum and its deliberations tended to mean that it used official
channels to make its voice heard, typically such as writing a letter and

reporting back the response, although it also used local radio as a means of influence. One example that occurred during the course of the research related to the reduction of benefit payments for those in hospital for a certain period. One forum had written to the Minister for Pensions to object to this practice, and her (unsympathetic) response, when read out in the meeting, drew a number of outraged comments from members; but there were no realistic means for the group to channel this outrage. Unofficial protests – such as individuals writing to newspapers or speaking on the radio without the sanction of the committee – tended to receive official condemnation.

However, informal channels were also used, enabled by the way in which the committee was tightly networked into national and local policy bodies. This had consequences for its capacity to influence change for the benefit of older people, campaigning on particular issues and, at times, challenging particular forms of policy or practice. But this 'insider' status had important consequences; not least, it opened up the potential for 'capture' by policy or professional actors. For example, the role of the senior citizens' forum in City B in relation to the development of the National Service Framework for Older People meant that the committee of the forum was, in part, drawn into the nexus of health authority power, acting on its behalf. As such, it was discursively constituted as a 'partner' of government. But, despite its 'insider' status, this forum was well able to challenge local authority and health authority officials. For example, in relation to the implementation of the National Service Framework there was a challenge to the discovery that 'implementation champions' could only be appointed by service providers, and some dissatisfaction about their limited attendance at meetings. This roused strong feelings, but a rather weaker resolution, that members should "challenge the champions at the next meeting about their attendance, *while recognising that they were very busy*". Discussing the forum's new role of monitoring the implementation of the National Service Framework, there was a discussion with the community health trust official about the need for the forum to access data from the public bodies involved in delivering the initiative. Certain members, our observation notes suggest, were 'highly vocal' on the issue, and when the official commented that "the state of the technology would not permit this at present", the dissatisfaction of the forum was made clear and there was a strong call for 'culture change' in the organisations concerned. This suggests that the forum members were politically aware enough to realise that this was not a matter of technology, but of the willingness of statutory bodies to share information with 'outsiders'.

The women's centre saw itself not as a campaigning organisation seeking to represent all women, but as a means of channelling issues raised through the work of the centre into official policy and service debates. For example, the experience of women who had been the subjects of domestic violence, and who had contacted the centre for help and advice, had helped influence change in the city's housing policy. Following an active campaign on behalf of a Pakistani woman, threatened with deportation following the breakdown of her marriage, the group took on a wider role publicising the flaws in immigration policy at the time, though with less successful outcomes. A key strategy was the organisation of conferences on particular issues:

> "One example we used, a really powerful one again, was a woman called [name]. She was murdered along with her four children on a contact visit. So we did a workshop on contact. What we did at the conference, we had a ballot box, and we made these cards. You send people away with things [to follow up] and they don't do things. We had something like 80 people at this conference. We got them to fill in these cards at the time asking [the Home Secretary] to look at the law around the one year rule, slotted them all into the ballot box."

During the period of the research we saw some of the implications of groups such as this becoming closer to official bodies – working in partnership, meeting regularly – as well as the potential for new counter publics to form. One example was an occasion in which the (local authority) chair of the domestic violence forum failed, in many members' eyes, to deal adequately with issues of 'race'. A second related to an incident where the minutes of a meeting with council officials had, it was felt, distorted what had been agreed and where there was evidence of decisions having been made 'behind closed doors' after the meeting had taken place. Following an unsatisfactory resolution to concerns about how far European funds secured to support disadvantaged women in the region were reaching the women most in need, several members of that forum – including the coordinator of the women's centre – resigned to form a new network, described as a 'virtual organisation', with the aim of ensuring "that women's experience informs practice, policy and legislation". This would explicitly not seek funding in order to ensure its independence. Another was the way in which the group supported the development of cross-national networks, securing funding to send delegates to international political events and forums. A much less tangible outcome can be traced in the ways in which our respondents spoke about their involvement, and the transformative effect on the self: "I feel I am part of a little snowball, or like ripples in a pool".

The lesbian and gay forum also appeared successful in balancing the need to sustain a 'safe space' in which issues and experiences could be shared against the aspiration of engaging with and influencing official bodies. Although drawn into partnership with the police service, there was a refusal to adopt the institutional features that might have rendered them more 'manageable' partners:

> "A number of us are very reluctant to get into that game. We have seen too many organisations becoming an existence for themselves.... We don't want to spend all our time running an organisation.... You know we want to see things happen. We don't want to spend all our time having to apply for grants and things like that."

The reference to the effects of 'running an organisation', 'applying for grants' and so on refers to the experience of groups in close relationships with the city council or health authority (see Chapter Five). Instead the members of the lesbian and gay forum tended to work through networks, going into chat rooms and listening to what was happening on the street and in gay venues. The guarantee of anonymity to those wanting to complain about police practice was highly valued and closely protected. Although there had been some positive outcomes of their interaction with the police service it was acknowledged that there were a number of constraints, not least the discriminatory nature of much of the legislation that the police were expected to enforce. However, some of the issues that the forum were working towards involved changes within the lesbian and gay community itself: more willingness to report hate crimes, more capacity to raise issues for public debate.

The forum, although initially set up as part of the city council equality policy, had become disillusioned about their capacity to work with the city, not least because of the way it had moved towards an area committee structure (the effects of which were explored in Chapter Six). Community, then, came to be defined in terms of locality or neighbourhood. The dwindling of contact between the gay and lesbian community forum and local authority B was attributed in large part to the local authority's switch to an area committee strategy, with the result that consultation and involvement on the basis of socially differentiated publics became relatively neglected. One of those interviewed commented on "a complete lack of any strategy for involving and consulting us". The police service, too, was increasingly focused on neighbourhood consultations – but here there was a deliberate attempt to transcend the limitations produced in terms of raising identity-based issues:

> "The police held forums within communities as a matter of course. Throughout the whole of [conurbation name]. And obviously the gay community is spread out through the whole of [conurbation name], and although they may well come along to the neighbourhood forum, they more often than not wouldn't bring up any gay issues. So it was decided that hard to reach groups like the gay community, and in some cases the black community etc, would have their own set of forums." (police respondent)

But related issues were now being raised in terms of the reorganisation of the police service into smaller geographical units. This, in the view of one of our respondents, made them more vulnerable to the attitudes and responses of individual operational unit heads. And specific initiatives – for example the proposal to set up a 'hate crime' telephone line in one area – were seen as cutting across the gains made: "I think it will mean failure because I know that gay and lesbian people are not going to ring a general hate crime line".

Despite hints about the problems of articulating a gay and lesbian identity in public arenas, with references back to the problems caused by Section 28 (see note 2 at the end of this chapter), the comparative success of the lesbian and gay forum can perhaps be attributed to the positive alignment between the new emphasis on issues of diversity in police services seeking to legitimise themselves in the post-McPherson climate, and a climate of increasing – albeit still highly conditional – tolerance that enabled gay and lesbian police officers to come out to their colleagues.

The impact of the forum was described in terms of a 'pressure group' whose effectiveness was in part due to one of its gay members becoming an independent member of the Police Authority:

> "So you get a lot of oomph, you know. He can sort of bring things up to high levels, he meets with the chief constable. If he wanted to meet with any of the senior

> officers he would be able to do so by making a 'phone
> call."

There appeared to be some considerable influence on policy making. A hate crime policy was presented back to the forum, who commented "It's very good", largely since a forum member had been on the committee that shaped it. As such, this was a forum that appeared to be relatively effective in creating the possibility of gay and lesbian voices being heard – and acted on – by a key public body. However, the voices concerned were predominantly those of gay men rather than lesbians, and of younger rather than older generations. "Very few lesbian issues are brought up.... The issues ... tend to be surrounding the social scene. And a lot of gay women don't go to the social scene."

Despite the effectiveness of the forum, however, participation alone was viewed as unable to overcome the lack of trust between the gay community and the police, or to address the difficulties and discrimination faced by gay and lesbian officers within the police service. Nor was it capable of resolving the tensions inherent in the policing of areas in which gay sexual activity takes place:

> "It's difficult for senior officers to tell people not to deal
> with that sort of thing when it is an offence. [So] you use
> the sensitivity thing, I mean when's public and when's
> private [in terms of where sexual encounters take place]?...
> And they [senior officers] are seeing the point. But until
> the law has changed it's difficult."

Lack of trust was also a key issue in the *youth forum*. Here there was a strong perception that considerable sums of money had been secured by the council and partnership bodies on the strength of deprivation in the area, including reference to the situation of young people, and yet young people had relatively little voice in how this was spent. Youth workers described the emerging hostility or frustration in terms of the unwillingness of young people to understand the constraints under which they worked. For example one described how youth forum members wanted more youth work in the local park, but this was difficult because of health and safety regulations that prevented them from working alone. They also attributed hostility to the general impatience of youth:

> "Young people were getting frustrated.... They would make
> comments and then leave the meeting, saying 'we want

this and it's not happening, OK see you'. People [the youth forum members] were unwilling to understand the frustration. Young people are expecting and wanting things bigger. And the delivery process – it must be immediate delivery process, not 'OK, we'll take it to so-and-so committee'. A lot of young people don't understand that."

Another commented:

"One of the things I think young people need to understand is that some processes take a long time. They have to go through certain mechanisms before it gets approved. Such as myself who works for the city and other officers, we have to follow certain measures, certain guidelines, and until these guidelines are met, we can't deliver. Young people think 'you've got the money to do this. Why don't you do it now?'."

As well as attempting to take on the planning of the youth conference, members of the youth forum were pushing for representation on local bodies such as neighbourhood councils and participation in local health forums. And some of the officers were exploring routes to influence through the local Labour Party, as councillors were seen to exercise considerable power over the local delivery of services. At the same time, however, there was a perception that putting forward strong arguments for young people, particularly where this involved criticising the status quo, would not lead to advancement.

Conclusion

As we noted in the introduction to this chapter, the attempt by public bodies to engage in deliberation with particular publics characterised by social difference raises a number of difficult issues. In trying to reach out to such publics, public bodies may assume a 'community' of identity that suggests a cohesiveness of identifications and interests within a particular category – here older people (defined as 'senior citizens'), women, lesbians and gays, or young people. What we have tried to show in this chapter is that such categorisations may not reflect the complexity of the identifications of individuals or groups. This intersects with problems of representation and representativeness experienced by each of the groups we have discussed here – the marginalisation of some categories of senior citizen, the focus on particular issues affecting younger, rather than older, lesbians and gays, the difficulties of working across both class and 'race' experienced by the women's centre, and the tensions between different youth organisations seeking to 'represent' young people in a specific locality. The idea of identity-based groups as 'counter publics' – publics operating in a space apart from the state, with strong mutual identifications and the capacity to form and articulate alternative political agendas – sits uneasily with the desire of public bodies to engage with 'representative' groups. And in seeking to consult or engage with representative organisations or individuals within a forum, public bodies may be understood as 'constituting' its publics rather than simply engaging with pre-existing social formations. This was recognised by one of the local authority officers we interviewed:

> "In the 1990s they [the council] realised they were not going to develop and regenerate unless they took communities with them. They started to get strategic and to get exclusive – they engaged with odd people, in a very particular way. They engaged with people who became the great and the good, who then became another level of bureaucracy as far as the community went.... The concept and understanding of what involvement was about was absent from that strategic framework." (local authority equalities officer)

The way in which the old style of consultation worked had had, she argued, either no impact or a detrimental impact: "It was an engagement in which officers were not nurturing the engagement, they were sucking it dry". This process was also highlighted by 'lay' respondents, in this case of the lesbian and gay forum:

> "Every bit of evidence I have seen suggests that they [officials] involve those who are already involved. So they liaise with a few key people who often they know anyway. Therefore it's relatively easy for them to work with. And the whole thing goes round in circles."

We can see the impact of this process of constitution in some of the case studies discussed in this chapter. The senior citizens' forums, although having their roots in campaigning organisations such as the National Pensioners Convention, were formed in partnership with statutory organisations. Both enjoyed high level support, with, in City A, strong involvement on the part of the council leader influencing its perceived legitimacy by council officers. This partnership had come to shape the kinds of work they undertook, acting as a consultative body and becoming invested with forms of responsibility that enabled it to take on activities on behalf of state organisations. However, their formal independence, and the campaigning and activist roles that formed the background of many members, meant that they could still challenge the actions of officials, and frequently did so. It is perhaps not surprising, then, that during the period of research a new body (an advisory council of older people) was being proposed in City A to more directly meet the needs defined by officers and members of the local authority. That is, a new, perhaps more 'manageable', public was being constituted. And we can see, in the example of the youth forum, how a clash between the self-constituted Kashmiri-Pakistani group and the attempt by youth workers to constitute a more inclusive and 'representative' group led to considerable conflict, producing a mutual hostility between the city council and an important part of its public – one which, in the current climate of potential distrust between Muslim and non-Muslim groups, may have long-standing consequences.

The examples of the women's centre and the lesbian and gay forum are rather different. Both comprised loose networks whose origins lay in the shaping of the new social and political movements of the 1970s, and both had established norms and practices that supported the possibility of voicing alternative agendas: that is, both had the potential to act as 'counter publics'. Although not representative, and not seeking to be so, both were drawn into policy-shaping forums by official bodies seeking to become more 'responsive' and to enhance their legitimacy with particular publics. In both cases a (mostly) positive climate of engagement was enabled by 'insiders' who shared some, at least, of the identity of the public concerned. 'Insider' and 'outsider' identities also tended to blur as members of the senior citizens' forum, women's centre, lesbian and gay forums were drawn into networks with officials and policy actors. Insider and outsider identities, then, are not fixed categories but are situational and may be mobilised strategically, both by officials and by forum members themselves. Indeed in many examples there is evidence of the tension between insider and outsider identities being displaced from the lay members of forums onto officials managing the interface between organisational norms and expectations and those of the groups to which they become informally attached.

In contrasting the 'alternative' norms that may be created or sustained within groups or movements based on presumed commonality of identity with the rules and norms of state agencies there is, then, a danger of creating a too clearly delineated boundary between public officials and 'counter publics'. As in the cases discussed in Chapter Five, many of the officials we interviewed had backgrounds and motivations not so dissimilar from those of the group members, and were active in creating the spaces in which new voices might emerge that might challenge existing organisational practice. There were close alliances between gay and lesbian police officers and members of the liaison group. The gender equalities manager of the city council was tightly embedded in community organisations, and was working to create a new network of women's groups that could inform policy but that could also be 'consulted' on issues that might provide levers for organisational change within the city council itself. At the same time, many members of the senior citizens' forums were long-standing activists who were deeply familiar with the power dynamics of official bodies, and who were well able to form appropriate alliances with key officials (in one case, with the council leader).

The mediation role of officials does, however, present different kinds of challenge that have to be negotiated. Our analysis of the youth group highlights the importance of the mediation roles played by officials in defining legitimate membership. The youth workers charged with securing young people's involvement in planning the youth conference had to negotiate both the wider regeneration initiative that was to sponsor it and with the young people themselves:

> "On the one hand it's about young people being, if you like, attached to their community and when I say attached I suppose participation becomes the important word within that, that they see an opportunity in order to be able to make some sort of difference within the community and so on. On the other hand it's also in this particular instance about those elected members, particularly, being aware of what young people's views are around certain things."

They demonstrated their willingness to actively involve members of the youth forum in decision making and planning, but could not surrender control to the forum itself. This was partly due to their difficulties in relinquishing professional control (for example over agenda setting and managing the processes of deliberation within meetings), but also to tensions between the self-identity of the forum and the way in which public officials structured notions of legitimate membership. Cutting across these was a particular dynamic associated with constructions of youth itself, in which young people are viewed as needing to learn – from adults – how to be 'proper' citizens.

In the case of the lesbian and gay forum, in contrast, there was an ambiguity about whether the police constable we interviewed was attending the forum as a representative of the police service or as a lesbian member of the 'gay community'. Similar issues arose in the identities of staff from minority ethnic groups in the MEGC discussed in Chapter Five. In the lesbian and gay forum the police constable commented "in the first 12 months I was on the committee I think he [a 'lay' forum member] thought I was very much a police officer and not a member of the gay community ... but that has changed. Because every time we have had an upset about something that he has told me has happened we have sorted it out, eventually, I think he is realising now that there is a genuine desire to do this right". But her effectiveness in negotiating this relationship is not the same as her adopting a closer identification with the gay community rather than the police. When asked about this dual identity she talked about her prime loyalty as being towards the job: "I am a member of the initiative, in my sort of belief, as a police officer first and then a gay person". As such she felt that she had to defend the police when accused of practices that this respondent saw as conflicting with her own perceptions of policing. "I mean that's a problem you have in policing generally, not just the gay community. I have stood up and argued until blue in the face with somebody, saying well that's not the procedure we use so what you are telling me couldn't have happened like that".

Certainly she was under considerable pressure as one of the few 'out' police officers on the force: "you know, they are trying to sort out the diversity policy, training etc. So they want you there to discuss what you think about it. You know, 'such and such a thing is happening, we need a gay officer there. Oh, she will do'.... It's all for positive reasons, [and] I'm quite happy to do it, [but] it does tend to get a little bit, you know, when you are looking at your desk and thinking good heavens, what am I doing taking on that lot". Organisational support for her role was limited: while she enjoyed considerable freedoms in terms of how she used her time, she stressed that if it interfered with her job as a unit post holder, "somebody would be speaking to me and saying no, at times". But "it's a ducked issue at the moment".

Bridging roles were played by both the women's centre coordinator and the gender equality manager of the city council. The former described her role in terms of "sticking her head above the parapet", negotiating with officials in order to protect the safe space for women in the group to shape their own agenda and find a collective voice that could then be fed into policy forums. The latter saw one of the purposes of her unit as building the capacity of organisations to provide commentary on policy decisions, and as trying to ensure that women were inserted into all the places where relevant debates were taking place. To that end she was active in creating new networks as well as drawing on existing groups and individuals already known to the council.

Here, then, we emphasise the need to pay attention to the nature of the boundary between members of particular groups characterised by their place in a differentiated public, and those working for, funded by or attached to state agencies. Our data illustrate how such boundaries may be mediated, and the extent of solidification or blurring of the boundaries themselves. This shapes the ways in which it is possible to delineate new spaces arising at the interface between a socially differentiated public and public bodies, and the extent to which this enables 'new voices' to emerge. By new voices we do not simply wish to denote the ways in which identity-based publics may become the focus of consultation and participation attempts; rather, we mean how far such publics can raise alternative or competing agendas, to speak in a different kind of voice and to be heard, and for this to shape public policy and the practices of public bodies.

Notes

[1] The McPherson Report of 1999 reported on an enquiry following the death of a young black teenager, Stephen Lawrence. It was heavily critical of the police response to the murder and introduced the concept 'institutional racism' into public discourse.

[2] In particular Section 28 of the 1988 Local Government Act had barred local authorities from 'promoting' homosexuality. This had a profound effect on education practice but also influenced other local authority services, and its ripple effects produced a cautionary stance towards explicitly engaging with lesbian and gay issues across the public sector (Cooper, 2004).

EIGHT

Issues and expertise

In the previous chapter we saw how publics constituted by reference to particular identities may find it hard to secure space for public deliberation in the context of official participation discourses and policies that prioritise community as 'place'. In this chapter we consider two examples of initiatives that have even less of a profile within contemporary democratic practice: initiatives that are based around campaigns and policy making in relation to specific issues. The fact that we only studied two such examples, one in each of the case study cities, is in itself evidence of the much lower profile of such initiatives in local policy making. As we will see, these examples illustrate many similar issues in terms of the dynamics of the relationship between autonomous SMOs and the official sphere of local policy making. However, their origin in issue rather than identity-based action also leads to some different factors affecting not only issues of membership, but also the nature of the deliberation in which they are engaged. Such issues reflect, in part, the analysis that has been made of differences between 'instrumental' movements and both 'sub-cultural' and 'counter-cultural' movements (Kreisi et al, 1995). In different ways the logic of action of sub-cultural and counter-cultural movements is focused on identity: the constitution of collective identities within group interaction in, for example the women's movement, and the generation of collective identity from conflictual interaction with other groups in terrorist organisations and some ethnic movements. Instrumental movements, in comparison, have more of an external orientation and action logic; their aim is to impact on the external environment. The ecology movement and peace movement have been identified as examples of instrumental movements. The lower profile of such actions also reflects the way in which policy 'problems' are currently constructed and thus the potential for opening up deliberative spaces within which policies can be debated.

The first example grew out of community action focused around poverty. The particular focus of the action we studied was a campaign relating to fuel poverty, which had emerged from a broader-based poverty action group in City B. It was evident in the early stages of our research that our references to 'social exclusion' when we introduced the research to local stakeholders prompted rather different responses in the two cities. In City A the response reflected the profile of 'race' and ethnicity in a city with a black and minority ethnic population well above the national average, and comparatively well-organised and high profile minority ethnic community organisations active in the area. When we said 'social exclusion' in City A, the response often assumed the necessity to focus on minority ethnic groups. In City B, in contrast, reference to social exclusion generated comments about poverty. It has been argued that one consequence of the emergence of the social exclusion discourse has been to 'hide' the significance of material deprivation (Levitas, 2005). In an area with high levels of such deprivation and in which the local political culture had often been characterised by an oppositional stance towards national government, an explicit recognition of the significance of poverty for the health of the local population as well as in relation to broader issues of social relationships characterised approaches towards policy issues in both the official and community spheres.

The identification of collective action that came to be described as *new* social movements marked the emergence of action for social change based not around class-based issues relating to material injustice, but in a desire for cultural transformation. While much action within social movements is prompted by experiences of oppression and disadvantage, within the UK class-based identities, and identities as people living in poverty are rarely what defines the basis for action, and even less often cited by officials as defining the particular publics they wish to engage. For example, many disabled people are poor, but it is the experience of disabling barriers rather than poverty per se that provides the basis for action (Campbell and Oliver, 1996). Elsewhere, many indigenous people's movements involve people whose lives are characterised by extreme poverty, but their objectives relate as much to recognition of their cultural distinctiveness as to redistributive outcomes (for example, Ruiz, 2005). Beresford et al (1999) identify a number of groups and campaigns involving poor people in the UK, but also argue that it has been harder for poor people to get their voices heard within policy forums than it has been for other groups of welfare recipients. The Child Poverty Action Group and other campaigning groups have largely involved academics, politicians and other campaigners who are not themselves poor. The fuel poverty group is thus a comparatively rare example of collective action in which people living in poverty are key players and it is poverty rather than other aspects of identity or experience that is the basis for action.

Fuel poverty group

The fuel poverty group was a coalition of individuals, voluntary and community groups from the environmental and poverty sectors that was initially formed to lobby for the passage of the 2000 Fuel Poverty and Energy Conservation Act, and to give increased prominence to the issue of fuel poverty within that. The lobbying had resulted in considerable support from local MPs and was considered highly successful. Its local development was decided following consultation with people living in poverty undertaken by a local anti-poverty campaign group and, following the passage of the Act, the group turned its attention to pressurising local authorities in the region into developing and implementing their own fuel poverty strategies. The aim was for a regional approach that would enable local authorities to learn from each other. The authorities themselves had formed a regional consortium to address this, although at the time of the research only one local authority in the region had a strategy in draft.

Any individual with an interest in fuel poverty issues in the region could join the group and members of the broader anti-poverty group were invited to attend. In practice, all individual members were from the anti-poverty group and all had direct experience of poverty. They had also all had considerable experience of community group, trades union or political campaigning. Environmental pressure groups were also represented although they had a much less active role after the success of the parliamentary campaign. In contrast, the active representation of local authorities increased and the head of the regional consortium was a regular attendee at group meetings. Other groups regularly sending representatives included regeneration partnerships, a pensioners' group and the Unemployed Workers Centre. An individual member chaired meetings and the anti-poverty group provided administrative support.

Sustainability forum

The environmental movement has been the subject of considerable research and is often considered an 'archetypal' new social movement. Brulle (1995) describes it as "one of the major political and cultural actors that is now originating and acting to enable an alternative social order" (p 309). It operates at an international and neighbourhood level and exhibits many of the network characteristics that have been argued to constitute the organisational structure of social movements (Diani and McAdam, 2003). Within the movement are highly focused groups with very specific objectives, such as those campaigning for an increase in cycle routes and organisations that have developed recycling projects, and those with much broader objectives relating to environmental protection. Thus it operates across a number of policy domains as well as at very different levels of the policy system. Although it is usually considered as an example of an 'instrumental' social movement with an external orientation focused on policy change, this is embedded within cultural values that generate often passionate commitments that are an important dimension of activists' personal identities.

The second case study considered here was a sustainability forum that provided opportunities for dialogue between activists in the environmental movement, local interested and concerned citizens, and council officers in relation to issues of environmental sustainability. The forum was set up by the city council in City A in 1992 following the Rio Environmental Summit. This had identified a range of organisations that needed to take forward the environmental agenda, including local authorities that were encouraged to commit to what became known as Local Agenda 21. The principle locations for dialogue were quarterly forum open meetings, normally held at the council house, and organised around specific themes – for example, more environmentally friendly buildings, meeting local needs locally, and recycling. Recommendations for action from these meetings were collated and circulated to relevant departments and organisations. Subjects for meetings were decided at smaller agenda-setting forums that met regularly in between forum open meetings. In addition to open meetings, the forum had also sponsored a set of working groups on topics such as poverty, water, pollution, land use and equality and discrimination.

The forum was chaired by an elected member who also chaired the council's environmental advisory team and under his tenure, the forum had established more formal links with that committee. Membership was not particularly formal. The least active level of membership involved simply being placed on the mailing list and there were a huge number of individuals and organisations in this category. Those attending meetings were asked to sign an attendance sheet and this generated the mailing list. Membership of the agenda-setting forum involved a greater level of commitment and required individuals to attend roughly monthly meetings. Membership of this group was by election at the time of this study.

Open forum meetings comprised a speaker session with questions, followed by a number of workshops on sub-areas of the meeting's headline topic. Workshop subjects were chosen by officers in the environment department, having regard to discussions in the agenda-setting forum. Recommendations from groups were fed back into the main meeting at a plenary session and were noted to be used in approaching relevant bodies following the meeting. At the forum observed for this research, there were recommendations to six city council departments, central government departments and agencies, housing associations and private sector manufacturers, regeneration partnerships, the utilities and the European Union.

Policies, discourses and political opportunity structures

One way in which the emergence and sustainability of social movements has been understood relates to the policy and political context that creates an environment that is more or less conducive to action intended to lead to social change, and to the specific policy or service developments that both demonstrate and contribute to the process of transformation that this implies. In both these case study examples the origins of the action that was the focus of the research can be linked to specific aspects of the policy context. The fuel poverty group was a direct response to proposed legislation (which started out as a Private Members' Bill) relating to energy conservation. The broader anti-poverty group within City B drew on consultation with their members to identify the significance of the proposed legislation and the need to extend this to recognise that energy conservation measures would be likely to impact disproportionately on poor people. Thus they argued that energy conservation could not be addressed without also considering the issue of fuel poverty. Their success in achieving an extension to what eventually became the Warm Homes and Energy Conservation Act of 2000 reflected the support they were able to secure from MPs in the city and region – which in itself reflected the profile given to poverty here, unlike in City A. The continuation of the group was encouraged by the willingness of the city council to take seriously the implementation requirements of the legislation and their preparedness to acknowledge the expertise of the fuel poverty group in doing so. This grew out of a history of close working between the wider campaigning group and the anti-poverty unit in the city council. Group members felt that their knowledge enabled them to come up with very practical proposals for implementation and that the regional focus supported opportunities for learning as well as helping to sustain a level of attention to the issue.

The position of health service organisations in the city was also helpful. At a time when the term 'health inequalities' was not recognised as a legitimate element of health policy discourse, the local health authority had been engaged in action to address the considerable health problems in the city from a perspective that explicitly acknowledged the relationship between poor health and poverty. In the more sympathetic environment created following the election of the New Labour government in 1997 the city was part of a regional initiative to address health inequalities in the context of the HAZ programme (see Barnes et al, 2005).

One member of the group spoke directly about the opportunity offered by the campaign around the legislation to shape the group's activities in a particular way:

> "Strategically it allowed us to branch across the region and also allowed us to focus on health and poverty related issues as they related specifically to affordable warmth ... give it a momentum and to give us a separate identity and to link it very closely to the process of legislation."

Group members had also learned the language of social exclusion and this may have helped them to frame the way in which they approached their objectives within a broader policy context. For example: "we are very concerned that we help to contribute to the creation of the most inclusive affordable warmth strategy we can".

The sustainability forum in City A had its origins in the appeal to local authorities coming from the Rio Environmental Summit to play their part in environmental issues. One activist interviewed talked of the early 1990s as a period of the "greening of government". The city had itself undertaken an environmental impact assessment prior to Rio and the suggestion was that the local authority wanted to ensure that it was seen to be performing well in this area. Developing a Local Agenda 21 action plan had become the subject of a Best Value performance indicator. The city's environmental services department included a small team with responsibility for sustainability issues and some officers in this team identified themselves with the environmental movement. An activist suggested that the profile of environmental issues was lower at the time of the research than it had been in the early 1990s, although there was another view that the renaming of what had originally been the 'environmental forum' reflected "the continual process of renaming and reinventing subjects in order to keep them current".

In addition to the opportunities offered, in different ways, by particular policy contexts, participants in both initiatives recognised the significance of broader agendas relating to more participatory forms of policy making. Members of the fuel poverty group located this within the context of community development and community self-help initiatives that reflected the empowered public discourse also evident in the community health forum in this city. They also located the forum within network forms of governance (without using this term). This related not only to the role of the group in working across all local authorities in the region, but also in bringing together local authority and health service interests, as well as specialist environmental groups, such as Friends of the Earth, and other voluntary organisations with specific interests in fuel poverty issues – such as Age Concern because of the significance of the cost of fuel for many older people. Thus as well as a strong basis in a notion of an empowered public challenging their own oppression, there was also some recognition of the significance of engaging people and organisations by reference to their identities as 'stakeholders'.

The local authority officer who organised the sustainability forum self-consciously appealed to the 'consultation' rhetoric that was influential within the city council as a way of securing attention to environmental issues raised within the forum:

> "It was quite good because it was a consultation … because at the city council it's a buzzword, consultation, so we'd be at a meeting and we'd say 'sustainability forum, this idea came up' and we'd feed it in…."

The power of the participation or consultation discourse was also invoked by an activist member of the forum who also suggested that this is "better consultation than most local government consultation in the form it takes". Another thought that it was "very much council led", while the council officer described it as an "internal pressure group". We explore this 'insider/outsider' position below in relation to both the identities of participants and the nature of the deliberative process and its outcomes.

The council officer also located the sustainability forum within a 'partnership' discourse, although she recognised its ambiguous position in this respect:

> "So a big part of Local Agenda 21 has always been about partnerships and participation, so the forum was set up to

respond to that. I think that's why it was set up, partly because of that but also because the participants see it as a way of trying to influence the city council, and perhaps the majority of people see it more as that rather than being a partnership. We're [the local authority] always going to be the big players in the partnership. You can never have an equal balance...."

The sustainability forum was a city-wide initiative and there was no evidence of an appeal to the discourse of 'community' in defining the public to be engaged in this process. The council officer identified participants as people from small voluntary groups or 'just interested individuals'. At other points she referred to participants as 'stakeholders' or residents, albeit "they've got a lot more knowing about what's happening than most residents". For one activist member, however, the forum was a location in which a particular type of community could be formed:

"We are occupying, we are interrelating with each other ... we are a community or should be a community because we are attempting to interchange ideas between each other...."

This 'community of ideas' is very different from the way in which community is usually used in policy discourse, but does suggest the potential of the forum as a space in which dialogue between officials and citizens might be conducted as equals.

Motivations and identities

The key difference between these two case studies in terms of the nature of the participants was the deliberate objective of involving people with direct experience of living in poverty in the fuel poverty group. There was no similar experiential identity that could be appealed to in the context of the sustainability forum. In the latter instance a shared commitment to a broad value position provided a basis around which a collective identity might develop (Melucci, 1996), but this was rather different from the shared *experience* of deprivation and disadvantage associated with poverty. However, the fuel poverty group also included sympathetic officers from the local authority and the NHS. In both cases, therefore, we see further examples of participants who are negotiating their identities as citizens, as activists with commitments to the broad objectives of the group, and as officials with responsibilities for developing and implementing public policies. As well as negotiating these identities within the forums, these people also had important roles at the interface between these spaces in which ideas and proposals were being developed and the spaces in which decisions were being made.

The coordinator of the fuel poverty group was a paid worker in the broader campaigning group and his route into this position was through his own experience of unemployment and as a recipient of welfare benefits. His background as a trade unionist while in employment and as a volunteer community activist when he became unemployed as a result of an industrial injury had persuaded him of the value of collective action. Thus a key purpose of the campaign as he saw it was to build a collective voice based in direct experience:

> "I think that's where the confidence comes in of being included, and people joining in and not feeling marginalised, umm, and ideas are coming from the people who are directly affected by the day-to-day life experiences, that they are living."

In contrast with most 'community'-based initiatives he saw a key purpose of this group as to transcend place to bring together people from different places who had similar problems in order to work together and to learn from each other.

Motivations based in personal experience can interact with more altruistic appeals to social justice. Another member of the group who had also become involved in community action following being made redundant talked about seeing the inadequate housing, bad heating and damp faced by many people in an area where he worked for a faith-based organisation: "I thought this wasn't right". A similar perspective was offered by another member who became involved via the regional pensioners' liaison committee and who specifically identified the injustice of the number of pensioners dying of cold-related health problems. For others social justice concerns were linked to their professional identities or paid employment. One member, who located his involvement in his work for a health organisation using community development approaches to tackle health inequalities, also described his personal motivation "around my personal sense of injustice and my sense that, if you like, access to affordable fuel is along with access to decent water, accommodation, etc, as a basic human right and underpins individual wellbeing".

In common with many community groups there was an active core membership that attended group meetings regularly and took part in working groups, conference and discussions relevant to the development and implementation of a fuel poverty strategy in the region on behalf of the group. Others attended less regularly or were invited in order to offer a particular perspective considered important to include as the group developed ideas and practical recommendations for the strategy. There was an emphasis on drawing ideas from a wide range of sources, on encouraging people to talk about the problems they had in order to widen the understanding of the impact of fuel poverty, and on encouraging all those who came to meetings to play an active part within them. The well-defined focus for the group's activities, in particular during its early phase, was identified as a factor contributing to unity within the group: "And I think that gave us a cohesion and a purpose if you like, and a direction. So that we were very much united in that whole effort to ensure that the legislation was improved". This participant went on to say that if the group had also included people who saw the key issue as energy conservation, "then we would have had a barny every time we met". But this did not mean an overly narrow set of interests that were shared among group members. Because the concern with fuel poverty was located within broader involvement in issues related to poverty, such as health inequalities, this also helped to ensure unity within the group.

One participant who became involved as a result of a direct invitation because of her employment in an energy saving trust stood out as having a rather different relationship with the group. She referred to the group throughout her interview as 'they' rather than 'we' and, in spite of agreement with the group's objectives and of referring to her own previous involvement in work with community groups and campaigning around women's issues, did not evidence the same level of emotional commitment as other members. Thus, although she talked of her belief in equality and human potential, and in spite of making a decision to return from living in France to come to this part of England because she felt strongly about it and developing the community within it, her relationship with the group was primarily an instrumental one: "can you help me and I will help you".

The local authority officer who coordinated the sustainability forum spoke at considerable length about the dilemmas she experienced negotiating her personal commitment to the objectives of the forum and her role as a council officer. She described herself as being lucky to be appointed to a post that enabled her to pursue her personal interest and commitment to environmental issues, but identified contexts in which this created dilemmas. She was reluctant to take part in locality-based participation initiatives that could provide another forum in which to promote environmental issues because 'her bosses' – the councillors who chaired those forums – would not know if she was speaking from her perspective as "Ms Council or Ms Resident". Yet in other contexts she explicitly used her involvement in the forum and her insider position within the council to shape the direction of discussion within decision-making forums. We consider this in more detail below. For other council officers who came to the forum 'as members of the public' rather than as part of their paid role, things were more straightforward. One employee in the social services department was described as a "really huge activist on transport" who appeared to have no inhibitions in attempting a highly critical and unpopular takeover of a working group on transport.

Interviewees from the sustainability forum contrasted the apathy of most people in relation to politics and policy making with their own, often passionate, commitment to the cause of environmentalism:

> "Depressingly the average person doesn't seem to want to participate, so the people who go to the forum are people who work in the area, or a campaigning area, or are involved in the issues one way or the other. I suppose you could call them stakeholders, not the ordinary member of the public who has a more general interest in these things."

All those interviewed had come to the forum from previous involvement in other issue-based social movements: the environmental movement, the peace movement, the anti-apartheid movement or, in one case, the Pan-African movement that was considered to have close links with such issues. This member suggested it was only natural for anyone serious about African issues to concern themselves with the environment, especially given the disproportionate impact of such issues on African countries. However, beyond this individual there was an awareness and a concern that the forum was predominantly white, predominantly middle class and "it does tend to be the same old faces and has been the same old faces predominantly for 10 years". Participation in the forum reflected the broader nature of the environmental movement with many of those coming to meetings being engaged in specific areas of activity, such as allotments, recycling, or transport, and others coming from broader-based SMOs such as Friends of the Earth or voluntary organisations such as Community Service Volunteers. The value of the forum as a networking opportunity was stressed in addition to the significance of existing networks as a route in to participation within the forum. The importance of this as a social space in which to maintain and develop contacts was also identified. One participant talked about the amount of contact she had with core participants outside the formal meetings and ran through a number of named participants noting: "I helped organise his birthday party", "I went on holiday with her". This may be related to evidence of a continuing commitment to taking part in the forum, in spite of a recent review of the forum that had indicated a strong sense among those on the mailing list that it was not having any significant impact.

One explanation that was offered for the composition of the forum was that better educated people, who already occupy comparatively powerful positions, have an expectation that their voices will be heard and thus those who also have a commitment to environmental issues would use the opportunity provided by the forum to have their say – they would also have the confidence and the skills to take advantage of this. It was also suggested that people who were not already familiar with key environmental issues would be put off from taking part in the forum because the majority did appear very knowledgeable. However, there was also evidence of a conscious attempt to become involved in a variety of activities, including media stunts as well as developing responses to council planning papers, which might engage a broader range of participants. Attempts had been made to engage whole families and some success was claimed in work with schools as a means of reaching children and young people. The task of taking the forum out to diverse communities, both in terms of locality and to minority ethnic communities, was considered too great to attempt in such a large city.

Expert deliberation

A strong theme within both case studies was the significance of the knowledge and expertise of participants in these initiatives, knowledge that came from different sources but which placed participants in a strong position to claim legitimacy for the position they took on policy issues and to be heard and influential within policy-making circles.

The fuel poverty group placed considerable emphasis on accessing the experiential knowledge of people living in poverty, and on deliberately inviting participation from people who were seen to have a particular insight, which could include people with a specific health perspective, or people from Age Concern who understood the issues as they relate to older people. Participants talked of the way in which they used their networks – including group participants and broader contacts – to build up a substantial body of evidence on the extent and impact of fuel poverty. That enabled them to argue their case with some force on the basis of sound information that was not available to others. There were two effects of this. Firstly, it was suggested that the group was seen as a useful point of contact for a range of agencies with interests in this issue. Thus although they may not have formal power, "we are seen as the best group to be involved with". Secondly, the combination of detailed knowledge and understanding of the issue, coupled with a position that was independent of statutory agencies, enabled them to think "out of the box.... We can act as a sort of catalyst to promote new types of thinking. Because what we are conscious of is that people in the statutory bureaucracies they very much have to think within legislation, think within existing budgets ... we have got particular expertise in the impact of poverty ... we have got a unique contribution to make to that process".

The deliberative style of meetings within the group was designed to enable a wide range of contributions to be made. The style was described as 'participative and non-hierarchical': "We accept that wherever you are coming from, you have a unique perspective on things. And we value that. And we give equal status to that". The agenda was set by members, documentation (such as the council's draft fuel poverty strategy that was the main focus of discussion at the time of the research) was sent out well in advance so people could prepare what they wanted to say and when council or other workers were invited to attend meetings: "the person couldn't put themselves above, and [they] wouldn't be below. Everyone would come in and it would be a collective discussion". The role of the chair in ensuring everyone could take part was highlighted and, the significance of rituals that Young (2000) included as the 'greeting' necessary to facilitating deliberation were recognised by providing tea and coffee after meetings so that people stayed together and got to know each other better. One person summed up their approach as "business-like but relaxed".

When it came to dialogue with the city council and other agencies their knowledge about the area gave them the confidence to adopt a robust approach: "We have no taboos. We are not worried about anything, we don't care who we upset". Participants thought that their expertise was recognised and the group was regarded as highly credible, although it was acknowledged that this could also be seen as threatening. The stance they took was one of offering radical but practical proposals.

Descriptions of the way in which the sustainability forum operated illustrated the impact of this being a council-led initiative, although there were rather different perspectives on this. For the council officer who organised the forum and who had responsibility for feeding back the results of deliberations to the environmental advisory team and to other council and other agencies, the forum constituted an 'internal pressure group' that enabled her to "put weight behind some of the issues that we were already trying to push". She acknowledged that her role in the agenda-setting group enabled her to influence the agenda and her role in writing up and presenting the results of forum discussions gave her some power over the selection of issues to be highlighted. She used her insider knowledge of the way the council operated and of particular aspects of the current context to pursue issues. For example, she described taking advantage of a sympathetic Lord Mayor to include an exhibition about farmers' markets in the Lord Mayor's show and subsequently gain council support for introducing such markets across the city. She explicitly noted that she did not go the 'official way' on this issue and was able to bypass likely opposition from within the council as a result.

Her description of another, more publicly controversial, issue illustrated the way in which her position as a council officer constrained the position she took within debates and indicated her role in steering a course between what might be regarded as radical and realistic positions. The issue concerned the commissioning of a new waste incinerator. This was designed to produce energy that could be used for domestic electricity supplies, but was opposed by environmentalists urging more emphasis to be put on recycling. She said she could see both sides, thought what the council was proposing was the realistic solution, but also thought it was completely right for Friends of the Earth to campaign against it.

She summarised her approach to seeking change in response to issues raised in the forum:

> "The ones that work tend to be the ones we're personally committed to, so we push for them more. Maybe subconsciously we judge a bit as well about what we feel we might be able to achieve more easily than other things. I might feel very, very strongly that the incinerator closed down, but I wouldn't even try it, because I'd be wasting my time. So I'd go and do a little project on fair trade or something."

This view that the forum was more likely to engage with issues that were less likely to provoke substantial controversy was reiterated by activist members who identified a number of key environmental issues that had not made it to forum agendas. These included proposals for a major road development and green belt developments, both of which had both planning and economic development implications and were seen to be too 'hot' for the forum to touch. There was also a view that the city council was generally very sensitive to criticism from a body that it saw as evidence of its participative credentials:

> "... in the early years there was an attitude almost that we are doing something very pioneering here, we are going out into the community and doing something very good, and the last thing we want is for you to criticise us because it makes us look weaker to our colleagues...."

Nevertheless there was some ambivalence about the possibility of the forum becoming more independent of the council because of the loss both of resources and of a clear route into the policy process. The role of the forum chair who also chaired the environmental advisory team was also cited in this respect. He was seen to be keen to be able to demonstrate outcomes from issues for which he had responsibility and thus would ensure debate and action within the advisory team and beyond.

The question of expertise was discussed by interviewees primarily in relation to debates within the forum, rather than in relation to the credibility of the forum with officials. Although the officer who organised the forum distinguished the forum from other public participation initiatives precisely on the basis of the expertise of participants:

> "Sometimes you go to ward subs [committees] and there are some mad people there, they just turn up and they haven't necessarily thought through the issues. Generally people [at the sustainability forum] have thought through the issues and they can provide constructive comments, and they have an understanding of the way things work."

She reinforced this picture of a forum in which institutional knowledge and rational, informed debate shaped the deliberative possibilities:

"With the forum, people sort of get trained in what the city council can and can't provide, so they get trained, they know the process, they'll tailor what they are saying differently and they will have different opinions depending on who they are talking to."

While there were accounts of individuals using the forum to pursue particular interests and being quite passionate about these, most accounts stressed the absence of dissent, the time constraints on discussion and the strategies used to prevent people pursuing their own 'hobby horses'. The structure of forum meetings was designed to introduce topics then enable discussion of predetermined sub-topics. People were allocated to facilitated groups and those known to hold particular positions on an issue were often allocated to a group addressing issues other than their area of expertise. Some frustration was noted that this meant people could only talk about the issues to which they had been allocated, and those who considered themselves to be experts on a specific topic and who felt their voices should carry more weight as a result, could be particularly aggrieved.

Conclusion

These two case studies provide different examples of the way in which participants in SMOs engage in dialogue with public officials as one means of achieving their objectives. As we have seen here, this can result both from initiatives taken by the movements themselves (as in the case of the fuel poverty group) or, in the case of the sustainability forum, from activists deciding that it is worth their while to take up opportunities offered from within the official sphere of local government. In both cases the high profile of public participation was seen to have facilitated this even though the issues the groups were engaged in did not fit comfortably into current policy priorities.

The rather marginal position of both case study examples may be considered to have afforded them some room for manoeuvre since they were not operating within, for example, the context of officially determined decentralisation initiatives, or affected by service delivery imperatives. Nevertheless, the example of the sustainability forum demonstrates the power of institutional norms to shape deliberative processes and assumptions about the knowledge and capacity required to take part in these. This is reflected in the rather elite group of participants that virtually all our interviewees commented on. The networking opportunity this afforded was valued and motivated continuing participation in the face of what was perceived to be limited success in terms of policy influence. The fuel poverty group was more obviously able to create a space within which disadvantaged people were supported to make a contribution towards the development of collective action based in experiential knowledge and a commitment to social justice. Networking was important here as well. Their position as an autonomous group enabled them to offer robust and sometimes oppositional responses to local authority proposals.

Although the elite nature of the sustainability forum participants was noted, in neither case was there any suggestion that the composition of these groups undermined their legitimacy because they were 'unrepresentative'. In both cases the issue-based nature of the process appeared to emphasise the importance of the knowledge that could be brought to the process rather than the role of participants in 'representing' any putative community. Indeed, a characteristic of both examples was that they operated across quite wide geographical areas. The fuel poverty group had a much more limited constituency than the sustainability forum and a more limited sphere of interest, but the focus of their activity was on the issue and how it affected people living in poverty, rather than on any particular 'community'.

While there was evidence of high levels of commitment to the causes being pursued in both groups, neither relied on collective identity building as a basis on which to determine or express their claims. Thus it was comparatively easy for officials engaged in the forums to identify themselves with the objectives being sought – even if there were times when their official role meant they were unable to represent this position as forcibly as they might like.

Although the development and dynamics of these two case studies were influenced by the institutional context within which they operated, they can be seen as having had a rather looser connection with the particular public authorities to which they related than the other case studies we have examined in this book. This may suggest that the policy domains within which they operated were lower profile than in other cases and that they were perceived as less threatening as a result (Kreisi et al, 1995). There was certainly a suggestion that within the sphere of interest of the sustainability forum some issues were 'safe' and others would be likely to fracture the opportunities for dialogue that did exist. The fuel poverty group was addressing an issue on which battles had been fought and won in securing legislation and the issue at stake was how to develop an implementation strategy. More generally, as we suggested in the introduction to this chapter, the dominant emphasis on locality as a focus for policy and service development may have made it easier for officials to welcome the expertise both groups were able to offer, rather than experience this as a direct challenge to professional or bureaucratic authority.

NINE

Conclusion: power, participation and political renewal

The case studies in this book have not been presented as examples of 'good practice' in public participation. Rather, they highlight a set of issues and raise a series of questions that we argue might productively be addressed in future policy and practice. The value of the case study material lies in the detailed empirical work that underpins it: that is, our arguments and analyses go beyond normative approaches to public participation (this is what *should* happen, or this is what organisations *ought* to do to get the process right). There are already a host of practical guides and handbooks, and innovations designed to reach new audiences – through games, interactive technologies, television or radio broadcast – are appearing all the time. Rather, we have attempted to describe what actually happens when public bodies and publics engage with each other in the new participative and deliberative spaces that have been opening up as a result of the public policy developments described in Chapter Two.

But describing what happens is not enough. In Chapter One, we asked how we might understand the significance of the sheer range and diversity of the initiatives through which public bodies seek to engage in face-to-face encounters with the publics they serve. How far does this represent a fundamental change in governance? And what might be the potential of any such change to address inequalities of power, overcome social exclusion or to foster political renewal? To answer such questions we have, in the case study analysis, drawn on the bodies of theory set out in Chapters Two to Four: studies of policy discourse, social movement literature, theories of deliberative democracy, new institutional theory and theories linked to the cultural turn in social and public policy. This has, we think, enabled us to transcend the rather normative approach to questions of democratic renewal, social inclusion, user empowerment and so on that tend to pervade the literature. The interdisciplinary approach has also enriched the insights we have brought to the analysis of each case study. The three opening chapters drew rather solid boundaries around these different theories in order to present them with some degree of internal coherence. In practice, our analysis was informed by a highly productive engagement between and across different theoretical traditions. Elsewhere, we have discussed the intersection between governance theory and social movement theory that resulted from our project, highlighting the ways in which each could be inflected as a result of its engagement with the other (Newman et al, 2004). Here we want to reflect on other meeting points, collisions and engagements within and across disciplinary boundaries. Each of them has at its centre questions of power.

The case studies do not all tell the same story, so the learning that can be drawn from them is not simply a new set of policy prescriptions. Each has to be understood in its own institutional, policy and cultural context. And each can be read in terms of successes as well as limitations. But in departing from a normative stance our findings have often led us to be relatively pessimistic about the potential of new initiatives to overcome entrenched institutional or political forms of power. The excitement about the empowerment of service users and communities through new forms of participation and voice fails to sufficiently address the kinds of barriers to institutional change we have highlighted in previous chapters. However, the picture is not entirely negative. In a few cases successful outcomes – for example of the campaign to keep the health centre open (Chapter Five), or the success of the lobbying activity around fuel poverty (Chapter Eight) – led to a wish among citizens to continue to be engaged. And even where outcomes were less positive, we can trace new channels of communication opening up, and new understandings emerging between actors in different relationships to the policy or management process. But overall our data suggests that creating new spaces of participation does not necessarily mean that issues of public policy or service delivery are debated in new ways. This finding is replicated in other studies – for example analysis of the meetings of the deliberative forum established to support the work of the National Institute for Health and Clinical Excellence found a very low proportion of actual deliberation (Davies et al, 2006). And it is not only the process of deliberation that appears to be constrained; many of our case studies seemed to have achieved little in terms of challenging professional expertise or bringing about change in the ways in which services were delivered. Why do attempts to foster such engagement so frequently seem to reinforce, rather than to challenge, entrenched forms of power? And how might things be different? Such questions are the focus of this final chapter.

We begin by highlighting the sheer volume of initiatives and ways in which this might be understood as some kind of shift in state–citizen interactions. There is, of course, no 'one size fits all' solution to public participation ambitions: multiple objectives, methods and opportunities are important for providing a range of points of potential engagement. And our data vividly illustrate the range and diversity of purpose and methods. But across this range, we highlight the importance of examining the dynamics that shape the possibility of new freedoms and new configurations of power. This draws attention to what happens over time, stressing the importance of understanding why and how initiatives that start out with good intentions – the 'empowerment' of new social actors, the inclusion of new voices in the shaping of policy, or a shift in power relationships between public bodies and the public they serve – often end up as a process in which participants become captured in governmental fields of power.

However, this concept of capture is too blunt an instrument. In subsequent sections we focus on a number of different dynamics of power that were highlighted in our exploration of the micro-politics of deliberative forums themselves, opening up the box to see what happens as officials and lay publics come together and decide how to work with each other. We trace ways in which institutional power may constrain, or enable, the possibilities of social agency. We explore how deliberative forums may be sites in which social identities are mobilised and negotiated in ways that challenge the binary distinction between official and lay perspectives. We analyse concepts of representation and presence as forms of claims-making that are used to bestow legitimacy, both within forums and in the interface between forums and public bodies. And we highlight the constitutive power of discourses such as those of community, consumerism and neighbourhood. We conclude by turning to the question of how far the explosion of initiatives fostering public participation and/or deliberative democracy opens up the possibility of political renewal. What kinds of political engagement are being fostered? What forms of 'political imaginary' through which people understand their relationship to the wider polity are being developed or sustained? And what might this all mean for the future of political participation in its widest sense?

Collaborative governance and the dynamics of power

We began this volume (Chapter Two) by tracing the rise of new political discourses and policy imperatives that created an enabling climate for public participation. The sheer diversity and range of initiatives that has resulted suggests something important about changing relationships between public institutions and the publics they serve. Our cases seem to suggest that notions of what is a legitimate matter for public participation is quite wide ranging, spanning not only the delivery of public services but issues of public concern from environmental protection through to neighbourhood safety. This appears positive for our understanding of what 'the public realm' is all about and how we should be expected to engage with it. The proliferation of deliberative forums suggests a shift from an old order dominated by bureaucracy and hierarchy towards a more open, collaborative and innovative public policy system. Governance theorists as well as many writers on deliberative democracy would view this in terms of a fundamental political shift in which state–citizen interactions become more differentiated, enabling governments to respond to complexity and diversity as well as fostering the self-steering capacities of society (Kooiman, 1993; Amin and Hausner, 1997; see also Newman et al, 2004). Different views on the relationship between these new flows and engagements and the 'old' institutions of representative democracy are offered. Many social and political theorists argue that the demise of old cleavages and the alignment of interests through political parties means that established institutions are no longer fitted to diverse and complex societies and the emergence of more reflexive actors. Policy actors, however, tend to view the new processes of engaging citizens as complementing, rather than challenging, representative democracy by enabling more subtle feedback to politicians and to public institutions.

We do not take a normative position on this question. Rather, our data highlight what happens as 'old', professional or political forms of power confront a plurality of 'new' voices. This illuminates some of the struggles taking place as public bodies attempt to respond to new claims (from a differentiated public) and new criteria of legitimacy (from a government claiming to speak 'on behalf of' the public in its policies on public service involvement, choice and consumerism). But it also foregrounds the struggles on the part of the public, in its multiple forms, to be heard by professionals, managers and local politicians. This interaction produces a number of different dynamics. Our case studies present not only a snapshot at a particular moment of policy evolution, but also reveal something about the dynamics of change over time as initiatives were subject to pulls that tended to shift their primary purpose. One set of dynamics concerns the life span of specific initiatives – what influences their formation, what conditions enable them to thrive, and what produces their demise. Chapter Five noted concerns about the survival of one of the health-related groups it described as a result of failures in negotiations between the group and the NHS, while Chapter Seven traced the potential residualisation of one of the senior citizens' forums as the local authority with which it engaged decided to set up an alternative forum more tailored to the local authority's needs. It might be argued that the short life span of some initiatives prevents lay members from becoming institutionalised and so removed from the constituencies they speak for. However, we might also anticipate that, where their demise is a product of official marginalisation, failures of communication or stalled negotiations, the damage to trust and legitimacy might be extensive, potentially creating a 'vicious circle' in which public bodies encounter disaffected citizens who are unwilling to engage with them in future deliberations.

But a second, and we think more interesting, set of dynamics concerns the trajectories of change produced as publics that have their roots in voluntary organisations, grass-roots bodies or other forms of social agency, encounter public bodies seeking to engage in dialogue with them. For example, Chapter Five traced complex and multiple alignments of official action (as organisations sought to enhance their legitimacy or conform with new governmental norms on the importance of consultation) and of service user agency (exerting 'pressure from below'). These produce different trajectories of change. In the case of service users, in particular those who have often been excluded from decision making because of assumed lack of capacity or ability to take part, separate organisation had often enabled them to generate a collective voice and to challenge the way in which their identities as 'clients' or 'patients' had been constructed within professional discourses (see also Barnes, 1997; Barnes and Bowl, 2001). Some groups managed to remain rooted in autonomous action (for example the community health group); however, others became partly captured by professional and organisational fields of power. Chapter Seven traced processes of progressively closer engagement between groups who had their origins in campaigning or social movement groups and the officials who they sought to influence. Here we can trace how some acceptance of partnership discourses and practices – however unequal the power relations between partners – was, for the senior citizens activists, members of the women's centre, and lesbian and gay networks, a condition of their engagement with official bodies. Other literatures on collaboration and participation under the New Labour governments (for example, Newman, 2001; Taylor, 2003) have suggested that the overall shift towards partnership produces a closing down of diversity and autonomy. Much of our data might confirm this view.

However, situating initiatives in governmental policy is not just a question of them being drawn into new forms and fields of power as passive victims – organisations and individuals often work to position themselves in ways likely to maximise legitimacy, resources and other forms of power. We can see this process at work in the case studies discussed in Chapter Eight; for example the fuel poverty group retained its independence while drawing into its ambit officials the group recognised as occupying positions of influence within local authorities and the NHS. And we also need to be alert to the possibility that officially sponsored initiatives might produce new forms of active citizenship with the capacity to contest the rules and norms of engagement set by officials. Earlier we noted examples where deliberation was linked to campaigning activity that produced successful outcomes, and in both of the cases discussed in Chapter Eight, success led to a wish among citizens to continue to be engaged, but also to a change in the nature of what they were engaged in.

So what is it that shapes these dynamics to produce different trajectories of change? Clearly shifts in government policy may be influential: for example the role of the community health forum was reshaped by the opportunity to create Healthy Living Centres as a result of a new government policy during our research; and we might speculate that the creation of children's centres will imply a shift in the forms of local engagement established by the earlier Sure Start projects. It may be that the freedoms associated with pilot or locally initiated projects may be constrained when such projects are 'rolled out', and that this may have an impact on forms of deliberative engagement with publics. The local political culture is also significant, both in negotiations about initial purpose and in shaping trajectories of change. For example initiatives established under a single policy (including Sure Start) took different forms in the two cities from which we drew case studies as a result of complex overlaying of national policy goals and local authority political cultures. Local authority policies designed to devolve some forms of decision making to local or neighbourhood boards similarly took different forms across the two cities, but also within one of the cities itself, in part as a result of complex interactions between political, managerial and local activist goals. But equally important, we argue, is what happens within forums themselves. In the following three sections we explore this, drawing on different theoretical approaches to questions of power and agency.

Participation and power

Institutions and agency

The extent to which the processes of deliberation enable different publics to challenge existing power relationships depends, we argue, not only on the discursive framing of the process of participation (whether, for example, publics are viewed as consumers or partners, stakeholders or responsibilised citizens) but also on what happens in the deliberative process itself. Chapters Three and Four set out contrasting perspectives for analysing the capacity of deliberative forums to challenge social and institutional power. Social movement theory, in brief, offers ways of recognising the importance of public spaces in which social actors can bring their experience to voice and can have such voices heard. Institutional theory, in contrast, helps us recognise how such spaces might become the site of contest, accommodation or negotiation between different sets of rules and norms. Bringing these two different perspectives together has enabled us to explore in some depth the micro-politics of deliberation, especially the internal processes and practices through which particular publics may be excluded. This turns the usual question – who participates, and why 'socially excluded' groups tend not to participate as much as middle-class service users – into a question about how some voices get marginalised within the participative process itself.

Institutions, in this context, refer neither to the organisations that sponsor initiatives nor to the groups they engage with. Rather, they refer to the rules and norms that facilitate – or constrain – the process of engagement between them. Chapter Six characterised the institutional dynamics that shaped deliberative processes into three categories: institutions as a source of support; institutions as sites of challenge and opportunity; and institutions as prisons. The placing of case studies in these categories depended on how rules of membership were established, and who had power to shape and reshape these rules; how agendas were set; and what happened as challenges to rules and norms were negotiated.

Institutions as sources of support

We can see, across the chapters, some examples where institutional norms and rules supported the deliberative process in ways that enabled marginalised voices to be heard, experience to be recognised and validated as a source of expertise, and group interests to be shaped and expressed. It is interesting that most – perhaps all – of the case studies that fall into this group were those that had their origins in voluntary or community organisations; but also significant were the backgrounds of leading individuals in, for example, trades union or political action. Clarity and simplicity of purpose were viewed by some – for example the residents' group – as enabling factors, as was a clear separation between a forum itself and the public authorities or professional actors it sought to influence. Such a separation enabled forums such as the women's group and the lesbian and gay forum to act as a safe space characterised by norms and values that in many cases differed from those of public service bureaucracies or professional organisations. Despite the discourses of empowerment or capacity building espoused by public officials, it is in these forums, clearly bounded from official intervention, that we saw most evidence of those discourses being lived in practice.

Earlier in this conclusion we highlighted the importance of tracing the dynamics of change as such forums or groups became drawn into new forms of institutional power. In some cases this challenged their capacity to serve as alternative spaces, governed by their own values and norms. But in others the 'alternative' public spaces served to sustain individuals and groups in their interface with public bodies.

Institutions as sites of challenge and opportunity

Here we move to many of the case studies that were established as a result of government policy but that attempted to create opportunities for power sharing with specific publics. This created new opportunities for lay publics, with perhaps little experience of engaging in the public sphere, to participate, and new potential challenges to the sponsoring bodies. However, despite the 'official' discourses of empowerment or partnership, of consumerism or stakeholding, which pervaded the language of policy documents and, in many cases, of the 'strategic' managers we interviewed at the outset of the project, it seemed that public bodies managed to retain and even enlarge their power. This was evident in the power of public officials to constitute their public in a way that best fitted their needs (rather than to engage with pre-existing and more potentially troublesome groups); the power to set the rules and norms of engagement; and in many cases to set the agenda of what issues were, and were not, to be opened up to public deliberation. They also had the power to decide what legitimacy to afford to different voices and different modes of expression; and ultimately, of course, the power to decide whether or not to take account of the views expressed.

However, in this grouping the power base of different actors was the site of negotiation and challenge. In relation to the case studies considered in Chapter Five, the impact of challenges to the ways in which services were delivered was delimited by what service providers could accept without either incurring significant costs or making significant change to policies or procedures. The officials with whom these citizens engaged in dialogue supported the idea of user-prompted improvements, but either saw themselves as unable or were unwilling to question fundamentally what was possible in terms of service change. In some cases citizens modified or restricted their claims as a result of realisations about what was possible 'in reality' as a result of their closer engagement with officials. These dynamics were less evident in the more autonomous community health forum, but here the demands of negotiating with planning and funding bureaucracies tended to have a similar restraining impact.

The experience of Sure Start discussed in Chapter Six illustrates how established professionals and voluntary sector activists all found themselves somewhat 'off-balance' in relation to a scheme that none of them controlled directly but that required their cooperation, and that of local parents, if it was to work. The case studies reveal how interprofessional tensions provided the space for new developments in parent engagement to emerge, as community and user-oriented workers established ways of interacting with parents and managing meetings in a more inclusive way, while key professional groups battled with each other about professional codes and ways of working. At the same time these interprofessional tensions did act to condition the environment within which the initiatives operated, adding tension to the local deliberative atmosphere.

The case study material discussed in Chapter Seven provides good examples of ways in which institutional norms developed in alternative spaces – in the women's group, in lesbian and gay networks, in the trades union and political activity that many members of the senior citizens' forums had experienced, and, in the case of the youth group, on the street – confronted the normative expectations and formal rules of public bodies. The outcomes differed; but the 'supportive' institutions developed in alternative political spaces were in each case challenged and in some cases modified as a result of the need to secure legitimacy in the eyes of officials with whom they had to negotiate. Legitimacy was also a theme in both case studies discussed in Chapter Eight, but was inflected in different ways. The sustainability forum offers an example of an official recognising the potential of a public participation initiative to provide added legitimacy for policy positions she wanted to pursue. In addition to the general moral authority offered by the forum in the context of an espoused commitment on the part of the local authority to 'consultation', the officer with responsibility for supporting the forum quite deliberately cited positions argued within the forum to support her case for policy change. In the case of the fuel poverty group, both the networks and the knowledge that the group developed gave it both credibility and influence in relation to the very specific policy issue group members sought to affect.

Institutions as prisons

Where 'the public' are not engaged in setting the rules, they are more likely to be viewed as passive observers or troublemakers in public participation forums, producing the kind of institutional defensiveness that we characterise as 'institutions as prisons'. In a few examples the institutional rules and norms were so strongly entrenched that they effectively imprisoned all participants, officials and the public alike. One such example – a local authority area committee – was described in Chapter Six. We might speculate that such cases arise where public bodies are required to engage in public participation exercises but do so reluctantly – they are, if you like, dragged kicking and screaming to the deliberative table. The idea of institutions as 'myths' and 'symbols' that we introduced in Chapter Four is also relevant here. Public bodies may decide to go through the motions of public participation and involvement because they are likely to be judged on their record of doing so in some future performance ranking exercise, or because they are required to demonstrate public involvement in proposals for which they are seeking government funding. In such cases the term 'coercive isomorphism' (Powell and DiMaggio, 1991) neatly captures the symbolic characteristics of conformance to new discursive rules and logics of appropriate action. And the result is likely to be a thin veneer of symbolic conformance but with 'loose coupling' to the norms and practices of the organisation concerned. That is, the host or sponsoring organisation is unlikely to shift its existing dominant culture or norms of practice, leaving professional or bureaucratic logics of decision making unchallenged. It is perhaps no accident that the most extreme version of 'institutions as prisons' in our case study sample was a local authority, where devolution formed a new site in which the struggles between local ward councillors and the 'strategic centre' of political and managerial power were played out. But this was not just a case of individual resistance to a strong centre of power: the tensions between representative and participative democracy formed a site of both challenge and opportunity across each of the local authority case studies. Local authority elected members' conduct was often key to making or breaking the operation of a forum; 'bad behaviour', particularly in forums that privileged elected members' representative claims, alienated other participants and ultimately undermined the forum's potential effectiveness.

Elsewhere, for example in the patient participation group discussed in Chapter Five, we can see similar struggles between professional power and 'lay' forms of experience and expertise. Even in the creative spaces that have been opened up in the case studies cited earlier, we need to recognise the importance of the power of professionals and managers to mediate, interpret, deflect or accommodate 'alternative' norms and practices. But the picture may be slightly more complex than this suggests. Our empirical work highlights ways in which new norms of public participation and involvement render problematic a clear distinction between official and lay identities. We develop this theme further below.

Public participation and the negotiation of social identities

Preceding chapters have highlighted many examples of conflicting definitions of purpose between officials and lay actors: for example between health professionals and lay members of the multi-ethnic group described in Chapter Five; between residents and participation workers in the residents' group forum discussed in Chapter Six; between the youth forum and youth workers in Chapter Seven. But they have also noted examples where the goals of officials and lay members of forums became more closely aligned over time: for example in the lesbian and gay forum (Chapter Seven), or the fuel poverty initiative and sustainability forum (Chapter Eight).

Similarly, one of the issues frequently raised in the literature on deliberative democracy is that of how far 'lay knowledge' or 'ordinary wisdom' can challenge expert power. However, our case studies suggest the difficulty of dividing these different forms of knowledge into two mutually antagonistic categories. We can see how lay members themselves may become 'experts', reinforcing institutionally defined norms of engagement and building up their own knowledge of bureaucratic practice, funding regimes and power structures. Sometimes so-called 'lay' publics may bring expertise that may be lacking in public bodies – for example in the two case studies discussed in Chapter

Eight. Elsewhere we can see officials becoming more closely aligned with 'lay' perspectives, perhaps because of closer contact with the public through the process of deliberation, or perhaps because of their own experience or political allegiances. Similar processes are examined by Mayo et al (2007: forthcoming) in their study of officials involved in community development and regeneration work. This study focused on the values of officials working in such roles, but offers similar conclusions about the significance of shared values and experiences in the negotiation of professional identities in the context of public involvement work.

This suggests that we need frameworks that enable us to look at what happens across the lay/official divide, rather than seeing these as two mutually exclusive groups of participants. Our research has approached this in two ways. The first draws on ideas of motivation; that is, what is it that brings individuals to the deliberative table, and what sustains them to continue participating in dialogue even when this proves to be frustrating or even exclusionary? In relation to each case study we have had something to say about the motivations of those who participated, and noted points where the motivations of officials seemed to resonate with those of lay members. For example, in Chapter Five we considered the position of the minority ethnic group council official who was herself a Hindu and located her voluntary activity within the values of her faith. The sustainability forum (Chapter Eight), the Sure Start projects (Chapter Six), the community health forum (Chapter Five) and the women's group (Chapter Seven) all demonstrate the importance of the beliefs, values and commitments that individuals bring to creating new ways of engaging publics in shaping change.

The second perspective draws on notions of identity. As we argued in Chapter Four, identities cannot be viewed as 'fixed' – particular kinds of subjects and subject positions are called into being in policy discourse and in the claims to knowledge or power made by different groups of actors involved in public participation. And our attention to the internal dynamics of forums has enabled us to suggest ways in which deliberative spaces have the capacity to produce new relationships and identifications, rather than just reflecting pre-existing interests and identities. In many cases we noted how so-called 'lay' publics came to identify with the goals of public bodies as they became expert in official discourse and took on some of the characteristics of organisational 'insiders'. This dynamic is, however, uneven; it is likely to be the individuals who negotiate directly with officials on a regular basis who come to take on 'insider' roles or identities, in the process becoming further separated from the other 'lay' publics who they might seek to represent. Public bodies may be dismayed at finding themselves talking to what are often termed 'the usual suspects', often the very people who have developed close working relation ships with officials. However, what tends not to be recognised is the way in which insider identities are actually constituted by public bodies themselves, as they reach out to those that they know best and find it easiest to communicate with, or as they engage in capacity-building or training activities. Such individuals may also be viewed with circumspection by lay publics who retain a more distanced stance from official power because of the ways in which 'insiders' may become removed from the day-to-day experience of the publics they claim to speak for.

We can see very different types of relationship between citizens and officials across our case studies, and as we have argued at several points, the notion of 'partnership' is highly problematic as a means of characterising these relationships. However, it is not enough to simply point to an inequality in the power relationships involved. In Chapter Seven we developed this theme, noting how, in responding to a differentiated public, participation initiatives were frequently led by officials who shared some forms of identification with those they were seeking to engage with – here as women, as gay or lesbian. In these and some other case studies we found that officials who were sponsoring or leading on specific initiatives themselves had backgrounds in voluntary or community activity. As new governmental discourses become more significant to organisational legitimacy and success, so managerial and professional actors with experience of community engagement or service user involvement come to prominence. However, in moving from the margins to the mainstream of organisational hierarchies, perhaps leading on important new partnership initiatives, they may come into conflict with established power bases. Particular pressures and strains may result from having to face both inwards to the strategic centre of an organisation and outwards to service users or communities.

This 'bridging' role of institutional actors can act as both a source of policy learning but also as a site of tensions and ambiguities. Social identities have to be understood as complex rather than singular, and officials engaged in deliberation with the public may find themselves with multiple loyalties: loyalties to the organisation in which they are employed, to a professional or public ethos, to a local community, to a particular user group, to values associated with social or political activity, and so on. This produces particular conflicts for the officials concerned, not only in managing the tensions between insider and outsider identities, but also in negotiating the interface between organisational norms and the alternative norms fostered in 'counter public' spaces. How these processes are likely to be played out is of course highly context-dependent, being shaped in no small part by the quality of organisational or, in the case of local authorities, political leadership. What is of interest, for our purposes, is how social agency – on the part of officials as well as lay actors – negotiates, mediates or challenges institutional power.

Representation and presence

As we noted in Chapter Four, public participation and deliberative practices are viewed as more capable of accommodating questions of difference and diversity than representative democracy. But they open up important issues about how a diversity of social groups in a plural polity can be 'represented' in the kinds of forums we have been considering in this book. The importance of this question is highlighted by the way in which notions of representation and representativeness pervaded the discourse of both officials and lay members. But it is also indicated by the direct relationship our data suggest exists between processes of representation and perceptions of legitimacy. *Internal* legitimacy (that is, that bestowed by forum members on each other) was informed by perceptions of the 'representativeness' of particular individuals. Here debates about legitimacy often drew on the failure of forums to represent particular publics – for example, in one of the senior citizens' forums, concerns were expressed about the limited presence of black and minority ethnic representatives. And *external* legitimacy (that is, that bestowed on the recommendations or other outputs of a forum by officials and elected members) depended on the perceived representativeness of its members as a whole. Senior officials sponsoring, but not necessarily directly engaged in, deliberative forums highlighted the problems of legitimacy for groups that could not claim representative membership.

However, our data suggest the power of the idea, discussed in Chapter Four, of representation as claims making. Citizens expressed a number of different kinds of representative claim – for example the claim to represent 'people like me' is rather different from the claim to represent those who an individual had spoken to and discussed the issues with. And claims based on experience – for example those of service users in many of the case studies discussed in Chapter Five – are very different from claims based on knowledge of a particular locality (Chapter Six) or issue (Chapter Eight). We might also contrast formalised representation (through elections of some kind) with the more reflexive and limited claims of members of the women's group and of the lesbian and gay forum (Chapter Seven). Neighbourhood or area-based public participation initiatives were the source of various different claims to representation, with local authority elected members coexisting alongside other representatives whose claims were based on their attachment to an organisation, their reputation or their connection to a particular experience. These different claims were not necessarily sources of conflict, but could become so if the rules governing the participation initiative privileged one set of representative claims over others – as happened, for example, in the youth forum discussed in Chapter Seven. The issue-based case studies in Chapter Eight were less concerned with claims to representation based on any notion of participation constituting a 'cross-section' of the local population or a 'representative sample' of residents. Members of the sustainability forum were concerned that membership was drawn from quite a narrow spectrum, but this did not appear to undermine their perceived legitimacy. The fuel poverty group actively engaged people living in poverty in order both to draw on their experiential knowledge and to engage in community development.

Participants in local area forums tended to accept local authority elected members' privileged claims in initiatives that were part of the local authority's decision-making process, but were less amenable to such claims being made in forums linked to the Sure Start initiative. In forums that were established to elicit representation of a range of 'voices', participants expected that their different claims would compete with each other. Deliberation sometimes – but not always – secured a reconciliation of these different claims. However, the processes of deliberation also revealed the power dynamics underlying the operation of the forums and how this informed different groups' assumptions about the respective value of their representation claims. For example, in one of the Sure Start initiatives, the balance of power between professionals and parents on the management board was supported, at least initially, by assumptions about the greater value of the professionals' claims to representation. The way in which individuals conducted themselves in the forums also contributed to perceptions of their legitimacy as representatives among forum members. Participants who 'played by the rules' and were able to 'get on' with other participants were more likely to be perceived as legitimate representatives, while those who were 'difficult' could find their position challenged.

So across our case studies, a number of strategies were used to secure the representativeness of their membership. However, representation proved to be both a constructed and a highly contested concept, and one that interacted unevenly with concepts of social difference and diversity. We want to conclude this section, however, by departing from this rather relativistic stance. There is an important distinction to be drawn between bodily representation (the presence or absence of individuals from particular groups – women, black and minority ethnic groups and so on) and the representation of social identities, such as those formed in the 'counter public' spaces of social movements. Both of these are implicated in debates about a politics of 'presence' (Young, 1990) or, from a different perspective, a politics of 'recognition' (Fraser, 1989). However, Young and Fraser both emphasise the importance of social identity as the basis for political mobilisation. The distinction between bodily and social representation is formed in the space between the idea of deliberative forums as a means of securing governmental and policy goals (improving services, renewing communities, and so on) and the idea of deliberation as political praxis. Fraser argues that discursive politics is an essential strategy of political resistance. But the arguments of subordinated groups cannot be "translated into the dominant discourses without being redefined in ways that shed important meanings" (1989, p 165). We explore the potentially constitutive power of political and policy discourses further below.

Constituting 'the public'

A focus on representative claims within deliberative forums cannot be the whole story here: there is also a need to explore ways in which public agencies constitute their publics for the purpose of participation. This was a theme developed in Chapter Four, where it was argued that the process of constituting the public involves a particular dynamic of power – one that produces its own reality rather than simply reflecting a reality of a taken for granted public 'out there'. The discourses of empowerment, partnership, consumerism and responsibility that we outlined in Chapter Two – alongside other policy discourses such as social exclusion or community engagement – themselves suggest suitable subject positions for participants but also produce particular speaking and practice norms.

The case study chapters traced the interplay of different discourses in the negotiations about purpose, and suggested ways in which different discourses of 'the public' had implications for who should be involved and for what purpose(s). They also had important implications for implementing public participation schemes, as to be 'fit for purpose' required the appropriate participation 'architecture' to be constructed (rules, structures, processes, roles, resource support). This is not to say that only one discourse can exist at any one time – our evidence showed that this is not the case, but rather that policy makers, practitioners and the public were aware of the different objectives and design issues associated with each discourse. And these design issues and objectives were open to challenge; at several points (Chapters Five and Six) we noted how lay publics objected to or contested forms of consultation that positioned them as simply the consumers of public services. The 'stakeholder' discourse found in several case studies offered greater recognition of the power that particular publics – often publics already organised around a common purpose or identity – brought to the deliberative process. However, overall we noted the move towards 'partnership' and 'responsibilising' discourses in many case study sites, and the ways in which this positioned lay publics as non-antagonistic to public officials.

Thus discourse, as we argued in Chapter Four, is not just a matter of the niceties of language. It results from the mobilisation of different forms of expertise – especially, in our case, the forms of expertise that carry with them the power to classify and name particular population groups. As such it has implications not only for practice but for the shaping of individual subject positions. Discourses of public participation are pervaded with such namings – the 'socially excluded', 'hard to reach groups', the 'usual suspects', or 'unrepresentative individuals'. In these examples it is evident which voices are to be afforded legitimacy and which marginalised. But what about the discourse of 'community'? The constitution of 'local community', 'black and minority ethnic community', or other collectivities constituted as unitary for the purpose of participation, assumes a commonality of interest or identity and suppresses the possibility of more complex and fluid identifications.

Throughout the case study chapters, but especially in Chapter Six, we can trace the increasing prevalence of locality or neighbourhood as a focus for public participation – a trend likely to be further increased as a result of the increasing legitimacy of a 'new localism' among government ministers. This pattern of public participation, however, tends to focus attention on the parochial or specific – street furniture, traffic calming measures and so on – rather than more 'strategic' agendas such as health or education. It also assumes a unified, coherent voice that is seldom realised in practice. Clearly the emphasis on very local levels of involvement in decision making and delivery has merits, but the potential exclusivity of neighbourhoods (emphasising communities of place rather than identity), the danger of them becoming insulated against matters that occur 'outside' the neighbourhood, and of there being an insufficient link between the neighbourhood and the strategic, are important potential consequences. There is also a danger of the term 'neighbourhood' being employed in such a loose way that it simply becomes a replacement word for 'community', with no specific meaning. It also brackets the identities constituted from other possible mobilisations. The turn to consumerism and choice in public policy is currently a different, but highly significant, source of such bracketing of other possible identities and sources of mobilisation (Needham, 2003; Clarke et al, 2007: forthcoming). We have touched on this in Chapter Two, and in our discussion of several of the case studies, including the service-based forums (Chapter Five) and the senior citizens' forums (Chapter Seven).

Notions of the constitutive power of discourse – that is, its capacity to bestow subject and speaking positions – can be over-read. That is, it may offer too deterministic a view of individual subjectivity and identity (Newman, 2005a). What has been evident across many of our case studies is the capacity of publics to refuse to conform to the identities offered to them, and their willingness to challenge official rules and norms. And in the closer affiliations between some officials and the publics they engaged with we can trace the possibility of norms of action that originated in social movements being adopted within deliberative forums – and even in 'official' discourse in sponsoring organisations. Such observations raise the question of how far the new deliberative spaces open up the possibility of political renewal.

Power, participation and political renewal

The forms of power highlighted in previous sections have a significant impact on how far deliberative forums and other participation initiatives might have the capacity to deliver the kind of political renewal that is the aspiration both of deliberative democrats and of some policy advocates. Such a process of political renewal has become the focus of a range of new movements and initiatives promulgating democratic reform or innovation: for example, the sponsoring by the Joseph Rowntree Foundation of the Power Inquiry (Power Inquiry, 2006, www.powerinquiry.org); the development of a New Politics Network (www.new-politics.com); the formation of Involve (www.involving.org); the Open Democracy network (www.opendemocracy.net); Compass (www.compassonline.org.uk); the New Economics Foundation (www.neweconomics.org); and many others. Although the political inflections of these different initiatives and networks vary, they all explore techniques and processes that seek to involve citizens in new forms of social and political engagement in order to bring about democratic renewal.

We want to suggest that political renewal, as the Power Inquiry acknowledges, is not just a matter of introducing new techniques of participation and citizen engagement. It rests in part on the capacity of public voices – including lay publics, but also the voices of some of those leading change within public service organisations – to challenge dominant rules and norms and to question the ways in which the rules of the game are defined. But here we want to take the analysis a little further. 'Political renewal' implies not only the capacity to challenge 'old' institutions, but also, in Melucci's terms, to foster the new linguistic and symbolic resources from which such challenges might flow (see Chapter Three). This is a different formulation of the policy discourse 'creating social capital'; indeed it turns the whole idea of social capital on its head, referring to resources that enable those within alternative discursive spaces to challenge dominant representations and images. Such resources may be of value not only to those that create them, but also to other social and political movements. We can see such processes at work in, for example, the rise of European and World Social Forums, in which networks of political and social activists not only engage in specific forms of protest but also sustain and renew their work by drawing on the resources, both material and symbolic, of other groups. We can also, however, see processes in which such resources may be impoverished as they are applied to new contexts: for example the participative budgeting process initiated in Porto Alegre in Brazil has been incorporated into official practice in contexts in which its radicalism has been somewhat muted. Nevertheless the concept provides a language through which new claims and challenges can be voiced.

The concept of 'voice' discussed in Chapter Three is another way of expressing the existence of the kind of symbolic resources that enable individuals and groups to be heard by policy makers and those delivering public services. It suggests not only the capacity to speak, but also for what is spoken to be recognised, respected and even acted on. The concept of voice was influential in the formation of many of the service user movements discussed in Chapter Three. But although having a voice and being taken seriously were viewed as important outcomes for those participating in the initiatives we studied, in the end such outcomes were not enough to sustain participation over time: material and/or institutional change was also necessary. The evidence across our case studies suggests that such change is not much in evidence as an outcome of new deliberative practices. For example Chapter Six concluded that overall the impact that each of the 'community governance' initiatives was having on mainstream service providers appeared limited. We argued that this was in part because little power was invested in any of the initiatives: their status was almost exclusively advisory. Whether the emerging frameworks of neighbourhood governance planned in the 2006 White Paper (Department for Communities and Local Government, 2006) will bestow more material power on local publics is open to question.

However, political renewal also depends on the formation of new collective identities that can overcome what is often viewed as an impoverishment of the public sphere produced by growing individualism and consumerism. The social movement literature suggests that such collectivities are potentially formed by connections with others who share a particular social identity and are mobilised by shared frameworks of meaning and action, developed in alternative public spaces. It is notable that where groups with a prior existence (formed around community activism, social movement politics or in other alternative public spaces) were invited to participate as stakeholders in a particular policy or service area, deliberation was more likely to produce challenges to the status quo and some element of transformation – if not in terms of quantifiable outcomes, then at least in terms of attitudes and orientations of public officials. What is of interest in some of our case studies is what happens as the linguistic and symbolic resources that have been fostered in alternative public spaces – in the residents' group, the youth forum, the women's group, the lesbian and gay movement – confront other norms of speech and action in officially sponsored deliberative forums. We want to suggest that alternative discursive spaces need to be fostered to develop or sustain alternative ways of conceptualising and theorising social issues. They also form sources of collective identity and oppositional politics that have the potential to reinvigorate and renew the public sphere.

More importantly for our study, the ideas of representation and representativeness fail to accommodate the ways in which concepts of identity and interest may actually be produced by the process of deliberation itself. This has important implications for how we understand the politics of public participation, and what is – and is not – deemed a legitimate political institution. Fraser (1997) argues for the importance of the formation of 'counter publics' as an essential element of the democratic process. Such publics tend to be formed outside the officially recognised public sphere as those with identities or interests not recognised within that sphere, form a sense of oppositional identities and perhaps an oppositional politics. The women's movement and gay liberation politics are prime examples of the importance of such counter publics; more recently environmental and anti-globalisation movements – and of course anti-immigration or pro-life movements – are formed outside the officially constituted public domain but then seek to have a collective voice within it.

Public participation – especially in its deliberative form – is often viewed as a route to more formal political engagement, that is, individuals putting themselves forward to serve as local councillor or as an MP. We do not have enough evidence to suggest what proportion of those we engaged with in the research were likely to take this route. However, we do have evidence of a large number of individuals losing trust or becoming further distanced from the political process as a result of negative experiences. We might also suggest that the capacity of public participation in its present form – however complex and diverse – can only be a limited vehicle for widening understandings of, and engagement in, citizenship because of a series of paradoxes.

The first is that we may be witnessing more and more public participation but the neo-liberal programme of state reform means that such participation relates to an ever-shrinking public sphere. As such, despite the diversity highlighted earlier in this Conclusion, we can see a number of potentially highly contestable 'public' issues – the use of Public Finance Initiative schemes to build new hospitals, or the implications of local authority procurement practices for local economies – not subject to the kinds of participation we have described in this book. Some local authorities, in their community governance capacities, are beginning to establish ways of involving the public in wider scrutiny roles. But whether participation initiatives can be developed that encompass dialogue with commercial services or debate the processes of marketisation and privatisation itself is debatable.

A second paradox concerns the unsettled relationship between representative democracy, deliberative forms of public participation and consumerism. In the context of an increasingly plural polity, the proliferation of highly specific and/or localised forms of dialogue offers more limited, fragmented conceptions of the public domain. There were, of course, exceptions – some of the forums we studied were attended by those with wider affiliations and interests. But the 'political imaginary' that is fostered by public participation tends to deflect attention away from wider – transnational, national and local – issues and debates. The turn to consumerism also implies a narrowed and depoliticised social imaginary. Clarke et al (2007: forthcoming) suggest that despite the turn to consumerism, citizens may continue to identify themselves as 'members of the public' or 'members of the local community'. However, they are increasingly constituted as individuals whose interests are antithetical to those of service providers, and as such consumerism may marginalise other forms of relationship and identification as well as squeezing the capacity of citizens and officials to form the kinds of alliances highlighted earlier in this chapter.

This makes an emphasis on participation and deliberation as forms of democratic practice crucial. Many of the issues we have examined in these case studies carried out in two cities in England are reflected in a series of studies of 'new democratic spaces' undertaken in very different environments across the globe (Cornwall and Coelho, 2004, 2006). In Brazil, Bangladesh, South Africa, Canada and elsewhere, what Cornwall and Coelho call the 'participatory sphere' is enlarging, and in spite of the very different socio-political contexts that exist in these places there are considerable resonances in terms of the dilemmas and tensions associated with this. Negotiations about issues of representation and representativeness, the necessity to understand the micro-dynamics of deliberative processes, the uncertain relationship between the claims made within participatory forums and any response to these from those in positions to make decisions, are significant whether the forum is a health council in Sao Paulo, a community group seeking to have its voice heard in rural Bangladesh, or a large-scale consultation with the indigenous population of Canada.

The analysis of these experiences leads the authors to assert the need for a similar cautious optimism to that which we want to express. In the context of a plural polity and diverse society faced by increasingly complex problems, new forms of citizen communication and engagement are, as the deliberative democrats argue, vital. Public participation can help to equip people to become better at dialogue with others, enabling a greater understanding of different perspectives and a respect for others' positions. It also opens up the possibility of new forms of social agency that are crucial to the process of political renewal. Our evidence suggests that these processes were more likely to occur in forums that had their roots in social movements, community activism and service user struggles. But here we confront a final paradox. Governments – and not only in the UK – seem to be increasingly anxious to promote active citizenship and to build social capital. Yet they appear to be deeply uncomfortable with the forms of social action associated with community activism and the politics of new social movements. Our evidence suggests that there are real difficulties in reconciling the ways in which the process of participation tends to draw citizens and social groups into new fields of governmental power, or into the impoverished domain of 'community', with the importance of sustaining the capacity of publics to make challenges in the name of social justice. But despite the constraints and limitations we have highlighted, a return to a position in which all decisions are made in the closed enclaves of the council chamber, management meeting or professional network cannot be contemplated. There is a need to retain commitment to the transformatory potential of the 'spaces for change' we have described at various points of this book without being naïve about the effects of power relationships within them, or over-optimistic about their capacity to influence decisions in the public sphere.

References

Aars, J. and Offerdal, A. (2000) 'Representation and deliberative politics', in N. Rao (ed) *Representation and community in Western democracies*, Basingstoke: Macmillan.

Adam Smith Institute (1989) *Wiser counsels: The reform of local government*, London: Adam Smith Institute.

Allen, J. and Cars, G. (2002) 'The tangled web – neighbourhood governance in a post-Fordist era', in G. Cars, P. Healey, A. Madanipour and C. de Magalhães (eds) *Urban governance, institutional capacity and social milieux*, Aldershot: Ashgate, pp 90-105.

Altman, D. (1994) *Power and community: Organizational and cultural responses to AIDS*, London: Taylor and Francis.

Amin, A. and Hauser, J. (1997) *Beyond market and hierarchy: Interaction, governance and social complexity*, Cheltenham: Edward Elgar.

Anastacio, J., Gidley, B., Hart, L., Keith, M., Mayo, M. and Kowarzik, U. (2000) *Reflecting realities: Participants' perspectives on integrated communities and sustainable development*, Bristol: The Policy Press.

Atkinson, D. (1994) *The common sense of community*, London: Demos.

Barnes, M. (1997) *Care, communities and citizens*, Harlow: Addison Wesley Longman.

Barnes, M. (1999a) 'Users as citizens: collective action and the local governance of welfare', *Social Policy and Administration*, vol 33, no 1, pp 73-90.

Barnes, M. (1999b) *Building a deliberative democracy: An evaluation of two citizens' juries*, London: Institute of Public Policy Research.

Barnes, M. (2004) 'Affect, anecdote and diverse debates: user challenges to scientific rationality', in A. Gray and S. Harrison (eds) *Governing medicine: Theory and practice*, Buckingham: McGraw Hill/Open University Press, pp 122-32.

Barnes, M. and Bowl, R. (2001) *Taking over the asylum: Empowerment and mental health*, Basingstoke: Palgrave.

Barnes, M. and Prior, D. (1995) 'Spoilt for choice? How consumerism can disempower public service users', *Public Money and Management*, vol 15, no 3, pp 55-8.

Barnes, M. and Prior, D. (1996) 'From private choice to public trust: a new social basis for welfare', *Public Money and Management*, vol 16, no 4, pp 51-8.

Barnes, M. and Prior, D. (2000) *Private lives as public policy*, Birmingham: Venture Press.

Barnes, M. and Walker, A. (1996) 'Consumerism versus empowerment: a principled approach to the involvement of older service users', *Policy & Politics*, vol 24, no 4, pp 375-93.

Barnes, M., Prior, D. and Thomas, N. (1990) 'Social services', in N. Deakin and A. Wright (eds) *Consuming public services*, London: Routledge.

Barnes, M., Harrison, S., Mort, M. and Shardlow, P. (1999) *Unequal partners: User groups and community care*, Bristol: The Policy Press.

Barnes, M., Newman, J., Sullivan, H. and Knops, A. (2003) 'Constituting "the public" in public participation', *Public Administration*, vol 81, no 8, pp 379-99.

Barnes, M., McCabe, A. and Ross, L. (2004a) 'Public participation in governance: the institutional context', in *Researching civil renewal*, Birmingham: Civil Renewal Research Centre, University of Birmingham, pp 127-46.

Barnes, M., Knops, A., Newman, J. and Sullivan, H. (2004b) 'The micro politics of deliberation: case studies in public participation', *Contemporary Politics*, vol 10, no 2, pp 93-110.

Barnes, M., Bauld, L., Benzeval, M., Judge, K., MacKenzie, M. and Sullivan, H. (2005) *Building capacity for health equity*, London: Routledge.

Barnes, M., Newman, J. and Sullivan, H. (2006) 'Discursive arenas: deliberation and the constitution of identity in public participation at a local level', *Social Movement Studies*, vol 5, no 3, pp 193-207.

Barnett, A. (1997) 'Towards a stakeholder democracy', in G. Kelly, D. Kelly and A. Gamble (eds) *Stakeholder capitalism*, Basingstoke: Macmillan, pp 82-98.

Benhabib, S. (ed) (1996) *Democracy and difference: Contesting the boundaries of the political*, Princeton, NJ: Princeton University Press.

Beresford, P., Green, D., Lister, R. and Woodard, K. (1999) *Poverty first hand: Poor people speak for themselves*, London: Child Poverty Action Group.

Blakeley, G. (2002) 'Decentralization and citizen participation in Barcelona', in P. McLaverty (ed) *Public participation and innovation in community governance*, Aldershot: Ashgate, pp 77-98.

Blunkett, D. (2003) *Active citizens, strong communities: Progressing civil renewal*, London: Home Office.

Bradford, M. and Robson, R. (1995) 'An evaluation of urban policy', in R. Hambleton and H. Thomas (eds) *Urban policy evaluation: Challenge and change*, London: Paul Chapman.

Brenner, N. (2004) *New state spaces: Urban governance and the rescaling of statehood*, Oxford: Oxford University Press.

Brenna, A., Rhodes, J. and Tyler, P. (1998) *Evaluation of the SRB challenge fund: A partnership for evaluation*, Cambridge: DETR.

Brulle, R.J. (1995) 'Environmentalism and human emancipation', in S.M. Lyman (ed) *Social movements: Critiques, concepts, case studies*, Basingstoke: Macmillan.

Burns, D., Hambleton, R. and Hoggett, P. (1994) *The politics of decentralisation*, London: Macmillan.

Burr, V. (1995) *An introduction to social constructionism*, London: Routledge.

Burton, P., Goodlad, R., Croft, J., Abbott, J., Hastings, A., Macdonald, G. and Slater, T. (2004) 'What works in community involvement in area-based initiatives? A systematic review of the literature', Home Office online report 53/04, London: Home Office (available at www.homeoffice.gov.uk/rds/pdfs04/rdsolr5304.pdf).

Campbell, J. and Oliver, M. (1996) *Disability politics*, London: Routledge.

Carley, M., Chapman, M., Hastings, A., Kirk, K. and Young, R. (2000) *Urban regeneration through partnership: A study in nine urban regions in England, Scotland and Wales*, Bristol: The Policy Press.

Cattaui, M.L. (2001) 'The user in the information society: changing rules of the game?', *Telecommunications Policy*, vol 25, pp 285-90.

Chanan, G. (2003) *Searching for solid foundations: Community involvement and urban policy*, London: Office of the Deputy Prime Minister.

Church, K. (1996) 'Beyond "bad manners": the power relations of "consumer participation" in Ontario's community mental health system', *Canadian Journal of Community Mental Health*, vol 15, no 2, pp 22-5.

Clarke, J. and Cochrane, A. (1998) 'The social construction of social problems', in E. Saraga (ed) *Embodying the social: Constructions of difference*, London: Routledge.

Clarke, J., Newman, J., Smith, N., Vidler, E. and Westmarland, L. (2007: forthcoming) *Creating citizen-consumers: Changing relationships and identifications*, London: Sage Publications.

Cockburn, C. (1977) *The local state: The management of cities and people*, London: Pluto Press.

Coelho, V.S.P. (2004) 'Brazil's health councils: the challenge of building participatory political institutions', *IDS Bulletin: New democratic spaces?*, vol 35, no 2, pp 33-9.

Cohen, J.L. (1985) 'Strategy or identity: new theoretical paradigms and contemporary social movements', *Social Research*, vol 52, no 4, pp 663-716.

Commonwealth Foundation (1999) *Citizens and governance: Civil society in the new millennium*, London: Commonwealth Foundation.

Cooper, D. (2004) *Challenging diversity: Rethinking equality and the value of difference*, Cambridge: Cambridge University Press.

Coote, A. and Lenaghan, J. (1997) *Citizens' juries: Theory into practice*, London: IPPR.

Cornwall, A. (2004) 'New democratic spaces? The politics and dynamics of institutionalised participation', *IDS Bulletin: New democratic spaces?*, vol 35, no 2, pp 1–10.

Cornwall, A. and Coelho, V.S.P. (eds) (2004) *IDS Bulletin: New democratic spaces?*, vol 35, no 2.

Cornwall, A. and Coelho, V.S.P. (eds) (2006) *Spaces for change? The politics of citizen participation in new democratic arenas*, London/New York, NY: Zed Books.

Corrigan, P. (1997) *Shaping the future: Managing new forms of democracy, the mixed economy and service quality in local government*, Luton: LGMB.

Coulson, A. (ed) (1998) *Trust and contracts: Relationships in local government, health and public services*, Bristol: The Policy Press.

Craig, G. and Taylor, M. (2002) 'Dangerous liaisons: local government and the voluntary and community sectors', in C. Glendinning, M. Powell and K. Rummery (eds) *Partnerships, New Labour and the governance of welfare*, Bristol: The Policy Press, pp 131–47.

Creegan, C., Colgan, F., Charlesworth, R. and Robinson, G. (2003) 'Race equality policies at work: employee perceptions of the "implementation gap" in a UK local authority', *Work, Employment and Society*, vol 17, no 4, pp 617-40.

Crossley, N. (2002) *Making sense of social movements*, Buckingham: Open University Press.

Cunningham, F. (2002) *Theories of democracy*, London: Routledge.

Daemen, H. and Schaap, L. (eds) (2000) *Citizens and city*, Delft: Centre for Local Democracy, Erasmus University.

Dahl, R. and Tufte, E. (1973) *Size and democracy*, Stanford, CA: Stanford University Press.

Davies, C., Wetherell, M. and Barnett, E. (2006) *Citizens at the centre: Deliberative participation in healthcare decisions*, Bristol: The Policy Press.

Davies, S., Elizabeth, S., Hanley, B., New, B. and Sang, B. (eds) (1998) *Ordinary wisdom: Reflections on an experiment in citizenship and health*, London: The King's Fund

Davis, L.J. (1995) *Enforcing normalcy: Disability, deafness and the body*, London: Verso.

Della Porta, D. and Diani, M. (1999) *Social movements: An introduction*, Oxford: Blackwell.

Denters, B. and Klok, P. (2005) 'The Netherlands: in search of responsiveness', in B. Denters and L.E. Rose (eds) *Comparing local governance: Trends and developments*, Basingstoke: Palgrave, pp 65-82.

Department for Communities and Local Government (2006) *Strong and prosperous communities*, Cm 6939, London: The Stationery Office.

DETR (Department of the Environment, Transport and the Regions) (1998) *Modern local government: In touch with the people*, London: The Stationery Office.

DETR (1999a) *Local leadership, local choice*, London: The Stationery Office.

DETR (1999b) *New Deal for Communities: First year of the pathfinders*, London: The Stationery Office.

DH (Department of Health) (2000) *NHS Plan*, London: DH.

DH (2004) *Patient and public involvement – A brief overview*, London: DH.

Diani, M. and McAdam, D. (eds) (2003) *Social movements and networks: Relational approaches to collective action*, Oxford: Oxford University Press.

Dietz, T. (1995) 'Democracy and science', in O. Renn, T. Webler and P. Wiedemann (eds) *Fairness and competence in citizen participation*, Dordrecht: Kluwer Academic Publishers.

DiMaggio, P.J. (1991) 'Constructing an organizational field as a professional project: US art museums, 1920-1940', in W.W. Powell and P.J. DiMaggio (eds) *The new institutionalism in organizational analysis*, Chicago, IL: University of Chicago Press, pp 267-92.

Driver, S. and Martell, L. (1997) 'New Labour's communitarianisms', *Critical Social Policy*, vol 17, no 3, pp 27-46.

Dryzek, J.S. (1990) *Discursive democracy: Politics, policy and political science*, Cambridge: Cambridge University Press.

Dunkerley, D. and Glasner, P. (1998) 'Empowering the public? Citizens' juries and the new genetic technologies', *Critical Public Health*, vol 8, no 3, pp 181-92.

Edwards, J. (1995) *Local government women's committees*, Aldershot: Avebury.

Etzioni, A. (1998) *The essential communitarian reader*, Lanham, MD: Rowman and Littlefield.

Ferlie, E., Ashburner, L., Fitzgerald, L., Pettigrew, A. and Manzella, G.P. (1998) *The new public management in action*, Oxford: Oxford University Press.

Fischer, F. (2003) *Reframing public policy: Discursive politics and deliberative practices*, Oxford: Oxford University Press.

Fishkin, J.S. (1991) *Democracy and deliberation: New direction for democratic reform*, New Haven, CT: Yale University Press.

Flores, A. (2002) 'Tlalpan neighbourhood committees: a true participatory option', in P. McLaverty (ed) *Public participation and innovation in community governance*, Aldershot: Ashgate, pp 63-76.

Fortmann, L., Roes, E. and van Eeten, M. (2001) 'At the threshold between governance and management: community based natural resource management in Southern Africa', *Public Administration and Development*, vol 21, no 2, pp 171-85.

Foucault, M. (1991) 'Governmentality', in G. Burchell, C. Gordon and P. Miller (eds) *The Foucault effect: Studies in governmentality*, Hemel Hempstead: Harvester Wheatsheaf.

Fourniau, J.M. (2001) 'Information, access to decision-making and public debate in France: the growing demand for deliberative democracy', *Science and Public Policy*, vol 28, no 6, pp 441-52.

Fraser, N. (1989) *Unruly practices: Power, discourse and gender in contemporary social theory*, Minneapolis, MN: University of Minnesota Press.

Fraser, N. (1997) *Justice interruptus: Critical reflections on the 'postsocialist' condition*, New York, NY: Routledge.

Fung, A. (2004) *Empowered participation: Reinventing urban democracy*, Princeton, NJ: Princeton University Press.

Fung, A. and Wright, E.O. (2003) *Deepening democracy: Institutional innovations in empowered participatory governance*, London: Verso.

Gamson, W.A. (1975) *The strategy of social protest*, Belmont, CA: Wadsworth.

Gaster, L. and Squires, A. (2003) *Providing quality in the public sector*, Maidenhead: Open University Press.

Gaventa, J. (2004) *Representation, community leadership and participation: Citizen involvement in neighbourhood renewal and local governance*, London: NRU and ODPM.

Gibbon, P. (1992) 'Equal opportunities policy and race equality', in P. Braham, A. Rattansi and R. Skellington (eds) *Racism and antiracism: Inequalities, opportunities and policies*, London: Sage Publications.

Gilling, D. (1997) *Crime prevention*, London: UCL Press.

Groenewald, C. and Smith, A. (2002) 'Public participation and integrated development planning in decentralized local government: a case study of democratic transition in South Africa', in P. McLaverty (ed) *Public participation and innovation in community governance*, Aldershot: Ashgate, pp 35-62.

Gusfield, J. (1963) *Symbolic crusade*, Urbana, Il: University of Illinois.

Gutmann, A. and Thompson, D. (1996) *Democracy and disagreement*, Cambridge, MA: The Belknap Press.

Gyford, J. (1991) *Citizens, consumers and councils: Local government and the public*, London: Macmillan.

Habermas, J. (1970) 'Toward a theory of communicative competence', *Inquiry*, vol 13, no 4, pp 360-76.

Habermas, J. (1984) *Theory of communicative action, vol 1: Reason and the rationalization of society*, Boston, MA: Beacon Press.

Habermas, J. (1990) 'Discourse ethics: notes on a programme of philosophical justification', in J. Habermas, *Moral consciousness and communicative action*, Cambridge: Polity Press.

Hajer, M. (2003) 'A frame in the fields: policymaking and the reinvention of politics', in M. Hajer and H. Wagenaar, *Deliberative policy analysis: Understanding governance in the network society*, Cambridge: Cambridge University Press.

Hajer, M. and Wagenaar, H. (eds) (2003) *Deliberative policy analysis: Understanding governance in the network society*, Cambridge: Cambridge University Press.

Hambleton, R., Hoggett, P. and Razzaque, K. (1996) *Freedom within boundaries: Developing effective approaches to decentralisation*, Luton: LGMB.

Harris, F.C. (2001) 'Religious resources in an oppositional civic culture', in J Mansbridge and A. Morris (eds) *Oppositional consciousness: The subjective roots of social protest*, Chicago, IL: University of Chicago Press.

Hastings, A., McArthur, A. and McGregor, A. (1996) *Less than equal? Community organisations and estate regeneration partnerships*, Bristol: The Policy Press.

Hey, V. and Bradford, S. (2006) 'Re-engineering motherhood? Sure Start in the community', *Contemporary Issues in Early Childhood*, vol 7, no 1, pp 53-67.

Hirst, P. (1994) *Associative democracy: New forms of economic and social governance*, Cambridge: Polity Press.

Hirst, P. (1997a) 'From the economic to the political', in G. Kelly, D. Kelly and A. Gamble (eds) *Stakeholder capitalism*, Basingstoke: Macmillan, pp 63-71.

Hirst, P. (1997b) *From statism to pluralism*, London: UCL Press.

Home Office (2004) *Firm foundations: The government's framework for community capacity building*, London: Civil Renewal Unit, Home Office.

Hughes, G. and Mooney, G. (1998) 'Community', in G. Hughes (ed) *Imagining welfare futures*, London: Routledge.

Hutton, W. (1997) 'An overview of stakeholding', in G. Kelly, D. Kelly and A. Gamble (eds) *Stakeholder capitalism*, Basingstoke: Macmillan, pp 3-9.

Jones, R. (2002) 'With a little help from my friends: managing public participation in local government', *Public Money and Management*, April-June, pp 31-6.

Kearns, A. and Parkinson, M. (2001) 'The significance of neighbourhood', *Urban Studies*, vol 38, no 12, pp 2103-10.

Klein, N. (2000) *No logo*, London: Flamingo.

Konur, O. (2000) 'Creating enforceable civil rights for disabled students in higher education: an institutional theory perspective', *Disability and Society*, vol 15, no 7, pp 1041-63.

Kooiman, J. (ed) (1993) *Modern governance: Government–society interactions*, London: Sage Publications.

Kornhauser, A. (1959) *The politics of mass society*, Glencoe, IL: Free Press.

Kreisi, H., Koopmans, R., Duyvendak, J.W. and Giugni, M. (1995) *New social movements in western Europe: A comparative analysis*, London: UCL Press.

Kuttner, R. (1997) 'An American perspective', in G. Kelly, D. Kelly and A. Gamble (eds) *Stakeholder capitalism*, Basingstoke: Macmillan, pp 29-34.

Leach, M., Scoones, I. and Wynne, B. (eds) (2005) *Science and citizens: Globalization and the challenge of engagement*, London/New York, NY: Zed Books.

Leadbeater, C. (2004) *Personalising public participation*, London: Demos.

Levitas, R. (2005) *Inclusive society*, Basingstoke: Palgrave.

LGMB (Local Government Management Board) *Citizens' juries in local government: Report for LGMB on the pilot projects*, London: LGMB.

Loney, M. (1983) *Community against government: The British community development project 1968-78*, London: Heinemann.

Lovenduski, J. and Randall, V. (1993) *Contemporary feminist politics*, Oxford: Oxford University Press.

Lowndes, V. (1999) 'Management change in local governance', in G. Stoker (ed) *The new management of British local governance*, Basingstoke: Macmillan.

Lowndes, V. (2001) 'Rescuing Aunt Sally: taking institutional theory seriously in urban Politics', *Urban Studies*, vol 38, no 11, pp 1953-71.

Lowndes, V. and Sullivan, H. (2004) 'Local partnerships and public participation', *Local Government Studies*, vol 30, no 2, Summer, pp 51-73.

Lowndes, V. and Sullivan, H. (2007: forthcoming) 'How low can you go? Rationales and challenges for neighbourhood governance', *Public Administration*.

Lowndes, V. and Wilson, D. (2001) 'Social capital and local governance: exploring the institutional design variable', *Political Studies*, vol 49, pp 629-47.

Lowndes, V., Stoker, G. and associates (1998) *Enhancing public participation in local government*, Research Report, London: Department of the Environment, Transport and the Regions.

Lowndes, V., Pratchett, L. and Stoker, G. (2006) 'Local political participation: the impact of "rules-in-use"', *Public Administration*, vol 84, no 3, pp 539-61

McIver, S. (1997) *An evaluation of the King's Fund Citizens' Juries Programme*, Health Services Management Centre, Birmingham: University of Birmingham.

McLaverty, P. (ed) (2002) *Public participation and innovations in community governance*, Aldershot: Ashgate.

McPherson, W. (1999) *The Stephen Lawrence Enquiry*, London: The Stationery Office.

Mainwaring, R. (1988) *The Walsall experience: A study of the decentralisation of Walsall's housing service*, London: HMSO.

Mansbridge, J. (2001) 'The making of oppositional consciousness', in J. Mansbridge and A. Morris (eds) *Oppositional consciousness: The subjective roots of social protest*, Chicago, IL: University of Chicago Press.

March, J. and Olsen, J. (1989) *Rediscovering institutions*, New York, NY: Free Press.

Marris, P. and Rein, M. (1972) 'Preface to the Second Edition', *Dilemmas of social reform: Poverty and community action in the United States*, London: Routledge and Kegan Paul.

Marsh, D. and Rhodes, R.A.W. (eds) (1992). *Policy networks in British government*, Oxford: Clarendon Press.

Martin, S. and Davis, H. (2001) 'What works and for whom? The competing rationalities of "Best Value"', *Policy & Politics*, vol 29, no 4, pp 465-75.

Mayo, M., Hoggett, P. and Miller, C. (2007: forthcoming) 'Ethical dilemmas of front-line regeneration workers', in S. Balloch and M. Hill (eds) *Care, citizenship and communities: Research and practice in a changing policy context*, Bristol: The Policy Press.

Melucci, A. (1996) *Challenging codes: Collective action in the information age*, Cambridge: Cambridge University Press.

Meyer, J. and Rowan, B. (1991) 'Institutionalized organizations: formal structure as myth and ceremony', in W.W. Powell and P.J. DiMaggio (eds) *The new institutionalism in organizational analysis*, Chicago, IL: University of Chicago Press.

Monbiot, G. (2000) *Captive state*, London: Macmillan.

Mulgan, G. (2005) 'Introduction', in Involve, *People and participation: How to put citizens at the heart of decision making*, London: Involve.

Murray, C. (1990) *The emerging British underclass*, Choice in Welfare Series, No 2, London: IEA Health and Welfare Unit.

NAO (National Audit Office) (2004) *Getting communities involved: Community participation in neighbourhood renewal*, October, London: English regions, NAO.

Narayan, D., Chambers, R., Shah, M.K. and Petesch, P. (2000) *Voices of the poor: Crying out for change*, Washington, DC: World Bank.

Newman, J. (2001) *Modernising governance: New Labour, policy and society*, London: Sage Publications.

Newman, J. (2005a) 'Introduction', in J. Newman (ed) *Remaking governance: Policy, politics and the public sphere*, Bristol: The Policy Press.

Newman, J. (2005b) 'Participative governance and the remaking of the public sphere', in J. Newman (ed) *Remaking governance: Peoples, politics and the public sphere*, Bristol: The Policy Press.

Newman, J. and Vidler, E. (2006) 'Discriminating customers, responsible patients, empowered users: consumerism and the modernisation of health care', *Journal of Social Policy*, vol 35, no 2, pp 193-209.

Newman, J., Barnes, M., Sullivan, H. and Knops, A. (2004) 'Public participation and collaborative governance', *Journal of Social Policy*, vol 33, no 2, pp 203-24.

Newton, K. (1989) 'Is small really so beautiful? Is big really so ugly? Size, effectiveness, and democracy in local government', *Political Studies*, vol 30, no 2, p 203.

North, D.C. (1991) 'Towards a theory of institutional change', *Quarterly Review of Economics and Business*, vol 31, pp 3-11.

North, D.C. (1993) 'Institutions and credible commitment', *Journal of Institutional and Theoretical Economics*, vol 149, no 1, pp 11-23.

Nutley, S. and Webb, J. (2000) 'Evidence and the policy process', in H. Davies, S. Nutley and P. Smith (eds) *What works?*, Bristol: The Policy Press.

ODPM (Office of the Deputy Prime Minister) (2002) *Public participation in local government: A survey of local authorities*, London: ODPM.

ODPM (2006) 'Empowerment and the deal for devolution', Speech by Rt Hon David Miliband MP, Minister of Communities and Local Government, February, London: ODPM.

ODPM/DfT (Department for Transport) (2006) *National evaluation of LSPs: Formative evaluation and action research programme, 2002-2005*, Warwick/Liverpool/London: Warwick Business School/Liverpool John Moores/ODPM/University of the West of England: ODPM.

ODPM/HO (Home Office) (2005) *Citizen engagement and public services: Why neighbourhoods matter*, London: ODPM.

Oliver, M. (1995) *Understanding disability: From theory to practice*, Basingstoke: Macmillan.

Osborne, D. and Gaebler, T. (1992) *Reinventing government: How the entrepreneurial spirit is transforming the public sector*, Reading, MA: Addison-Wesley.

Ostrom, E. (2000) 'Crowding out citizenship', *Scandinavian Political Studies*, vol 23, no 1, pp 3-16.

Peterman, W. (2000) *Neighbourhood planning and community based development*, London: Sage Publications.

Peters, G.B. and Pierre, J. (2001) 'Developments in intergovernmental relations: towards multi-level governance', *Policy & Politics*, vol 29, no 2, pp 131-6.

Peters, T.J. and Waterman, R.H. (1982) *In search of excellence: Lessons from America's best run companies*, London: Harper and Row.

Petts, J. (1997) 'The public–expert interface in local waste management decisions: expertise, credibility and process', *Public Understanding of Science*, vol 6, pp 359-81.

Petts, J. (2001) 'Evaluating the effectiveness of deliberative processes: waste management case studies', *Journal of Environmental Planning and Management*, vol 44, no 2, pp 207-26.

Phillips, A. (1995) *The politics of presence*, Oxford: Clarendon Press.

Powell, W.W. and DiMaggio, P.J. (eds) (1991) *The new institutionalism in organizational analysis*, Chicago, IL: University of Chicago Press.

Power Inquiry (2006) *Power to the people*, York: Joseph Rowntree Trust.

Pratchett, L. (1999) 'Defining democratic renewal', *Local Government Studies*, vol 25, no 4, pp 1-18.

Pratchett, L. (2004) 'Local autonomy, local democracy and the new localism', *Political Studies*, vol 52, no 2, pp 258-75.

Prior, D., Stewart, J. and Walsh, K. (1995) *Citizenship: Rights, community and participation*, London: Pitman.

Putnam, R.D. (1993) *Making democracy work*, Chichester: Princetown University Press.

Putnam, R.D. (2000) *Bowling alone*, New York, NY: Simon and Schuster.

Ranson, S. and Stewart, J. (1994) *Management for the public domain*, London: Macmillan.

Rao, H., Morrill, C. and Zald, M.N. (2000) 'Power plays: how social movements and collective action create new organizational forms', *Organizational Behaviour*, vol 22, pp 239-82.

Renn, O., Webler, T., Rakel, H., Dienel, P. and Johnson, B. (1993) 'Public participation in decision making: a three step procedure', *Policy Sciences*, vol 26, pp 189-214.

Renn, O., Wiebler, T. and Wiedermann, P. (eds) (1995) *Fairness and competition in citizen participation*, Dordecht, Kluwer Academic Publishers.

Rhodes, J., Tyler, P., Brenna, A., Levas, S., Warnock, C. and Otero-Garcia, M. (2002) *Lessons and evaluation evidence from 10 SRB case studies*, mid-term report, London: DETR.

Rodriguez, M.S. (2001) 'Cristaleno consciousness: Mexican-American activism between Crystal City Texas and Wisconsin, 1963-80', in J. Mansbridge and A. Morris (eds) *Oppositional consciousness. The subjective roots of social protest*, Chicago, IL: University of Chicago Press.

Rogers, B. and Robinson, E. (2004) *The benefits of community engagement: A review of the evidence*, London: Active Citizenship Centre, Home Office.

Rose, N. (1996) 'Governing advanced Liberal democracies', in A. Barry et al (eds) *Foucault and political reason*, London: UCL Press.

Rose, N. (1999) *Powers of freedom*, Cambridge: Cambridge University Press.

Rose, L. and Ståhlberg, K. (2005) 'The Nordic countries: still the "promised land"?', in B. Denters and L. Rose (eds) *Comparing local governance: Trends and developments*, Basingstoke: Palgrave, pp 83-99.

Ruiz, C.C. (2005) 'Rights and citizenship of indigenous women in Chiapas: a history of struggles, fears and hopes', in N. Kabeer (ed) *Inclusive citizenship*, London: Zed Books.

Russell Commission (2005) *A national framework for youth action and engagement*, London: Russell Commission.

Russell, H., Dawson, J., Garside, P. and Parkinson, M. (1996) *City challenge – Interim national evaluation*, London: The Stationery Office.

Rustin, M. (1997) 'Stakeholding and the public sector', in G. Kelly, D. Kelly and A. Gamble (eds) *Stakeholder capitalism*, Basingstoke: Macmillan, pp 72-81.

Saward, M. (2005) 'Political representation and governance', in J. Newman (ed) *Remaking governance: Peoples, politics and the public sphere*, Bristol: The Policy Press.

Scott, W.R. (2001) *Institutions and organizations* (2nd edn), Thousand Oaks, CA: Sage Publications.

Seidman, S. (1998) *Contested knowledge: Social theory in the postmodern era*, Oxford: Blackwell.

SEU (Social Exclusion Unit) (2000) *National strategy for neighbourhood renewal: A framework for consultation*, London: The Stationery Office.

SEU (2001) *A new commitment to neighbourhood renewal: National strategy action plan*, London: The Stationery Office.

Sevenhuijsen, S. (1998) *Citizenship and the ethics of care: Feminist considerations on justice, morality and politics*, London/New York: Routledge.

Sevenhuijsen, S. (2003a) 'The place of care: the relevance of the feminist ethic of care for social policy', *Feminist Theory*, vol 4, no 2, pp 179-97.

Sevenhuijsen, S. (2003b) 'Trace: a method for normative policy analysis from the ethic of care', Paper for the seminar 'Care and Public Policy' Centre for Women's and Gender Research, University of Bergen, 9-11 November.

Smith, G. (2005) *Beyond the ballot*, London: Power Inquiry.

Squires, J. and Wickham-Jones, M. (2004) 'New Labour, gender mainstreaming and the women and equality unit', *British Journal of Politics and International Relations*, vol 6, no1, pp 81-98.

Stewart, J. (1999) *From innovation in democratic practice towards a deliberative democracy*, Birmingham: University of Birmingham, School of Public Policy.

Stockdill, B.C. (2001) 'Forging a multidimensional oppositional consciousness: lessons from community-based AODS activism', in J. Mansbridge and A. Morris (eds) *Oppositional consciousness. The subjective roots of social protest*, Chicago, IL: University of Chicago Press.

Stoker, G. (1996) 'Redefining local democracy', in L. Pratchett and D. Wilson (eds) *Local democracy and local government*, Basingstoke: Macmillan.

Stryker, S., Owens, T.J. and White, R.W. (eds) (2000) *Self, identity and social movements*, Minneapolis, MN: University of Minnesota Press.

Sullivan, H. (2001a) 'Modernisation, democratisation and community governance', *Local Government Studies*, vol 27, no 3, pp 1-24.

Sullivan, H. (2001b) 'Maximising the contribution of neighbourhoods – the role of community governance', *Public Policy and Administration*, vol 16, no 2, pp 29-48.

Sullivan, H. (2002) 'Modernisation, neighbourhood management and social inclusion', *Public Management Review*, vol 4, no 4, pp 505-28.

Sullivan, H. (2003) 'New forms of local accountability – coming to terms with "many hands"?', *Policy & Politics*, vol 31, no 3, pp 353-69.

Sullivan, H. and Howard, J. (2005) *Below the LSP*, Issues Paper, National evaluation of LSPs, London: ODPM.

Sullivan, H. and Skelcher, C. (2002) *Working across boundaries: Partnerships in public services*, Basingstoke: Palgrave.

Sullivan, H., Root, A., Moran, D. and Smith, M. (2001) *Area committees and neighbourhood management*, London/York: LGIU/JRF.

Tam, H. (1998) *Communitarianism*, Basingstoke: Palgrave.

Taylor, M. (2003) *Public policy in the community*, Basingstoke: Palgrave.

Taylor, M., Ardon, R., Carlton, N., Meegan, R., Purdue, D., Russell, H., Syed, A. and Wilson, M. (2005) *Making connections: An evaluation of the community participation programmes*, Cities Research Centre, University of the West of England, Bristol, COGS, European Institute for Urban Affairs, Liverpool John Moores University.

Taylor-Gooby, P., Hastie, C. and Bromly, C. (2003) 'Querulous citizens: welfare knowledge and the limits to welfare reform', *Social Policy and Administration*, vol 37, no 1, pp 1-20.

Thompson, S. and Hoggett, P. (2001) 'The emotional dynamics of deliberative democracy', *Policy & Politics*, vol 29, no 3, pp 351-64.

Toynbee, P. and Walker, D. (2005) *Better or worse? Has Labour delivered?*, London: Bloomsbury.

Vari, A. and Kisgyorgy, S. (1998) 'Public participation in developing water quality legislation and regulation in Hungary', *Water Policy*, vol 1, pp 223-38.

Wainwright, H. (2003) *Reclaim the state: Experiments in popular democracy*, London: Verso.

Wakeford, T. (1999) *Citizen foresight: A tool to enhance democratic policy making: 1. The future of food and agriculture*, London: Centre for Governance, Innovation and Science.

White, R. W. and Fraser, M.R. (2001) 'Personal and collective identities and long-term social movement activism: Republican Sinn Fein', in S. Stryker, T.J. Owens and R. W. White (eds) *Self, identity and social movements*, Minneapolis, MN: University of Minnesota Press.

Wilson, D. (1999) 'Exploring the limits of public participation in local government', *Parliamentary Affairs*, vol 52, no 2, pp 247-58.

Yanow, D. (2003) 'Accessing local knowledge', in M.A. Hajer and H. Wagenaar (eds) *Deliberative policy analysis*, Cambridge: Cambridge University Press.

Young, I.M. (1990) *Justice and the politics of difference*, Princeton, NJ: Princeton University Press.

Young, I.M. (2000) *Inclusion and democracy*, Oxford: Oxford University Press.

Young, J. (1999) *The exclusive society*, London: Sage Publications.

Index

A

Aars, J. 42
accessing participation 39, 67, 89-90, 189
  and social movements 48-9, 49-51
accountability and neighbourhood groups
  108-10
active citizen concept 9, 12, 188, 204-5
  'consuming public' discourse 13-15, 19
  'responsible public' discourse 19, 20-1
Active Citizenship Centre 28
Active Learning for Active Citizenship
  initiative 26
activism and participation 175, 204-5
  identity-based groups 141-2, 144
  neighbourhood initiatives 116-17
  service user groups 72-3, 86, 91, 92
advocacy initiatives 55, 56
affective discourse 150
Age Concern 135, 136
agency
  and institutional context 61, 132-3, 189
  and power relations 81-3, 188, 189
  see also political agency; social agency
anti-poverty campaign group 165-6, 167,
  169
area advisory board 105-6, 107, 109, 112
  and identity 116
  and institutional rules and norms 120-1
  representation issues 127, 128-9
area committee 106-7, 109-10, 112, 131
  and identity 116, 117
  and institutional rules and norms 122-6
  motivations for participation 113-14
  representation issues 128-9
area forums 101, 131
  and accountability 109-10
  and collective identities 117
  and differentiated publics 156-7
  and diversity 129-30
  and institutional context 122-6, 132-3
  motivations for participation 113-14
  official roles 116
  representation issues 127, 128-9, 197
  and 'stakeholder public' discourse 112
area-specific initiatives 55, 56
associationalism 18
'associative democracy' 16, 34-5

B

Barnes, M. 20, 22, 29, 35, 50, 85, 93
Barnett, A. 17
beliefs and policy 41
Beresford, P. 166
Best Value programme 22-3, 55, 62

Blunkett, David 20
Brulle, R.J. 167
bureaucratic organisation 9, 34, 96

C

Campbell, J. 44-5
capacity building 11, 26, 27, 57, 126, 130-1
carriers of institutional rules and norms 61
case studies 3, 72-9, 93-4, 183-4
  see also identity-based groups; issue-based
    groups; neighbourhood and community
    governance; service users
Central Statistical Office (CSO) 12
Chanan, G. 29
change and participation 187, 188, 190
  see also transformation of views
Child Poverty Action Group 166
circumcision see Muslim male circumcision
  group
Citizen engagement and public services 26-7
'citizen panels' 67
Citizens Charter initiative 14
citizens' juries 36, 38
City Challenge 11
civic engagement see capacity building
civil renewal agenda 21
civil society groups 10, 19
claims-making and representation 65, 185,
  196-7
Clarke, J. 203-4
Coelho, V.S.P. 204
'coercive isomorphism' 192
collective action 20, 42-3, 166
collective identities
  and identity-based groups 139
  and neighbourhood strategies 116-17
  and political renewal 202
  and service user participation 88-91, 97
  and social movements 46-7, 165, 166
collectivism 17-18, 21, 35
communicative competence 37
communicative rationality 36-8, 44
communitarianism 19, 20, 21, 57
communities
  capacity building 11, 26, 27, 57, 126,
    130-1
  'empowered public' discourse 10-13, 80,
    81, 84-5, 171
  'engaging communities' objective 57
  as partners 8, 11-12
  and 'responsible public' discourse 20-1
  and 'stakeholder public' discourse 83-5,
    171
  and sustainability forum 172, 173
  use of 'community' 10, 67-8, 132, 199

see also community health forum; identity-based groups; neighbourhood and community governance
'communities of identity' 57-8, 67-8
community development 11, 110-11
Community Empowerment Fund (CEF) 26
Community Empowerment Network (CEN) 26
community governance *see* neighbourhood and community governance
community health forum 71, 72-3, 78, 171, 184, 188
  and institutional rules and norms 94, 96, 191
  legitimacy of members 91-2
  motivations for participation 85-6, 87, 194
  purpose of 80-1
  and stakeholder discourse 84-5
'community of ideas' 172
Community Participation Programme (CPP) 30
Compass 200
complex societies and democracy 50-1, 204
Conservative governments 18, 100
  and 'consuming public' discourse 14-15, 19, 22
'constitutive rules' 60, 61
'consuming public' discourse 9, 13-15, 19, 21, 56
  as dominant discourse 81, 97, 200
  inadequacies of 71, 79, 82
  and paradox of participation 203-4
  and participation in local governance 22-3
  and senior citizens' forums 139
Coote, A. 35
Cornwall, A. 204
Corrigan, P. 14
'counter-cultural' movements 165
'counterpublics' 43-4, 135, 160, 161-2, 196, 198, 202-3
  see also identity-based groups
cross-cutting initiatives 55
Crossley, N. 43
cultural-cognitive pillar of institutions 59

D

'daily care' and policy 40-1
Davies, S. 35
Davis, L.J. 44
decentralisation 21
  neighbourhood initiatives 101, 102, 105-7
  and 'stakeholder public' discourse 16, 17, 18

decision-making
  neighbourhood initiatives 101
  participation and public services 33-42
deliberative democracy 2, 33-52, 184, 186
  critical analysis 35-41
  'lay' and 'expert' knowledge and power 193-6
  and representative democracy 41-2, 59-60, 61
  and social movement theory 42-51
Della Porta, D. 48-9
democracy *see* 'associative democracy'; deliberative democracy; 'participatory democracies'; representative democracy
'developmental capacity' 57
Diani, M. 46, 48-9
Dietz, T. 34
differentiated publics *see* identity-based groups
DiMaggio, P.J. 61
disability movement 44-5
disadvantaged groups *see* marginalised groups
discourses of participation 9-22, 53-4, 56, 138, 198-9
discursive practice and power 66-7, 69-70
diversity
  and 'empowerment' of marginalised groups 12-13
  and identity-based groups 143-4
  and neighbourhood initiatives 102, 126, 129-30
  see also identity-based groups
Driver, S. 21
Dryzek, J.S. 35

E

Economic and Social Research Council 2
Education Action Zones (EAZs) 55
education priority areas (EPAs) 11
elderly people *see* senior citizens' forums
elected assemblies
  attitudes towards participation 41-2, 122-6, 179
  and representation of public groups 39, 128
  see also local authorities; representative democracy
emotional discourse 150
employees and 'stakeholder' discourse 17
employment sub-group 76-7, 78, 83, 93
'empowered public' discourse 9, 21, 56
  and communities 10-13, 80, 81, 84-5, 171
  and identity groups 137
  neighbourhood initiatives 100-1, 111-12, 130-1
  and participation in local governance 24, 25, 26
energy conservation 169, 174
'engaging communities' objective 57

environmental movement 167-9, 170,
175-6
see also sustainability forum
ESRC Democracy and Participation
programme 2
ethnic minority groups
representation issues 142-3, 146-7, 196
and social exclusion 166
see also minority ethnic group council;
Muslim male circumcision group; youth
forum
Etzioni, A. 20
European Social Forum 201
evaluation of participation 28-30
effectiveness of identity-based groups
153-9, 161, 187
participation in public services 71-97
expansion of government 34
experiential knowledge 83-4, 90, 112, 145,
176-7
'expert' knowledge
and deliberative democracy 34, 36,
179-80
and governmentality 65-6, 69
'lay' and 'expert' knowledge and power
193-6
'expert user' discourse 81, 83-4, 112
external legitimacy 196

F

feminism 44, 49-50
feminist ethics of care and policy 40-1
Fischer, F. 40, 65, 66
Fishkin, J.S. 35
Foucault, M. 65, 66, 69-70
Fourniau, J.M. 60-1
Fraser, M.R. 47
Fraser, Nancy 37, 38, 42, 43, 198, 202
fuel poverty group 165-6, 167, 184, 188,
197
and institutional rules and norms 176-7,
181-2, 192, 193
motivations for participation 172-5
and policy context 169-70, 171, 180
funding and public participation 30
identity-based groups 137, 138, 149-50,
155-6
neighbourhood initiatives 103, 104, 105,
109, 111, 118, 129-30
service user groups 72, 73, 76

G

Gaebler, T. 13
Gamson, W.A. 48
Gaster, L. 15
Gaventa, J. 7-8, 12-13, 30
gay forum *see* lesbian and gay forum
governance 33-42, 186

see also democracy; local governance;
neighbourhood and community
governance; state
governmentality discourse 65-6
grant applications: advisory board 105-6,
109
'greeting' mode of speech 38
Groenewald, C. 13
Gusfield, J. 45-6
Gutmann, A. 34
Gyford, J. 8-9, 12, 19-20

H

Habermas, J. 36-7, 66
Hajer, M. 68
Harris, F.C. 44
Health Action Zones (HAZs) 29, 170
health services *see* community health
forum; minority ethnic group council;
Muslim male circumcision group; NHS;
primary care groups
healthy living centres (HLCs) 72, 73, 78,
81, 85, 91, 188
Hirst, P. 15-16, 17, 18, 34-5
Hoggett, P. 38
Home Office 26, 30
Housing Action Trust (HAT) 102-3,
116-17, 117-18
human resources sub-group 76-7, 78, 83,
93
Hutton, W. 17

I

identity
'insider/outsider' duality 145, 154, 161,
178, 194-6
and new social movements 166
and service user groups 86-7, 88-91
see also collective identities; identity-based
groups
identity-based groups 67-8, 135-64
effectiveness and capacity to challenge
153-9, 161, 187
institutional context 147-53, 190, 191,
193
level of engagement 135, 139-40, 154,
155-6, 159, 160-1, 195-6, 204-5
and neighbourhood initiatives 115-16
and new social movements 166
and objectives of participation policy
57-8
and political renewal 202-3
representation issues 136, 139, 140,
141-7, 158, 159-60
'improving services' objective 57
see also reform
inclusiveness of public groups 67
independent groups *see* identity-based
groups

India: 'empowerment' and representation 12-13
'insider/outsider' duality 145, 154, 161, 178, 194-6
institutional rules and norms 53, 58-63, 69
  and agency 189
  and capacity building 27
  and identity-based groups 135, 136, 138, 147-53
  institutions as prisons 122-6, 192-3
  institutions as sites of challenge and opportunity 119-22, 190-2
  institutions as support 117-18, 189-90
  issue-based initiatives and expertise 176-80, 181-2
  neighbourhood and local governance forums 101-2, 107, 117-26, 132-3, 189
  and power relations 189-93
  and representative democracy 60, 61
  and resistance to participation 30, 31, 61, 74, 123-6, 192-3
  and service user groups 93-6
  see also new institutional theory; power relations; public bodies
'instrumental' movements 165, 168
'interactive governance' 18
interim advisory boards (IABs) 103-4, 110
internal legitimacy 196
Involve 200
issue-based groups 55, 56, 58, 165-82, 188
  membership and representation 167, 168, 181, 197
  motivations for participation 172-6, 194
  and policy context 169-72, 180, 181-2, 191-2, 193

J

Jackson, Jesse 44
'joined up' services 24, 101, 107, 111, 131
Joseph Rowntree Foundation 200

K

knowledge
  and deliberative democracy 34, 35-6
  'lay' and 'expert' knowledge and power 193-6
  experiential knowledge 83-4, 90, 112, 145, 176-7
  see also expert knowledge
Kornhauser, A. 45-6
Kuttner, R. 17-18, 18

L

Labour governments 100
  see also New Labour
language 64, 65, 109-10, 121-2, 199
  speech 37, 38, 44, 201, 202

'lay' and 'expert' knowledge and power 193-6
legitimacy of representatives 91-3, 196-8
Lenaghan, J. 35
lesbian and gay forum 135, 137-8, 140-1
  effectiveness 156-7
  and institutional context 150-1, 190, 193
  and level of engagement 140, 161
  membership and representation 144-5, 158, 162
limits on public participation 203-4
Local Agenda 21 action plans 170, 171-2
local authorities and participation 25-6, 28-30, 55
  domination of council culture 121-6
  and identity-based groups 135-64
  and issue-based groups 167, 168, 169-72, 174-5, 177-80
  participation and shrinking public sphere 203
  political cultures 188
  resistance to participation 74, 123-6, 192-3
  see also area forums; local governance
Local Exchange Trading Systems (LETS) 28
local governance
  Citizens Charter initiative 14
  decentralisation
    and neighbourhood initiatives 101, 105-7
    and 'stakeholder public' discourse 17, 18
    and 'empowerment public' discourse 12-13
  institutional environment 62-3, 69, 132-3
  New Labour and public participation 22-30
  see also local authorities; neighbourhood and community governance
local knowledge and policy 41
Local Strategic Partnerships (LSPs) 24, 26, 29-30, 104
locality 56, 181-2, 199-200
  see also communities; neighbourhood and community governance
Lovenduski, J. 49-50
Lowndes, V. 27, 61, 99

M

McAdam, D. 46
McPherson Inquiry 140
Major, John 14
managerialism 22
Mansbridge, J. 47
mapping public participation initiatives 54-8
March, J. 61, 62

marginalised groups
  and 'empowerment public' discourse
    12-13, 21
  institutional support 189-90
  lesbian and gay forum 140
  and objectives of participation policies
    57-8
  representation issues 39, 189
  see also social movement theory
market approach to public services 13-15
Martell, L. 21
Mayo, M. 194
Melucci, A. 43, 45-7, 49, 50-1, 88, 201
membership *see* representation of publics
minority ethnic group council study 72,
    76-7, 78, 80
  and collective identity 89, 163
  and institutional rules and norms 94-5,
    193
  legitimacy of representatives 93
  motivations for participation 86-7, 194
  and stakeholder discourse 83-4
minority groups *see* identity-based groups;
    marginalised groups
monitoring role of identity-based groups
    140
motivations for participation 194
  issue-based groups 172-6
  neighbourhood initiatives 101-2, 112-15
  officials 86-8, 113, 114, 173, 174-5
  and service user participation 85-8
  and social movement theory 45-8
  and social networks 45-6, 175-6, 180-1
Mulgan, G. 1
multilevel governance 26
Murray, C. 19
Muslim male circumcision group 72, 75-6,
    78
  and collective identity 88-9
  and institutional rules and norms 94, 95
  motivation and identity 87
  and partnership discourse 79-80
  and stakeholder discourse 84
'myth' of institutional context 62, 192

N

National Audit Office 30
National Commission of Public Debate
    60-1
National Framework for Youth Action and
    Engagement 26
National Health Service *see* NHS
National Institute for Health and Clinical
    Excellence 184
National Pensioners Convention 135, 136
National Service Framework for Older
    People 140, 154
National Strategy for Neighbourhood
    Renewal (NSNR) 26, 62, 100

neighbourhood and community
    governance 99-133, 199-200, 202
  and accountability 108-10
  and claims-making 197
  and identities 115-16
  and institutional rules and norms 101-2,
    107, 117-26, 132-3, 189
  motivations for participation 112-15, 194
  Sure Start boards 103-4, 104-5, 107, 191
  use of 'neighbourhood' as term 131-2,
    200
Neighbourhood Council movement 101
Neighbourhood Management Pathfinder
    initiative 24
neighbourhood renewal agenda 26-7,
    99-100
networks *see* policy networks; social
    networks
New Deal for Communities programme
    25, 27
'new democratic spaces' 204
New Economics Foundation 200
new institutional theory 2, 53, 58-68, 189
  publics and public groups 63-8
  rules and norms of public bodies 58-63,
    69
  see also institutional rules and norms
New Labour 22-30, 54-8, 100-1
  and 'consumerist public' discourse 15,
    200
  critiques 27, 31, 187
  and 'empowered public' discourse 11-12
  and 'responsible public' discourse 20-1
'new localism' 199-200
New Opportunities Fund (NOF) 72
New Politics Network 200
new public management 14
New Right 19
new social movements 48, 135, 166, 167,
    204
NHS
  public participation 23-4
  see also primary care groups
NHS Plan 78
normative pillar of institutions 59
norms *see* institutional rules and norms
North, D.C. 60, 61

O

Offerdal, A. 42
Office of the Deputy Prime Minister
    (ODPM) 29
official discourses of participation 9-22,
    53-4, 56, 138, 198-9
officials in participation initiatives
  and collective identities 88-93, 116-17
  and constitution of groups 93-4
  and identity-based groups 161-4, 195-6

lesbian and gay forum 137, 144, 145,
150-1, 157-8
women's group 144
youth forum 138, 146-7, 151-3, 158-9,
162-3
'insider/outsider' duality 145, 154, 161,
178, 194-6
and institutional context 93-6, 117-26,
132-3
rigidity of roles 116, 122-6
and issue-based initiatives 178, 191-2
'lay' and 'expert' knowledge 193-6
motivations 86-8, 113, 114, 173, 174-5
and neighbourhood groups 110-12,
116-17, 117-26, 191
privileging of 9
service user groups 71, 73, 74-5, 76, 77-8
and purpose of partnerships 79-83,
198-9
see also institutional rules and norms
'old' social movements 48
Oliver, M. 44-5, 49
Olsen, J. 61, 62
Open Democracy network 200
'oppositional consciousness' 47, 202-3
Osborne, D. 13
Ostrom, E. 7

P

paradoxes of public participation 203-4
participative budgeting 201
'participatory democracies' 16, 21-2, 27
participatory planning initiatives 16-17
partnerships 8, 97, 187
and 'empowered public' discourse 11, 80,
81, 84-5
and identity-based groups 141, 154, 156,
160-1
and issue-based groups 171-2
power relations in 79-81, 88, 89-90, 195,
199
'passive recipients' 8-9, 12
Patient Advice and Liaison Services (PALS)
15, 23
patients' participation group (PPG) 71,
77-8
balance of power 74-5, 80-1, 81-2, 88,
193
constitution of group 93-4
motivations for participation 86
Peters, G.B. 26
Peters, T.J. 13
Phillips, Anne 39, 42
Pierre, J. 26
place *see* neighbourhood and community
governance
planning: participatory planning 16-17
police and lesbian and gay forum 137-8,
140-1, 144, 145, 151, 156, 157-8

policy
and identity-based groups 57-8, 153-9
and issue-based groups 169-72, 180,
181-2
and social values 40-1
and trajectories of change 188
policy networks 64, 171
political agency 56
political movements 56
political participation 25, 33, 126
political renewal strategies 200-5
post-structural theory 54, 63, 65-8, 132-3
poverty
and 'empowered public' discourse 10-11,
171
and participation 7, 166-7, 172-3, 197
see also fuel poverty group
Power Inquiry 200, 201
power relations 184, 185-205
and deliberative democracy 37, 51
and discursive practice 66-7, 69-70
in identity-based groups 148-9, 151-3,
154
and institutional rules and norms 189-93
knowledge and expertise of government
65-6, 69
'lay' and 'expert' knowledge and power
193-6
symbolic power of institutions 62, 192
unequal relations 81-3, 90-1, 97, 172
partnerships 79-81, 88, 89-90, 195, 199
patients' participation group 74-5, 80-1,
81-2, 88, 93-4, 193
'presence', politics of 198
primary care groups (PCGs) 54-5
see also community health forum;
Muslim male circumcision group;
patients' participation group
Prior, DE. 14-15
privatisation and participation 203
professionals *see* officials in participation
initiatives
public bodies and initiatives 56-8
declining public sphere 203
and identity-based groups 135-64, 191
conflicts 135-6, 138, 146-7, 161
impact on policy and practice 153-9,
191
level of engagement 135, 139-40, 154,
155-6, 159, 160-1, 195-6, 204-5
range of initiatives 54-8, 183, 184-5,
185-7
see also institutional rules and norms; local
authorities; officials in participation
initiatives; publics/public groups
public services
'consuming public' discourse 9, 13-15,
200
decline in public sphere 203-4

governance and deliberative democracy 33-42
participation and reforming effects 71-97
  motivations for participation 85-8
resistance to participation 30
see also service users
publics/public groups
  collective identities 88-91, 116-17, 139, 166
  constitution of case study groups 72-9, 93-4, 198-9
  and deliberative democracy 38-9
  discourses of participation 8-22, 53-4, 56, 138, 198-9
  and discursive practices 66-7, 69-70
  institutional context 63-8
  motivations for participation 85-8
  range of initiatives 56-7, 183, 184-5, 185-7
  as 'stakeholder public' 83-5
  see also accessing participation; communities; identity-based groups; issue-based groups; marginalised groups; neighbourhood and community governance; representation of publics; service users
Putnam, R.D. 7

R

Randall, V. 49-50
Rao, H. 41-2, 49
rational choice theory 45, 46
rationality and deliberative democracy 36-8, 44, 65
recognition, politics of 198
reform
  effectiveness of identity-based groups 153-9, 161
  and service-user participation 71-97, 204
regeneration policies 11-12
  see also neighbourhood and community governance
regulative pillar of institutions 59, 60
Renn, O. 36
representation of publics 68, 196-8
  accessing participation 39, 89-90, 189
  as claims-making 196-7
  and 'empowerment' discourse 12-13
  identity-based groups 136, 139, 140, 141-7, 158, 159-60
  issue-based groups 166, 167, 181
  legitimacy of representatives 91-3, 196-8
  and neighbourhood initiatives 126, 127-9
  politics of presence/recognition 198
  service user groups 91-3
  and social movement theory 198
representative democracy 2, 9, 16, 21, 35
  and deliberative democracy 41-2, 59-60, 61, 102

and difference 67
problems of representation 68
and public participation 27, 186, 203-4
residents' group 100, 102-3, 107, 131, 132
  and accountability 108
  and collective identity 116-17
  communication with professionals 110, 112
  and institutional rules and norms 117-18, 132, 190, 193
resistance 30, 31, 61, 74, 123-6, 192-3
'responsible public' discourse 9, 19-22, 199
  and neighbourhood initiatives 56, 101, 112
  and participation in local governance 25
rhetoric and deliberative democracy 38, 65
Rose, L. 14
Rose, N. 65, 66
rules *see* institutional rules and norms
Russell Commission 26
Rustin, M. 15, 18

S

'Safer and Stronger Communities Fund' 30
Saward, M. 68
Scott, W.R. 59, 60, 61
Seidman, S. 44, 45
self-governance 19, 20, 140
self-help 19
senior citizens' forums 56, 135, 136
  and 'consuming public' discourse 139
  effectiveness 153-4, 161
  and institutional rules and norms 147-9
  level of engagement 140, 154, 160-1
  membership and representation 141-3, 162, 196
service users
  and access to participation 49, 50
  'consuming public' discourse 13-15, 200
  participation initiatives 71-97, 187
  'expert user' discourse 81, 83-4
  and identity 86-7, 88-91
  institutional rules and norms 93-6, 191
  motivations for participation 85-8, 194
  purposes 79-85, 198-9
  representation issues 91-3
  as partners 8
  service-specific initiatives 55, 56
Sevenhuijsen, S. 40-1
Single Regeneration Budget (SRB) 11, 100
Smith, A. 13
social agency 56, 59, 69-70, 132, 187, 196, 204
social capital 7, 27, 57, 201, 204
social constructionism 39-40, 49, 54, 63-5, 68
social entrepreneurship 24
social exclusion 165-6, 167, 170
  see also marginalised groups

social inclusion 12, 57-8
social justice 37, 41, 173, 205
social movement theory 2, 10, 33, 42-51,
    64, 202
    and identity-based groups 135, 138
    and issue-based groups 175-6, 180
    and public forums 56-7, 88, 189
    and representation 198
    see also collective identities; identity-based
        groups; issue-based groups
social networks 45-6, 175-6, 180-1
social services user group 71, 73-4, 79
    and collective identity 89-90
    constituency of group 92-3
    and institutional rules and norms 94, 95
    power and agency 80, 82-3
social values and policy 40-1
sociocultural motivations 45
speech 37, 38, 44, 201, 202
Squires, A. 15
Stahlberg, K. 14
'stakeholder public' discourse 9, 15-18,
    21-2, 56
    and communities 83-5, 171
    as dominant discourse 81, 82, 83
    and identity-based groups 139-41
    and neighbourhood initiatives 101, 112
    and participation in local governance 22-
        3, 25, 26
'stakeholder society' 17
state and participation 7-8, 53-70, 186
    and identity-based groups 135, 139-40,
        154, 155-6, 159, 160-1, 204-5
    official discourses 9-22, 53-4, 56, 138,
        198-9
    as regulator 13, 14
Stewart, J. 35
storytelling 38, 65
'sub-cultural' movements 165
subordinate groups 47, 198
Sullivan, H. 99
Sure Start initiative 25, 55, 56, 188
    and capacity building 130-1
    communication between professionals
        110-12
    and community health forum 87, 88
    and diversity 129
    and 'empowered public' discourse 111-12,
        130-1
    identities and roles 115
    institutional context 119-20, 191, 197
    motivations for participation 114-15, 194
    neighbourhood case studies 100-1, 103-4,
        104-5, 107
    representation issues 127-8, 197
sustainability forum 55, 56, 168-9, 197
    and institutional rules and norms 177-80,
        181-2, 191-2, 193
    motivations for participation 175-6, 194
    and policy context 170-1, 171-2, 180

symbolic power of institutions 62, 192

T

Tam, H. 20
target group initiatives 55, 57, 67
Taylor, M. 10, 30
technical knowledge 34, 35-6
technologies of power 65-6
tenant participation programmes 16-17, 24
Thompson, D. 34
Thompson, S. 38
Together We Can initiative 26
trajectories of change 187, 188, 190
transformation of views 37, 39, 47-8, 202,
    205
trust and expertise 62

U

underclass scenario 19
users *see* service users

V

values: social values and policy 40-1
voice 15-16, 25-6, 67, 200, 201
    identity-based groups 153-9, 164, 186
    see also representation of publics; speech
voluntary sector 111, 190
    and 'associative democracy' 16, 34-5
    and identity-based groups 135, 187
voting innovations 25, 33

W

Waterman, R.H. 13
'we-ness' 47, 91
Webler 37
White, R.W. 47
Wilson, D. 27, 28
women's centre 56, 135, 137
    effectiveness 155-6
    institutional context 149-50, 190
    level of engagement 140, 155-6, 161,
        164-5
    membership and representation 143-4,
        162, 163-4, 194
World Bank 13
World Social Forum 201

Y

Yanow, D. 41
Young, Iris Marion 37-9, 42, 44, 177, 198
Young, Jock 40
young people in public forums 106-7, 129
youth forum 141
    conflict 135-6, 138, 146-7, 161, 197
    effectiveness 158-9
    and institutional context 151-3, 193
    and level of engagement 159
    membership and representation 145-8,
        162-3